9.95

A REGIONAL HISTORY OF
THE RAILWAYS OF GREAT BRITAIN

General Editors: DAVID ST JOHN THOMAS and J. ALLAN PATMORE

VOLUME VIII
SOUTH AND WEST YORKSHIRE

Frontispiece: West Riding railways personified. The Manchester &
Leeds Railway of 1840 forces a path through the narrow confines of
the upper Calder Valley at Todmorden and crosses the Rochdale
Canal by Gauxholme viaduct, still largely in its original condition. In
this 1968 view, 'Britannia' class 4–6–2 no 70013 *Oliver Cromwell*
heads an enthusiasts' special in the closing weeks of steam on British Railways

A REGIONAL HISTORY OF
THE RAILWAYS OF GREAT BRITAIN

Volume VIII

SOUTH AND WEST YORKSHIRE

(the industrial West Riding)

by

David Joy

WITH 33 PLATES
7 ILLUSTRATIONS IN TEXT
9 MAPS
AND FOLDING MAP

DAVID & CHARLES

NEWTON ABBOT LONDON NORTH POMFRET (VT) VANCOUVER

ISBN 0 7153 6883 4
Library of Congress Catalog Card Number 74–20464

Set in 11 on 12pt Baskerville and printed in
Great Britain by Latimer Trend & Company Ltd Plymouth
for David & Charles (Holdings) Limited
South Devon House Newton Abbot Devon

Published in the United States of America
by David & Charles Inc
North Pomfret Vermont 05053 USA

Published in Canada
by Douglas David & Charles Limited
132 Philip Avenue North Vancouver BC

Contents

Illustrations

PLATES

7

IN TEXT

MAPS

Introduction

Yorkshire's industrial West Riding had arguably the most complex railway network in Britain. It is true that other areas had equal or even greater rail concentration, but they evolved in a more straightforward manner. The London network for all its vastness is basically a series of radiating spokes. South Wales was unequalled for its profusion of independent lines, but virtually all of them performed the same function of moving coal from pit to port and neatly followed parallel valleys. Of the other areas of railway abundance, Birmingham, South Lancashire, Glasgow and the Derby/Nottinghamshire Coalfield, not one was dominated by more than three companies.

By contrast the West Riding sported no less than seven major railway companies, an eighth hovering on the outside ever eager to gain entry, eleven significant joint lines and a small but interesting group of minor systems. They formed no overall pattern, either of territory or of route, but instead incessantly vied with one another for supremacy. They fought long battles, waged major campaigns and usually only co-operated when no other course remained. They indulged in wasteful competition, lapsed into frequent bouts of complacency and in many cases were woefully inefficient. Where one went another was sure to go, so that over twenty-five of the area's towns and villages had two passenger stations while others had three or even four. Yet, despite all their faults, they boldly took the harsh topography of the West Riding in their stride, creating a magnificent legacy of monumental engineering works. To link industrial Yorkshire with its Lancashire counterpart, they pierced the Pennine watershed by four tunnels, three of which at their opening were the longest in Britain while the fourth has remained second only to the Severn tunnel. Even more spectacularly, they strode across river valleys by mighty viaducts such as Conisbrough, Lockwood or the ninety-nine arches at Wakefield. The region had in total over 30 miles (48km) of line in tunnel, claimed to possess both the highest embankment and the deepest cutting in the country (respectively at Pudsey and Chevet) and was famed for its ferociously steep gradients.

Crowded into some 1,800 square miles were 850 route miles (1,360km) of railway. Much of this colourful network has now vanished and so too has the West Riding as an administrative unit. In April 1974 its urban portion was split into two metropolitan counties, West Yorkshire and South Yorkshire, their boundaries approximately according with those of this volume: the river Wharfe and then the river Aire to the north, the river Don and then the Nottinghamshire boundary to the east, the Derbyshire border to the south and the new Lancashire boundary to the west. The hallowed name of the West Riding will however take time to erase, and it is retained in these pages whenever the sense is historical.

How and why did the area come to have such a uniquely complex railway network? The answer largely lies in the physical and economic geography of the region, which fundamentally consists of an east-facing slope of the great Pennine chain broken by the valleys of four major rivers—the Wharfe, Aire, Calder and Don—and numerous tributary valleys. It was once entirely a countryside of great beauty, dramatic and craggy uplands with their tussocky grass, heather and gaunt grey rocks giving way first to richly wooded valley slopes, then to rolling green foothills and finally to the plains and marshland to the east. Had that been all much of the area might today have been designated a National Park, but apart from its own impressive quality the landscape contained three elements which were ultimately to result in its desecration.

There was the fast-flowing water rushing down from the hills in innumerable streams, becks and small rivers. It was soft, lime-free and ideal for cleansing the wool from sheep which thrived on the upland pastures. Hence fulling mills by the streams and domestic weaving in the hill-top villages were established from the thirteenth century, and three hundred years later Halifax, Leeds and Wakefield had become important centres for woven cloth. There was coal, mined in the area by the twelfth century and from Elizabethan times increasingly worked and transported for household purposes. And there was ironstone, extracted from the 1300s and smelted with charcoal obtained by plundering the native woodland. It gave Sheffield its famous cutlery industry, again helped by running water for powering the grinding mills and drop-hammers.

The interdependence of these three natural resources was dramatically altered from the late eighteenth century when steam superseded water power. Coal came into its own, transforming both the cutlery and weaving trades. The woollen industry moved down from the hills as the domestic system of cottage weaving gave way to harsh and impersonal factories built as close as possible to workable coal seams. Expansion created a demand for better transport facilities, and led to turnpike roads, a network of canals and primitive railways for moving coal from pit to barge. These last were normally only a few miles in length, with rails initially of wood and worked by rope or horse haulage.

The West Riding had all the prerequisites of industrial boom: water transport; good quality stone to build factories and back-to-back houses; coal and fast-flowing streams to provide power; and iron to construct machinery. It is not surprising that, together with Lancashire, it led Britain and the world into the Industrial Revolution. The boom conditions, coupled with an ability for hard work on the part of local inhabitants, brought about a classic example of industrial migration—the movement of Britain's focus of worsted manufacture from East Anglia to the area between the Aire and Calder valleys. Factory towns and colliery villages appeared to merge into one great urban sprawl, and indeed many contemporary observers saw the region as such. But in reality the area was too rugged and the Yorkshireman too individual for this to happen. Each community clung tenaciously to its own ideals and independence, creating what has been described in thesis jargon as 'a unique multinodal conurbation'—a region teeming with people and industry and yet having no single clearly defined centre. It was this fragmentation, coupled with the rich rewards offered by the coal, iron and textile industries which led to such complexities with the onset of the railway age. There was plenty to attract railways into the area but no single golden goal, and so once established a company strived to put out tentacles which soon became interwoven with those of its competitors.

The first line in the area—and in Britain—to be constructed under an Act of Parliament was the Middleton Railway of 1758, and the first company to be incorporated was the Heck Bridge & Wentbridge Railway of 1826. Both were basically waggonways, the former of great historical importance and the latter an almost total failure. The first railway in the modern sense to be incorporated in the region was the Leeds & Selby of 1830, although still performing the traditional waggonway function of connecting with a navigable waterway rather than another line. Its genesis was strongly influenced by the success of the 1825 Stockton & Darlington Railway and the subsequent promotion of the Liverpool & Manchester, two lines which created sufficient confidence to help bring about the first wave of railway promotion on a national scale in 1835–7.

Five lines which formed the basis of the West Riding rail network emerged in this period. The most important was the North Midland, stretching from Derby to Leeds and forming a trunk route by connecting at its southern end with lines from London and Birmingham. To keep gradients to a minimum it avoided Sheffield, which reluctantly had to make do with a connecting line, the Sheffield & Rotherham Railway. A second and more significant off-shoot was the York & North Midland, joining the trunk route with lines to the north so that ultimately it extended on to Newcastle and Edinburgh. This link was also important in another sense for it was the first line with which George Hudson, the 'railway king', was associated. Often ridiculed as a common swindler, he nevertheless master-minded the first major railway amalgamation by welding the North Midland with two other companies to form the mighty and magnificent Midland

Railway. He was in many ways creator of the first East Coast route, running north via Derby, Normanton and York.

The other two lines formed in the first promotional rash both ran from west to east. The Manchester & Leeds pierced the Pennines by the first railway tunnel through the watershed, at Summit, and then pursued a sinuous course along the Calder Valley to reach Normanton. Here is was pipped at the post by the North Midland, and woefully forced to share the latter's tracks on to Leeds. On 22 July 1847 the Manchester & Leeds became the Lancashire & Yorkshire Railway, for years an appalling line which earned the description of 'probably the most degenerate railway in the kingdom'. Also breaking through the Pennines, by a far more notorious tunnel at Woodhead, was the Sheffield, Ashton-under-Lyne & Manchester Railway. It was the last of the five to be opened, in 1845, by which time Leeds and Sheffield were linked with London, Manchester and Gateshead (Newcastle). The basic outline was complete, notably similar to that later to be formed by the M1, M62, M18/A1 and the projected Sheffield–Manchester motorway.

The national promotion of 1835–7 was undoubtedly a success, but owing to economically difficult times there was a ten-year interval before a marked surplus of ready capital triggered off the frenzied Railway Mania of 1845–7. This saw virtually all places of any importance receive the benefits of railway communication. In the northern half of the industrial West Riding, Halifax had already been reached by a branch of the Manchester & Leeds and this was extended by a satellite company to the key textile centre of Bradford. Hudson promoted a company to build a link along the Aire valley between Leeds and Bradford and an extension to Colne. At Skipton it connected with a line running through to Lancaster, creating the first rudimentary connection for northbound traffic between the West Riding and the West Coast route to Scotland. Also providing new outlets from the region were the Leeds & Thirsk and Wakefield, Pontefract & Goole railways. Of paramount importance was a more direct link between Leeds and Manchester passing through Dewsbury and Huddersfield. Promoted by two independent companies it was quickly taken over by the London & North

Western Railway, thus giving that famous company its primary access route into the region. The 'Premier Line', as it styled itself, was the largest joint-stock corporation in the world, and achieved majestic eminence personified by the egotistical description on its postcards: 'The London and North Western Railway is noted for Punctuality, Speed, Smooth Riding, Dustless Tracks, Safety and Comfort, and is the Oldest Established Firm in the Railway Passenger Business.'

Further south Barnsley was linked with Wakefield, and Huddersfield with Penistone and thence Sheffield. An important exception to the general pattern of West Riding railways, in which most lines were promoted outside the county as if plundering its riches from afar, was provided by the South Yorkshire. Projected by local coal-owners, it too served Barnsley by connecting the town and its pits with Sheffield and, more important, Doncaster. Sheffield gained a coastal outlet when the line from Manchester was independently extended eastwards to Grimsby, the various companies amalgamating to form the Manchester, Sheffield & Lincolnshire Railway.

Among the most significant of Railway Mania promotions was the Great Northern Railway, a brand new trunk route striding boldly and directly north from London to Doncaster. In terms of both mileage and capital it was the largest single railway scheme to come before Parliament, and was bitterly but unsuccessfully opposed by Hudson as it rendered obsolete his existing East Coast route via Derby and Normanton. The Great Northern had to fight every inch of the way in order to gain running powers into Sheffield, Wakefield and, by virtue of Hudson's double-dealing, Leeds and York. This treachery was a factor in events culminating in the 'railway king's' dethronement in 1849, although removal of the former arch-enemy by no means eased the Great Northern's growing pains. No sooner had he departed than the London & North Western co-erced the three other major companies in the West Riding, the L & Y, MS & L and Midland, to combine in an all-out attempt to strangle the new giant at birth. For seven years the Euston Square Confederacy, as it was termed, placed every obstacle in the newcomer's path, but to no avail. The Great Northern survived and became indeed great.

The Railway Mania, despite its excesses of wildcat schemes and speculation, did provide the essential links between all major towns in the West Riding, and gave the region's three basic industries adequate rail outlets. From now on the pattern was to be one of consolidation and, as can be seen from the reference section, new lines were of lesser importance. A major post-Mania event came in 1854 when Parliament for the first time gave its blessing to an amalgamation conferring an area monopoly. This was the formation of the North Eastern Railway, having as two of its three major constituent companies the Leeds Northern (until 8 August 1851 the Leeds & Thirsk) and the York & North Midland which had already absorbed the Leeds & Selby. North Eastern penetration into the industrial West Riding came to take the form of a series of projecting fingers, reaching or giving access to such points as Ilkley, Leeds, Normanton, Knottingley, Doncaster and Thorne. It also entered into a sensible arrangement with the Midland for joint construction of the Swinton & Knottingley line, so that the two companies respectively had access to Sheffield and York.

The Midland overcame the malpractices of Hudson's reign and maintained a policy of sustained expansion, transforming itself from a provincial company into an Anglo-Scottish trunk route by means of its 1868 extension into St Pancras and the scenically superlative Settle–Carlisle line of 1876. As a preliminary, it had earlier absorbed the lines extending north-west from Leeds to Colne, Ingleton and Morecambe. The company's rolling stock and stations became second to none, and after the North Eastern it carried more coal than any other railway. In the West Riding the Midland went on to build lines to Barnsley and into Wharfedale, and also rather belatedly put Sheffield on a direct route to the south. Its swan-song, which never achieved fruition, was a cut-off from Royston through Dewsbury and Bradford to Shipley with an offshoot to Huddersfield and Halifax. For an expenditure of over £2 million it would have shortened the company's route to Carlisle by $5\frac{3}{4}$ miles (9·2km), bringing the total distance from London down to 302½ miles (484km) compared with the L & NW's 299 miles (478km) over Shap.

Attempted expansion by the 'Premier Line' in the West Riding was well contained by the other companies. Its strenuous efforts to reach Bradford, extend beyond Leeds into the heart of North Eastern territory and penetrate the southern half of the region by a Buxton–Sheffield line were all foiled. Instead, the L & NW for once had to take a subservient role and be content with obtaining running powers, although these at one time or another gave it access to every major centre except Barnsley. Another company even more frustrated in its ambitions was the Great Eastern, formed in 1862 by amalgamation of the Eastern Counties Railway with a number of smaller undertakings and at no point remotely near a coalfield. It thus saw the West Riding as an Eldorado on a tantalisingly distant horizon, spending almost twenty years trying to gain its own route into the area before finally capitulating and reaching Doncaster by means of a joint line with the Great Northern. It also managed to obtain access to Sheffield by devious means, but never really took advantage of these hard-won powers.

The Lancashire & Yorkshire was so impoverished and penny-pinching after the collapse of the Railway Mania that for years it indulged in little major construction, even throwing away the last opportunity of reaching Leeds over its own metals. Once recovered it still fought shy of promoting additional through routes, but almost alone among the major companies in the West Riding it did build some delightful rural branches serving mill communities in tributary valleys of the Colne and Calder. The Great Northern, by virtue of its enormous promotional and constructional costs, also found itself critically short of funds, but followed a more ambitious policy. Having so tenaciously gained access to Wakefield and Leeds, it sought to expand westwards by encouraging the promotion of local companies and then absorbing them once they had proved themselves. By this ploy it came to have access to Bradford, Halifax, Morley and Batley over the basis of what became the only true suburban passenger network in the West Riding. Serving a large number of textile centres in a relatively small area, it gradually expanded to embrace further towns such as Dewsbury, Pudsey, Shipley, Queensbury and Keighley. Oddly, the company never managed to obtain its own exclusive access to this network, and had to be content initially with running powers over the Lancashire & Yorkshire and then joint ownership of the West Riding & Grimsby Railway between Doncaster and Wakefield.

Its partner in this case was the Manchester, Sheffield & Lincolnshire, a line condemned by many of its shareholders who averred that its initials stood for 'Money Sunk and Lost'. In the West Riding the MS & L's main rival was the Midland, the two companies almost completely dominating the southern portion of the region. In positive vein, the MS & L absorbed the South Yorkshire Railway, placed Barnsley on direct routes to Manchester and Wakefield and forged a vital link north-east from Doncaster to the north and south shores of the Humber. The company was making steady progress when in the closing decade of the century it suddenly indulged in a giddy metamorphosis, rechristened itself the Great Central Railway on 1 August 1897 and built an enormously expensive extension through the Midlands to the Metropolitan near Aylesbury and hence to a London terminus at Marylebone. Alas, it was too late in the day for such flights of fancy and there was simply not enough traffic to support a fourth trunk route between London and the North. The poor shareholders became even poorer and now held that the new initials meant 'Gone Completely'. The other spectacular failure which impinged on the West Riding was the Hull & Barnsley, the last major company in the area to be incorporated. Conceived largely with the idea of breaking the monopoly which the North Eastern Railway held at Hull, it remained in dire financial straits until it came to terms with the company it had set out so resolutely to oppose. Plans for reaching Huddersfield, Halifax and centres even further afield were never realised, and the line settled down quietly to the routine task of conveying coal from South Yorkshire pits to its own dock at Hull.

How did the growth of the railway network and its consolidation into these major companies affect the West Riding? Unlike so many other parts of Britain, this was not an area where railways created a new industrial economy.

Rather did they cause an expansion of the already existing framework of mills, mines and furnaces and accelerate trends that had for some time been apparent. Improved transport facilities helped to create more sharply defined zones of industry. In the northern textile belt the mills spread out from the towns and cities alongside the railway lines where they could conveniently receive supplies of coal and dispatch their products. With the greater ease of transport there was an increasing tendency for them to split into separate spinning and weaving units. An even more profound change came to the pattern of coal mining, which at the start of the railway age consisted of a large number of small pits scattered over the whole of the region but concentrated close to the mills around Leeds and Bradford. Railways rendered obsolete the old mill and pit system and, coupled with technical advances, enabled coal to be worked at fewer but larger mines which no longer needed to be on the doorstep of the factories. The industry thus left behind the relatively shallow coal measures in the textile zone and with the aid of some intense railway promotion became concentrated on the deeper and richer seams around Barnsley. Towards the end of the century it began to move still further east into the concealed coalfield, causing a scramble for domination by every railway company in the area and creating a new wave of construction which did not completely subside until the late 1920s. To the south railways transformed the heavy steel industry centred on Sheffield, not only by easing distribution of its weighty products but also in creating a new market for the supply of rails and materials for locomotives and rolling stock. Here too the foundries spread out alongside the railway lines, quickly forming a near-continuous chain between Sheffield and Rotherham.

The rapid growth of industrialisation in the West Riding during the railway age meant that the population more than doubled between 1841 and 1891. Yet for several reasons railway passenger movements remained subservient to those of freight. What the Victorians termed the labouring classes generally continued to live close to their place of work, creating few daily passenger movements and having neither the leisuretime nor the money to make other regular journeys. Any tendency to travel to the mill or mine by train was discouraged by the failure of the West Riding companies to issue cheap workmen's tickets. What we would now term the upper middle classes opted for living in residential quarters in or just outside the big cities, often on high ground clear of the smoke-filled valleys and therefore difficult of rail access. It was thus the real horse rather than the iron horse which provided the backbone of public transport in the respectable suburbs of Leeds, Bradford, Huddersfield and Sheffield, although detached residential communities such as Eccleshill and Upper Batley did gain the benefits of rail communication. Long distance commuting was most marked in the textile zone with its numerous dark, satanic and, for the owners, extremely prosperous mills. Wealthy woolmen fled as far as possible from the neo-slavery they had created, daily travelling into Bradford from Harrogate, Ilkley and even Morecambe. Elsewhere such commuting occurred only in isolated instances as for example from the fringes of the Peak District into Sheffield.

The nineteenth century attitude of the West Riding railways towards passengers can be summed up as one of complacency. They had a virtual monopoly, and in any event their prime purpose was the movement of freight and minerals. This laissez faire policy was destined to continue with regard to medium and long distance traffic, but suburban passenger movements were transformed in the first decade of the twentieth century by the advent of the electric tramcar. The hilly West Riding with its fragmented settlement pattern was peculiarly suited to this new form of transport which rapidly became all-conquering. Typically for Yorkshire, the various systems adopted different gauges but nevertheless all the major centres of the textile zone were quickly inter-connected as were Sheffield and Rotherham, and later Barnsley. Tramcar stops, unlike so many stations, were sited at points convenient for the user, and the railways found it difficult to compete. One of the few attempts to do so was that made by the Lancashire & Yorkshire on its Stainland and Rishworth branches, both partially paralleled by tram routes, where steam rail-motors were introduced and new halts built. Elsewhere both train formations and density of services were reduced, particularly hard-hit being the Great Northern with its fairly respectable suburban network inter-linking the textile towns. In 1904 it estimated that it was losing £20,000 per annum as a result of tramcar competition in the West Riding.

The railways' attempts to meet the challenge were generally unadventurous, and neither the impact of World War I nor the subsequent advent of the trolleybus brought major changes. The Grouping of 1923 might have been expected to end wasteful over-provision of facilities stemming from almost a century of cut-throat competition, but in fact lamentably failed to do so. The London & North Western, Lancashire & Yorkshire and the Midland became part of the London, Midland & Scottish Railway, while the Great Central, Great Northern, Hull & Barnsley and North Eastern were absorbed into the London & North Eastern Railway (the L & Y in fact amalgamated with the L &NW just prior to the Grouping as did the H & B with the NE). This meant that all major centres in the area except Huddersfield and Doncaster were still catered for by two companies providing duplicate and usually unco-ordinated services. On the freight side, despite the advent of the motor lorry, virtually nothing was done to implement rationalisation and increase efficiency. Some duplicate passenger services such as that over the former Hull & Barnsley main line, and a few unnecessary stations such as Dewsbury Market Place, were eliminated, but these were the exception rather than the rule. In criticising it must be remembered that economically this was not a time for innovation and also that considerable progress was made in ways not obvious to the general public. For instance, pooling of passenger and goods receipts between common points was effected on a large scale. In addition, the coming of the motor bus and the private car prodded the companies into adopting a more competitive fare policy. As an example, the cost of a day return fare from Leeds to Castleford fell from 2s 3d in 1923 to 9d in 1938, and at the same time the number of trains per day was increased. Another development indicative of the times was the establishment of bus services jointly operated by the railway companies and the respective municipality at Halifax, Huddersfield, Sheffield and Todmorden. In some cases these services ran in competition with parallel railway routes!

Further progress towards rudimentary transport integration was cut short by World War II. Nationalisation of the railways followed in 1948, but such is the complexity of the West Riding network that it was some time before any radical changes were evidenced. For instance, the two closely parallel routes between Sheffield and Barnsley were now for the first time under a single administration, yet it was not until 1953 that one of these was closed to passengers. Mounting financial losses finally drove home the need for a complete reappraisal which gathered momentum following the publication of British Railways' modernisation plan in 1955 and then the Beeching proposals of 1963. Duplicate lines were eliminated, wayside stations and their accompanying goods depots abandoned and unprofitable services curtailed. Major passenger withdrawals have occurred on the direct route from Leeds to Thirsk through Ripon, the Queensbury lines, much of the Calder Valley main line, the major part of the former Great Central's London extension and, only sixteen years after electrification, the link from Sheffield to Manchester via Woodhead.

On the surviving suburban lines the initial modernisation policy was to replace steam hauled non-corridor stock with diesel multiple units (DMUs). In the first $3\frac{1}{2}$ months of operation in 1955 the diesel trains running between Leeds and Bradford attracted an additional 80,000 passengers and netted an extra £4,558 in revenue. These results encouraged a rapid and widespread introduction of such services, although in many cases receipts were not sufficient to cover the full costs of providing the new trains. It quickly became obvious that DMUs could not resuscitate such unprofitable lines as Ilkley–Skipton or the Worth Valley branch, but it took longer for the railways to realise that local services as a whole were best surrendered to the roads unless grant-aided. It was not until the mid-1960s that this tenet was generally accepted and regular through trains withdrawn between such important centres as Halifax and Huddersfield, and Wakefield and Bradford.

With long-distance services it was a different story, the

so-called Inter-City network being developed to a point where it was far superior to road transport in terms of comfort and speed if not cost. By 1973 Sheffield and, even more creditably, Leeds had been brought within 2½ hours of London. Both these West Riding cities gained enormously from having their passenger facilities concentrated in a single modernised station, as was done on a smaller scale at Barnsley, Castleford, Rotherham and, in effect, Bradford.

On the freight side outmoded siding layouts were replaced by vast new marshalling yards at Healey Mills and Tinsley. Over £250,000 had reputedly been spent on preliminary works for a third at Stourton when it became apparent that the railways were rapidly switching from single wagon loads to block liner trains, and this project was sensibly abandoned. The accent changed to the provision of freightliner terminals and centralised goods depots, and ambitious rationalisation programmes were put in hand for all the major centres, especially Sheffield and Rotherham. A complete remodelling of the area's railway network, which ideally would have been put in hand fifty years earlier, was at last coming to fruition.

ARRANGEMENT OF THIS VOLUME

The main text of the work splits into two portions, chapters one to five covering what is now the county of West Yorkshire and chapters six to eight the county of South Yorkshire. In each portion the initial chapter describes the dominant centre (respectively Leeds and Sheffield/Rotherham), and because of the relative compactness is arranged entirely on a chronological basis. Other chapters are sub-divided by area, although within these divisions the treatment is chronological.

With a subject as complex as the West Riding railways, a text which gave sufficient data for the dedicated historian would quickly become indigestible for the more casual reader. In an attempt to overcome this problem, a detailed reference section has been provided in order to list in concise form the basic historical facts of every section of railway in the region. Many of the dates that have to appear in the body of the book are therefore given to the year rather than the day, the hope being that this will be sufficient for many general readers and at the same time minimise numerical interruptions to the flow of the text. The more fastidious user requiring dates to the actual day can readily turn to the reference section, which also contains a key to the company abbreviations used in the text.

Another facet which could easily get out of hand is that of lines proposed but not built. The number of these in the West Riding ran into hundreds, and to mention them all would be wearisome indeed. The approach adopted has been to refer, either in the text or the reference section, to all railways authorised by Act of Parliament. Proposals which succumbed at or before the Bill stage are only described if especially noteworthy. Other subjects not covered comprehensively are the widening (generally quadrupling) of existing lines and the history of the region's waggonways, although in both cases developments of special significance are recorded.

The maps depict the network at its maximum size rather than at any particular date. Names are shown as at the Grouping, and therefore spellings may differ slightly from those given in the reference section. In order to save space some station suffixes have been omitted.

CHAPTER I

Leeds

THE MIDDLETON RAILWAY

Leeds owes its rise to importance to influential merchants, once abundant supplies of local coal and a position geographically favourable to the development of inland communications. It was natural that a village should grow up at the point where the river Aire leaves the Pennines and begins to enter the Vale of York and, as the river valley then formed the easiest route between Yorkshire and Lancashire, Leeds had become an important settlement by the later Middle Ages. It was thus in a favourable position to attract cloth merchants driven westwards by the restrictive practices of guilds in York and the East Riding towns. These merchants made Leeds the focal point of the West Riding's domestic cloth industry, and stimulated the community's growth by obtaining a charter of incorporation in 1626 and an Act for making the Aire navigable down to Goole in 1699. This important link with the sea was completed in 1704 and led to further expansion. In 1730 Leeds was described by Gonzales as 'one of the largest and most flourishing towns in the country'.

Three years earlier Defoe had referred to 'inexhaustible stores' of coal at Leeds. Soon after the Aire had been made navigable small collieries were established near its banks, although for the first half of the eighteenth century the coal was transported from pit to barge by horse and cart. At this time wooden waggonways were flourishing on Tyneside, and when Charles Brandling of Gosforth Hall, near Killingworth, inherited estates and collieries at Middleton in 1749 it was logical that he should attempt to improve the output of the pits by means of this proved form of transport. Accordingly, a waggonway was constructed from Middleton down to the Aire at Thwaite Gate, and was in existence by 1755 when an indenture makes an early reference to 'a bredth' of 4ft 8in (1·42m).

Brandling would realise that an obvious development was to construct a waggonway into the centre of Leeds, thus avoiding payments of dues to the navigation proprietors. The necessary agreements were made with landowners, but to ensure the validity of these he obtained on 9 June 1758 the first Act of Parliament authorising a railway. The waggonway, to a gauge of 4ft 1in (1·25m) and unusual in having double track, extended from Middleton to Casson Close near Leeds Bridge. It was opened on 20 September, when the town's 'Bells were set a ringing, the Cannons of [its] Fort fired, and a general joy appear'd in every face'. It immediately gave Brandling a monopoly of the supply of coal to Leeds and, together with the opening of the Leeds & Liverpool Canal as far as Skipton in 1777, fostered the rapid industrialisation of the town. The Leeds Pottery was built alongside the waggonway and became something of a national institution from 1781 until the 1820s, while Kirkstall Forge was established in 1779. Thirteen years later Benjamin Gott introduced steam power into a mill in the town and within a decade had become one of the largest factory employers in the world. The population of the town grew from an estimated 16,380 in 1771 to 30,669 by 1801. The Middleton waggonway did not retain its monopoly without a struggle, and in 1781 Brandling inserted this gem in the *Leeds Intelligencer*: '. . . great Impositions have been put on the public as well as Charles Brandling Esq by the Vendors of Coals in the Neighbourhood of Leeds, several of whom have sold an inferior sort to their customers as and for Mr Brandling's coals. . . .' Some of the opposition was eliminated in 1789 when Beeston New Colliery was linked to the waggonway, making a network which by 1808 totalled 4¼ miles (6·8km). From about 1809 the track was improved by laying cast-iron plates on top of the wooden rails.

It was at this stage that outside influences became decisive. The Napoleonic wars increased the price of horses and

An ACT *for Eſtabliſhing Agreements made between* Charles Brandling, Eſquire, *and other Perſons, Proprietors of Lands, for laying down a Waggon-Way, in order for the better ſupplying the Town and Neighbourhood of* Leeds, *in the County of* York, *with Coals.*

Whereas *Charles Brandling,* Eſquire, Lord of the Manor of *Middleton,* in the County of *York,* is Owner and Proprietor of divers Coal-works, Mines, Veins, and Seams of Coals, lying and being within the ſaid Manor of *Middleton,* and Places adjacent ; and hath propoſed, and is willing to engage and undertake, to furniſh and ſupply the Inhabitants of the Town of *Leeds* with Coals for their neceſſary Uſe and Conſumption, at the Rate or Price of Four Pence Three Farthings a Corf, containing in Weight about Two hundred and Ten Pounds, and in Meaſure Seven thouſand Six hundred and Eighty cubical Inches, for the Term of Sixty Years, to commence from the Second Day of *January* One thouſand Seven hundred and Fifty-eight, and for ſuch further Term, or longer Time, as the ſaid Mines, or any of them, ſhall continue to be uſed and wrought ; and, at his own Charge and Expence, to carry and convey, or cauſe to be carried and conveyed, from

A   his

The title page of the first Act of Parliament authorising a railway—the Middleton waggonway of 1758

fodder to such an extent that John Blenkinsop, appointed agent at Middleton in 1808, forthwith started to experiment with the then embryo steam locomotive. A paramount difficulty was the poor quality of cast-iron rails, and with a view to overcoming this problem and securing improved haulage Blenkinsop obtained an important patent on 10 April 1811. It involved an engine with a cogged driving wheel which worked into projecting semi-circular lugs cast on the external face of one of the pair of edge rails forming the track. He was fortunate in that among the men of genius attracted to Leeds was Matthew Murray, who walked into the town from Stockton with a bag of tools on his back in 1789 and soon became the leading partner in the pre-eminent engineering firm of Fenton, Murray & Wood of the Round Foundry. Murray, known as 'the father of Leeds engineering', was one of the few men capable of putting Blenkinsop's ideas into practice, and he did so swiftly, for the first of his locomotives designed to work on the rack rail was tested on 24 June 1812. *Prince Regent* seems to have gone into immediate daily service, steam traction formally being inagurated on 12 August.

Blenkinsop claimed that each of the two initial engines replaced fourteen horses, saved one-sixth of his transport costs and would draw twenty-seven waggons at $3\frac{1}{2}$mph on the level. They were the first locomotives in the world to be used commercially on rails, and attracted enormous interest, one of them forming the subject of what is claimed to be the first illustration of a steam locomotive in the *Leeds Mercury* on 27 June 1812. They cost £350 each. Blenkinsop was obviously well satisfied, for it appears that two further engines were placed in service in 1813, and certainly a record output of about 100,000 tons was achieved the following year. That steam power was still in its infancy is shown by an incident in 1818, later referred to by George Stephenson: 'The driver had been in liquor and had put a considerable load on the safety valve, so that upon going forward the engine blew up and the man was killed.'

The position of Leeds as a pioneer in the realms of railway transport was brief. By the early 1830s the Stockton & Darlington and Liverpool & Manchester railway openings had completely eclipsed the early experiments at Middleton. The Brandling collieries were suffering from increasing competition and passed into the hands of trustees in 1834, while the locomotives were due for replacement and the price of fodder had fallen sharply. Under such circumstances it is perhaps understandable that the clock was turned back and horse haulage reinstated by 1835. One of the locomotives was exhibited in a shed at Belle Isle until about 1860, but unhappily was then broken up.

In 1862 the Brandling Estates were sold and steam traction reappeared. In 1881 the line was converted from the 4ft 1in (1·25m) gauge which had existed since 1758 to standard gauge, but shortly afterwards the system slowly began to contract until total closure seemed likely in 1958. Then it became the first standard gauge line to be successfully preserved by amateurs, the Middleton Railway Preservation Society running its first train on 20 June 1960 and on 1 September commencing regular freight services from the connection with the Midland main line at Balm Road to various private sidings. The main line section from Hunslet Moor to Middleton Park was reopened on 30 June 1969.

Another important system in this area started life as a wooden waggonway about 1755, running from the Aire at Thwaite Gate towards Temple Newsam. It was rebuilt in iron in 1816 on the opening of Waterloo Colliery, which developed to such an extent that probably the first colliery village in the West Riding was built nearby before 1821. A decade later there were seven pits, a complex network of waggonways and an ironworks. About 1860 the whole system was adapted for locomotive working, while 'paddy' trains were run for the colliers until as late as 22 August 1959. Most of the line closed on 1 December 1968.

THE LEEDS & SELBY RAILWAY

Doubts over forms of motive power remained to the fore until after 1830 and loomed large in the promotion of the West Riding's first passenger-carrying line, initially put forward in 1821 as the abortive Leeds & Selby Rail-road. By 1824 technical developments and national availability of capital were both sufficiently buoyant to encourage the conception of numerous rail links including one across England from Liverpool to Hull. In the following year Joseph Locke, working under the direction of George Stephenson, surveyed the section east of Leeds, recommending a route which included three inclined planes to be worked by stationary engines. But in the event the whole scheme east of Manchester was allowed to lapse so that experience gained in constructing a line to the more populous Liverpool could be carefully assessed.

By this time the number of people in Leeds was soaring above the 100,000 mark, the 1831 census figure for the Borough totalling 123,393. The town had become the acknowledged woollen capital of England and its trade with Europe was rapidly expanding. The existing roads were inadequate, and the pressure on the inland waterways was only eased by the opening in 1826 of an improved route to the Humber in the form of the Knottingley & Goole Canal. This development alarmed shareholders who had subscribed to the 1824 project and also threatened to deprive Selby of much of its trade. Thus in 1829 the decision was taken to build a railway to this point from Leeds, and to run a connecting service of fast steam packets down the river to Hull. James Walker's recommendation that the inclined planes proposed in 1825 should be abandoned was accepted, but a pamphlet by Thomas Hill urging horse haulage went unheeded with the promoters finally opting for locomotives. The company was incorporated in 1830, despite the most strenuous opposition from canal interests.

The Leeds terminus was on the north side of the Aire at Marsh Lane, then described as 'one of the most unpleasant and dirty parts of the town'. It was here that a crowd of over 40,000 greeted the first return train on the opening for passengers in 1834. The journey from Leeds to Selby was shortened from $29\frac{1}{2}$ miles (47·2km) by canal to 20 miles (32km) by rail, and an immediate result was that the Aire & Calder Navigation, hitherto making an annual profit of £70,000 on a capital of £26,700, reduced its tolls by an average of 40 per cent. The line, which cost £340,000, had as its most notable feature the 700yd (637m) Richmond Hill

Page 33 Early scenes: (*above*) a print of 1829 by N. Whittock showing the Middleton Railway's coal staith alongside the river Aire at Leeds. The artist mistakenly represented the locomotive as having two chimneys; (*below*) rail, road and canal intermingle at Charlestown, near Hebden Bridge

Page 34 Contemporary views of the North Midland Railway: (*above*) a 2–2–2 locomotive enters the original Barnsley station, renamed Cudworth in 1854. Like other intermediate stations on the line, it was designed by Francis Thompson and was architecturally distinctive; (*below*) the first Normanton station, junction for main lines from Derby, Manchester, Leeds and York. It was notable for its period in being connected directly to the hotel and refreshment rooms on the right by a covered footbridge

tunnel, just outside Marsh Lane, the first in the world through which passengers were drawn by a locomotive. Many of the early travellers were terror-stricken at the thought of a 'steam monster' in such stygian depths, and so the interior was whitewashed and copper plates installed at the foot of the air shafts in order to reflect light. It was claimed that a newspaper could be read in the tunnel. A far-sighted move was to make all bridges and earthworks on the line of sufficient width to accommodate four tracks.

A peculiarity was the timing of the main train from Selby to Leeds, which initially varied according to the tides determining the running of the packet boat. It is also noteworthy that the company played a pioneering part in promoting the idea of excursions by rail, one of the first 'cheap trips' of this kind in Britain being run in August 1835 from Leeds to Selby, from where coaches took passengers on to the York Festival. Similarly, connecting coach services were established with Batley, Bradford and Wakefield, while omnibuses conveyed travellers from Marsh Lane to the more central Kirkgate for the then extortionate sum of fourpence. During its first year the railway carried an average of 3,500 passengers a week compared with the former average of 400 on the stagecoaches, and there was a similar upward trend in the amount of goods traffic handled.

FIRST MAIN LINES

Three of the new companies incorporated in the 1835–7 wave of railway promotion played a vital role in creating south to north and west to east trunk routes serving Leeds. The North Midland and Manchester & Leeds railways had several similarities, one of the most important being that their common engineer was George Stephenson who in both cases applied his cherished concept that main line railways should have minimum gradients, ideally no steeper than 1 in 330, even at the expense of increased distances and avoidance of intermediate population centres. The M & L, a revival of the 1824 project and more fully described in chapter four, made use of the low-lying Calder Valley route through the Pennines, although this involved a total rail distance between

C

its two termini of 61¾ miles (98·8km) compared with 40
miles (64km) direct. As noted in the introduction, the two
trunk routes met at Normanton, the original intention being
for them to run into Leeds parallel to one another. Parliament did not favour such duplication, and provided for the
M & L to have running powers over the NM north of Normanton. The Manchester company could only have built this
section if the NM had failed to commence construction
within eighteen months of the passing of the Act.

It would at this stage have been logical for Leeds to have
become one of the key early railway centres with the NM
extending north towards Newcastle and also connecting with
the L & S which, as had been originally envisaged, would be
projected east to Hull. The Hull & Selby Railway was in
fact incorporated in 1836, but at this point logic was
thwarted by the increasing dominance of George Hudson
who was determined that his own city of York should rival
Leeds as a nodal point of railways. He perceived that a line
from York to Normanton would provide connections to Hull
(by a junction at the point where it crossed the L & S), Leeds
(by a spur at Normanton), Manchester and, above all,
London. Accordingly he persuaded George Stephenson to be
engineer to the project, which took the name of the York &
North Midland and was also incorporated in 1836. His
second move was to ensure that the Great North of England
Railway, then promoting a line to link Newcastle with both
York and Leeds, concentrated solely on York.

Thus the NM ended at a terminus in Leeds at Hunslet
Lane, almost as far from the town centre as Marsh Lane. It
was originally intended to be near Leeds Bridge, but continuing opposition from the Aire & Calder Navigation
brought about the re-siting of the station which was designed
by Francis Thompson, the NM architect. It was described by
Herapath's Railway Magazine as 'exceedingly handsome' and
comprised a two-storey building with a 179ft (54·5m) façade,
a central arcade and a train shed which was 267ft (81·3m)
long and had six lines of rails. In 1839 Leeds had been linked
by rail with York on the opening of the Y & NM as far as its
connection with the L & S at York Junction near Milford,
but one of the most important dates in the history of West

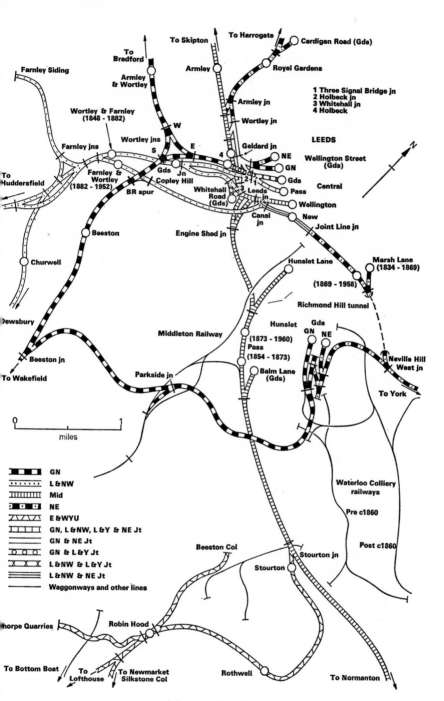

Map 1: Leeds

Riding railways was 1 July 1840 which saw the public opening of the NM through to Leeds, the Y & NM through to Normanton and the formal opening of the Hull & Selby. For the first time it was possible to go from Leeds to London in a day, although for another six years it would still be necessary to change en route.

Equally significant was the competition which became feasible for Hull traffic between the direct and already established L & S and the new and $4\frac{1}{2}$ miles (7·2km) longer NM/Y & NM approach. Hudson realised that this might well prove disastrous, but characteristically overcame the difficulty by persuading the L & S directors to lease their line to the Y & NM. They could hardly do anything but agree as long and serious competition with the Aire & Calder Navigation had weakened the company's position. Yet they certainly did not welcome Hudson's immediate and ruthless step which was to close the L & S to passenger traffic west of York Junction, both the lease and the closure coming into effect on 9 November 1840. The explanation given was that Marsh Lane did not allow for connections with the trains of other companies, but this was insufficient to prevent the deepest resentment in Leeds. One result was that the NM/Y & NM route to York became hopelessly congested, journeys in 1841 often taking as long as two hours. Much more serious was the inconvenience to Hull passengers who for almost another thirty years were to suffer seemingly interminable waits in changing at bleak Milford Junction, just to the south of York Junction.

Trains of the M & L began to run through from Manchester to Leeds on 1 March 1841, and plans for building a separate M & L station at Hunslet Lane were soon drawn up, although never put into effect. By the following year all was financially not well with the NM, partly owing to the colossal £$3\frac{1}{4}$m spent on construction as a result in significant measure of Stephenson's gradient philosophy. After several stormy meetings Hudson gained control of the company in November, and proceeded to institute drastic economies at the price of temporary traffic chaos. One field that continued to be developed was excursion workings, many interesting advertisements appearing in the contemporary press. Regular features were Whit Monday specials from Leeds to Ambergate in connection with boats for Matlock, while cheap week-end return tickets to London quickly became popular. An amazing procession must have been that of 12 September 1844 when 6,600 persons travelled from Leeds to Hull in four trains involving a total of ten engines and 240 carriages!

The same year saw the incorporation on 4 July of the Leeds & Bradford Railway. This company, and the way it contributed to the demise of Hudson, is more extensively referred to in chapters two and three, but it is of note that its Wellington station at Leeds was the first in the centre of the town. The terminus actually straddled the river Aire, and just outside a spur trailed off from a double junction to connect with what had by now become the NM section of the Midland Railway. The opening of these new lines in 1846 and the lease of the L & B to the Midland enabled the passenger services of this latter company and the Y & NM to be transferred to temporary buildings at the much more conveniently sited Wellington terminus. Hunslet Lane thus lost the bulk of its passenger traffic after only six years.

This point in time marked the nearest that Leeds was to come to having a single central station for more than a century. It also saw the town beginning to benefit from the wider effects of the coming of railways. Competition from elsewhere, particularly Bradford, caused the cloth trade to decline from 1837 onwards, but this was more than counteracted by a rapid growth of engineering industries. Peter Fairbairn had founded what was to become one of the greatest machine making businesses in the world at Wellington Foundry in 1829, while in the next decade the emphasis began to change from textile to railway machinery. In 1837 James Kitson utilised a mill in Hunslet to build the famous *Lion*, the first of an order of six 0–4–2s for the Liverpool & Manchester Railway, and reputedly had to pull down a wall in order to extract it. He thus laid the foundations of what was to become but one of many leading locomotive-building enterprises having their works in the town. What was now the firm of Fenton, Murray & Jackson reached their greatest heights in 1840–2 by constructing twenty 7ft single 'Firefly' class express engines for the broad gauge Great Western Railway. Less noticeable but most important was the way railways improved commercial services, marketing and retailing, thus bringing about an increase in the number of traders. The population of Leeds soared by almost 30,000 to a total of 152,054 in the ten years up to 1841, but the rate of growth eased off slightly to reach 172,270 in 1851. Part of the reason was the difficult times which inflicted the town in the late 1830s and early 1840s when, in 1839 for instance, an eighth of the entire population was unemployed. But by the mid-1840s a completely different picture had emerged for this period marked the onset of the Railway Mania.

THE RAILWAY MANIA AND AFTERWARDS

The origins of Leeds Central station have long puzzled transport historians for it was the end-product of perhaps the most complex series of events in the growth of the West Riding railways. Tyros may prefer to note that it evolved rather than opened, and was ultimately used by the GN and L & Y. A complete examination of the surviving minutes and correspondence of the station's management committee has still left some aspects obscure as the secretary, none other than Samuel Smiles, recorded only the barest details. Perhaps he was too pre-occupied with *Self-Help*.

A formidable number of new companies sought to serve Leeds during the Railway Mania but only four were to be incorporated. Two had the same prime purpose of providing a shorter route to Manchester than the roundabout M & L. The Leeds, Dewsbury & Manchester Railway of 1845 was promoted in association with the Huddersfield & Manchester Railway & Canal Company, the combined systems forming a very direct link which served two important West Riding towns en route. The West Riding Union Railways of 1846 had a turbulent origin as described in chapter three. Their incorporation Act compelled amalgamation with the M & L within three months, and authorised an ambitious network centred round a main line running from a junction with the Calder Valley route near Sowerby Bridge through Halifax to approach Leeds from the Bramley direction.

The Leeds & Thirsk Railway, incorporated in 1845, again filled an obvious need in providing the desirable direct link to the north which had hitherto been prevented by the activities of Hudson. At this time the 'railway king' was being greatly harassed by the promotion of a new trunk line from London to York which, as described in chapter eight, successfully came into being as the Great Northern Railway in 1846. Its plan for a branch from Doncaster to Leeds was thrown out in this session, but the chairman, Edmund Denison, remained firmly determined to serve the town.

The differing allegiances of the new companies caused considerable jockeying for position with regard to terminal facilities at Leeds. The LD & M route involved a high-level approach crossing over both the L & B and the Leeds & Liverpool Canal to a point just to the north-west of Wellington, and it was in this area that the four new companies agreed in September 1846 to construct a Central station. Initial suggestions for the structure envisaged a grand concept costing no less than £500,000. Demarcation disputes and disagreements over layout caused difficulties from the outset, while in 1847 the Bill for the station had to be suspended owing to the financial difficulties of the L & T. The Thirsk company was to have an independent entry to the site, running alongside and connecting with the former L & B before climbing up to the high-level terminus. On 1 May 1847 the GN had obtained running powers over the then Wakefield, Pontefract & Goole Railway as far as Methley and was now seeking to build a connecting line from there to the WRU at Wortley. This was rejected but only on a technicality, a result which led to Hudson granting the GN running powers over the Midland from Methley to Leeds by an historic agreement of 16 October 1847. A further development in the same year was the amalgamation of the LD & M and H & M with the powerful London & North Western Railway, keen to gain a foothold in the West Riding.

Early in 1848 a less ambitious plan for the new station drawn up by John Hawkshaw was adopted, although it still envisaged a structure 900ft (274m) long by 400ft (122m) wide stretching from Monk Bridge to Infirmary Street and costing an estimated £258,000. There would be separate arrival and departure platforms for each of the four companies which as a result of amalgamations were now the GN, L & NW, L & T and L & Y. By this time the LD & M main line was almost complete, and work had begun in April to convert a warehouse on the site into a temporary terminus. This was ready for the formal opening of the line on 31 July 1848 by the LD & M managing committee, a body clearly trying to maintain its independence to the last. It did not notify the L & NW of the ceremonies, and consequently the parent board loftily declared that it did not recognise the line as open. Stubbornly refusing to be crushed, the managing committee replied that it must do so from 7 August. The board's reaction to this insubordination was to dispatch Captain Mark Huish on a personal visit to Leeds, the outcome being the arrangement of an 'official' opening ceremony which took place on 18 September. Four days later the managing committee told the L & NW that the two engines it had sent to run the passenger trains 'were unfit to work'. Similar complaints were still being voiced in October and, as the H & M section was not yet finished, it was agreed that the L & Y should work the Huddersfield–Dewsbury–Leeds route as part of its own system. This arrangement came into operation on either 7 November or 1 December (official sources differ), although the L & Y had diverted some Manchester–Leeds trains over the shorter LD & M route from 18 September. It was a logical development for in 1845 the then M & L had gained running powers over the LD & M in return for abandoning its own projected line following approximately the same route.

After a period of uncertainty the Central station partners agreed in January 1849 to adopt a plan for the terminus which would cost a quarter of the amount envisaged in Hawkshaw's scheme and would not extend north of Wellington Street. It was to incorporate the works already carried out by the LD & M and therefore would be on the high-level, although space was to be left on the low-level for GN and L & T goods facilities. This space was reduced when the L & Y insisted on being provided with a high-level goods depot as it was under pressure from the Midland to vacate its accomodation at Hunslet Lane. The GN strongly opposed

such a move, but was unsuccessful and as a result gave notice
in March 1849 to withdraw from the station project. It was
subsequently agreed that the company be provided with
accommodation until May 1850. One is bound to wonder if
there was more in this dispute than contemporary evidence
reveals, for Captain Huish had now replaced Hudson as the
dominant power in the railway world and formed the Euston
Square Confederacy. It is therefore quite feasible that the
provision of extra goods space for the L & Y was an excuse
to deprive the GN of proper passenger facilities.

Construction of the station was now put in hand and made
sufficient progress for the incomplete terminus to be used
by the L & T from its opening to passengers on 10 July
1849 and by L & NW cross-Pennine traffic on completion of
the company's route from Manchester on 1 August. These
two lines shared the former LD & M goods depot, although
it was late August before the L & T began to run freight
traffic into Leeds. It worked over the Midland as far as
Rothwell Haigh with coal trains, and also opened a wharf
alongside the Leeds & Liverpool canal near St Annes Ing
lock. The L & Y continued to exercise its right to approach
Leeds over the LD & M route rather than its own indirect
main line as it was by now becoming evident that the WRU
project was basically a non-starter. This company also routed
its workings from Doncaster to Leeds via Wakefield into
Central instead of Hunslet Lane. The diversion was in operation by 20 August, and probably began on 10 July when the
L & T provided the necessary connection by means of its
junction with the former L & B. It was certainly short-lived
for it was agreed that all Doncaster–Leeds services would be
taken over by the GN as soon as the more direct route from
Pontefract to Methley was open for traffic. As explained in
chapter four this should have taken place on 4 September,
but owing to the 'Methley incident' the GN did not begin
to work its own trains into Leeds until 1 October when a
roundabout service from Peterborough via Boston, Lincoln,
Gainsborough and Retford was introduced. The company
gained access to the high-level terminus by running round
all trains from the south near Wortley junction and in the
opposite direction reversing traffic out of the terminus.

Further building work on the Central station continued, but during 1850 a total disagreement over apportionment of land caused construction to stop and led to a general exodus. The L & T built its own low-level goods depot on the north side of the station site at Wellington Street, and the GN purchased a half-share in L & T lines running from Holbeck junction to this depot so as to regularise access to its own low-level goods station erected alongside. It was not until 1 July that the company began to operate its own goods traffic from Doncaster to Leeds; prior to this date it was worked by the L & Y into Hunslet Lane. The GN also built a temporary passenger station on the same site, and moved to it from the high-level on 14 May. The L & T had likewise vacated the Central station on 1 May, but in this case had transferred to Wellington where it was to pay an annual rental of £2,250. Finally the L & NW also moved its passenger traffic to the Midland station on the opening of its spur between Copley and Whitehall junctions on 1 October. From 7 August two routes became available from Leeds to London with the completion of the southern end of the GN, and at once an intense rate war began. By July 1851, Great Exhibition year, the return excursion fare by the Midland route had come down to five shillings, while at the end of the month the GN advertised a Leeds to London excursion at a return fare of 4s 6d.

On 12 June 1851 it was agreed that the incomplete Central passenger station should be the joint property of the L & NW, L & Y and L & T (renamed the Leeds Northern Railway later the same year). But of the three only the L & Y was henceforth to use it, and indeed the only passenger trains running into Central from 1 October 1850 until 1854 were those on the company's service from Manchester to Leeds via Dewsbury. Even then certain of these went down the L & NW spur into Wellington until March 1854. Other L & Y services were transferred on or about 28 February 1851 from Hunslet Lane to Wellington, which thus became rather overtaxed in attempting to accommodate the Midland, Y & NM, L & NW, Leeds Northern and L & Y. The whole of this series of events, confusing enough in retrospect, must have been even more trying to the contemporary traveller, and affords a prime

An 1868 engraving of Leeds Central and adjoining goods depots. From left to right are the low level Wellington Street depots of the NE and GN, the high level L & NW and L & Y joint depot, and finally Central passenger station

instance of the results of a lack of central direction in the most important period of the growth of railways.

It should be stressed that with the Leeds Northern, as with the L & S and Y & NM, only details relevant to Leeds are given in this chapter. A more general account of their development is contained in Volume 4 of this series.

GREAT NORTHERN DEVELOPMENTS

Among the first of the local companies in the West Riding with which the GN was closely associated was the Leeds. Bradford & Halifax Junction Railway, formed as a result of the L & Y failure to build the WRU main line and following approximately the same route. This failure probably had its origins in the L & NW chairman, who did not want to see the establishment of a rival and reasonably direct line from Manchester and thus 'persuaded' the L & Y to give up what was to be its last chance of entering Leeds on its own metals.

The LB & HJ was incorporated in 1852 and its working by the GN authorised the following year. As it had the same high-level approach to Central station as intended by the WRU, and the GN was bottled up in its temporary low-level station, some difficult negotiations were obviously necessary. These became even more essential with the formation of a direct Wakefield–Leeds line, rather misleadingly titled the Bradford, Wakefield & Leeds Railway, and joining the LB & HJ by a double junction at Wortley. It provided the GN with a welcome opportunity to cease being dependent on the Midland for access to Leeds, and powers for it to work the new line were contained in the 1854 Act incorporating the BW & L. The GN now concluded arrangements enabling it to become the fourth partner in the high-level Central station and to buy a half-share in both the portion of the approach viaduct originally built by the M & L for the abortive WRU lines and the L & T spur from the low-level goods station to the upper level. The LB & HJ was opened in 1854, and used not only by GN services to Bradford and Halifax but also by expresses of the L & Y which had obtained running powers over the new route and thus ceased approaching Leeds via Dewsbury and the L & NW. The following year a serious accident at Central station, still in the incomplete state in which it had been left in 1850, resulted in a recommendation that extensive rebuilding would be necessary at a cost of £20,000. There was again a period of wrangling over who was to pay for the work, but this time reason prevailed. What was virtually a new station was due to be completed in 1855, but was not finished until two years later. Perhaps understandably in view of all that had transpired, it was almost totally bereft of architectural merit.

A new service from Leeds to London (Euston Square) at reduced fares was introduced on 1 February 1856, causing competition with the GN to reach its greatest heights until agreement was reached a month later, and prompting Edmund Denison to comment: 'If this goes on I should think the great majority of my West Riding constituents, washed and unwashed, will visit London in the course of next week.' The same year saw the breaking up of the Euston Square Confederacy, the Midland moving further away from the L & NW in 1858, when it instituted through passenger services on its new Leicester–Hitchin line and thence over the GN into King's Cross. On the other side of the scales the GN ceased to enter Leeds by courtesy of the Midland when on 1 November 1857 it commenced to run through trains over the BW & L, thus also eliminating the time consuming process of running round before entering Central. The final stage in the evolution of the GN route to Leeds occurred in 1866 when the opening of the West Riding & Grimsby line cut twenty minutes from the journey time from London, and eliminated the detour over L & Y metals via Askern and Pontefract. The previous year both the LB & HJ and the West Yorkshire Railway, as the BW & L was renamed on 21 July 1863, were amalgamated with the GN.

During this period the Hunslet district of Leeds became one of the most concentrated locomotive building centres in the world with the establishment of such famous firms as E B Wilson & Co (the Railway Foundry); John Fowler; Manning, Wardle; Hunslet Engine Co; and Hudswell, Clarke. The thirty acres of Hunslet ultimately produced over 10,000 steam locomotives, and among the famous

engineers employed at the various works in the earlier stages
of their career were John Chester Craven, Luke Longbottom
and Samuel Johnson, respectively locomotive superintendents
of the London, Brighton & South Coast, North Staffordshire
and Midland railways; Richard Peacock, locomotive superin-
tendent of the Leeds & Selby Railway and founder of Beyer
Peacock; and David Joy, inventor of the Joy radial valve
gear and designer of the famous 'Jenny Lind' class of 2–2–2s
built at the Railway Foundry. The engineering industry had
become the main large scale employer in the town by 1860,
but for the remainder of the nineteenth century diversifica-
tion was to be the key factor behind the growth of Leeds.
In the 1850s it began to lose its position as the capital of
the Yorkshire woollen trade, but this event coincided with
Isaac Singer's patenting of the sewing machine in 1851. Five
years later John Barran installed some examples in his Leeds
factory, and thus pioneered the local clothing trade which
was to become more dominant here than in any other town
in Britain. Its expansion was due in no small measure to the
by now largely adequate network of radiating railways, which
were particularly important in transporting the new and
cheap cloths of shoddy and mungo from the textile districts
lying to the west.

CONSOLIDATION

In one respect services from Leeds were still woefully
inadequate. Trains to York remained firmly rooted in the
Hudson era by still following the detour through Methley,
while travellers to Hull had more convenient facilities in
1840 than in the mid-1860s. A number of efforts had been
made to alleviate the problem. During the Railway Mania
the M & L backed a direct Leeds–York line, a threat which
Hudson regarded seriously for he put on a short-lived non-
stop service between the two centres covering the 31 miles
(49.6km) via Methley in fifty minutes. A rival Y & NM link
was authorised in 1846 only to get no further than building a
magnificent viaduct at Tadcaster. The result was the re-intro-
duction of stage coach services between Leeds and York. A
further retrograde step came in 1848 when freight services
were withdrawn from Marsh Lane and diverted via Methley

into Hunslet Lane. The former L & S was then completely closed west of York Junction except for mineral traffic from some intermediate collieries. The Y & NM Committee of Investigation, set up to examine Hudson's malpractices, criticised the virtual abandonment of this important route and recommended that services should be reinstated. A strike of porters at Hunslet Lane caused freight traffic to return to Marsh Lane in December 1849, although it seems it was July 1850 before such workings were placed on a permanent basis. Passenger trains appeared at the terminus for the first time in ten years when an experimental local service from Marsh Lane to the Old Junction station at Milford (formerly York Junction) was instituted early in November 1850. However, the accommodation remained very inadequate until enlargement and remodelling of the station was completed by February 1852. Another interesting move by the Y & NM at this time was its attempt to compete with the L & T for Harrogate traffic by running a service from Wellington via Castleford, Church Fenton and Wetherby. This was a journey of 40 miles (64km) compared with $18\frac{1}{4}$ miles (29·2km) direct, but the two trains each way managed to survive until withdrawn by mutual agreement on 1 November 1850.

It was the increasing congestion at Wellington which finally helped to bring about a long-overdue improvement for eastbound travellers from Leeds. The NE, as successor to the Y & NM, deposited Bills in 1864 for a line from Marsh Lane through the centre of the town to a new station on the north side of Wellington Street, but this would have involved such massive destruction of property and brought forth so much vitriolic correspondence in the local press that the company was compelled to withdraw its proposals. The following year it opted for a more southerly route constructed largely on viaduct and running through some of the worst slums of Leeds as well as the graveyard of St Peter's church. Elaborate and most unusual provisions were made in the Act of 1865 for laying rails on 'India Rubber' and using semaphore signals instead of whistling so as to minimise sacrilegious noise; for the reverent treatment of bodies; and for replacing gravestones on the slopes of an embankment where some still remain. The extension was to connect with Leeds New station, to be built jointly with the L & NW on the south side of Wellington.

Both developments came into operation in 1869 when all L & NW and NE services were transferred to Leeds New, covering 7½ acres and designed by Thomas Prosser. Few would disagree with the comment of W W Tomlinson that 'having practically no frontage, the station added nothing to the architectural embellishments of Leeds'. It did however have a distinctive Mansard-shaped roof with very light trusses resting on foliated columns. The station was built on what became known as the 'Dark Arches', an impressive array of vaulting spanning the river Aire and an underground arm of the Leeds & Liverpool Canal, and reputedly consuming 18 million bricks. The L & NW obtained sanction in 1870 to surrender its part-ownership in Central station, but never took up these powers and always diverted one train a year into the terminus in order to maintain its right.

The major point of congestion now in Leeds was the two-track section of the Midland from Leeds junction to Whitehall junction, used also by all L & NW passenger services and NE trains to Harrogate. To overcome this the L & NW took the bold step of promoting a line from the west side of New station to a junction with the existing route at Wortley, and again running extensively on viaduct. It was opened in 1882, regular passenger traffic between Farnley North and Whitehall junctions then ceasing. An ironworks was established at Farnley in 1844, and this grew to the extent that a branch connecting it with the former LD & M was opened in 1866. The branch faced towards Manchester, but this rather inconvenient arrangement was rectified in 1885 when a curve providing direct access to Leeds was opened and the original connection utilised as part of the new Farnley engine sheds. On 13 January 1892 a most destructive fire broke out in a tallow works in the 'Dark Arches', lasting for two days and causing serious collapse and the diversion of most of the New station traffic to Central for some weeks.

On the Midland the main changes in this era stemmed from the transformation of a provincial system into an Anglo-

Page 51 Railway companies in the West Riding—1: (*above*) the Midland had its most important terminus in the area at Leeds (Wellington), seen here about 1905. In 1938 it was combined with Leeds (New) to form Leeds (City); (*below*) Lancashire & Yorkshire 4–4–2 no 1494 prepares to depart from beneath the impressive roof of Bradford (Exchange)

Page 52   Railway companies in the West Riding—2: (*above*) the Great Northern gained access to Leeds (Central) after a severe struggle. An 0–4–4 well-tank takes water prior to departure from the station as a 4–4–0 arrives on a passenger train; (*below*) a Great Central light-weight express rushes through Darnall on the approaches to Sheffield

Scottish main line. In the early 1900s the company came up with a grand scheme to avoid reversing its expresses at Leeds, the idea being that trains would take the direct curve between Engine Shed and Whitehall junctions and then stop at Armley so that passengers could be taken by shuttle service to Wellington. The platforms were lengthened and additional lines from Wortley junction completed in April 1909, but the idea got no further. Until 1914, however, certain expresses ran past Leeds without stopping at either Wellington or Armley.

At Central station the GN and L & Y settled down to a relatively quiet existence after the tumultuous events of the 1850s. An interchange station between the high-level GN and the low-level Midland/NE was completed at Holbeck in 1862, but lost some of its importance as a transfer point when the through NE service from Harrogate to Bradford via Otley was introduced in 1877. The low-level Midland portion had the dubious distinction of topping a poll to find the most uncomfortable railway station in the country. On the NE the replacement of Richmond Hill tunnel by a cutting was completed in 1895 and new engine sheds opened at Neville Hill in 1904.

The need for a single central station at Leeds continued to be raised every few years, but it was not until 1938 that the first steps were taken when Wellington and New were inter-connected and unofficially renamed City North and City South. Six years later a report by the LMS and LNER concluded that 'it is not considered practicable or economic to combine the Leeds passenger stations', but obviously the determination to do so became stronger after nationalisation. A £4½ million scheme for concentrating all passenger services at a rebuilt Leeds City was commenced in 1959, but stopped in 1961 by a curtailment on capital expenditure. It was resumed in 1963 at a substantially reduced cost, the works including altering the layout at Copley Hill junction so that trains from the former GN Bradford route could descend to Whitehall junction and Leeds City. This approach would also again be used for all trains on the former L & NW route, the viaduct line of 1882 being modified at its western end so as instead to connect with the ex-GN Wakefield route

D

and thus provide an alternative and uncongested path for main line services. Leeds City North was converted into a parcels depot, and the greatly expanded City South together with the new track arrangements came into use on 1 May 1967 when two men and a computer took over the work of seventeen signal boxes. On the same date all Bradford services were concentrated on the GN route, while from 6 March all passenger services to the North East had travelled via York on the closure of the ex-Leeds Northern line beyond Harrogate. The rebuilt City South did not escape criticism, the *Financial Times* describing its roof as 'a gloomy tunnel with the light shut out at each end', but even so it represented one of the most important post-nationalisation developments in the West Riding. Operating difficulties and inconvenience to passengers stemming directly from cut-throat railway politics of more than a century earlier had finally been eliminated.

TRAIN SERVICES

An examination of the pattern of train services from Leeds after establishment of the main routes reveals intense and perhaps even wasteful competition between rival companies. To London, traffic was dominated by the GN until the opening of the Settle–Carlisle line, when the luxurious Anglo-Scottish trains introduced by the Midland tempted many passengers on to the St Pancras route. Several would be wooed back when the first dining car service in the country began regular operation on the GN line in February 1880, but on 1 June the Midland introduced vastly accelerated and improved schedules to London. As a result the GN temporarily cut its timings to $3\frac{3}{4}$ hours, but even so by October was forced to discontinue three of its London trains. Another serious round of competition broke out in 1901, and two years later the GC entered the field by putting on a through service to Marylebone. In the opposite direction the Midland offered through services to Edinburgh, but it was generally slightly quicker to travel by the NE and change at York.

To Sheffield the Midland was the obvious approach, but on 1 July 1879 the MS & L put on a service from Central station by means of running powers over the GN. It was taken off on 2 October 1893, re-introduced on 1 May 1903 and discontinued as a daily service on 19 March 1912. In 1880 the GN ran a Sheffield service on the same route, but it lasted only a few months. To Manchester the most popular route was the L & NW, although from the 1880s the L & Y services over the GN from Central were only about ten minutes slower. A Thursdays only cotton buyers' special from Hull to Manchester was introduced on 5 January 1888 and worked throughout by the NE, while an interesting if unsuccessful service was that run by the Midland from Leeds to Manchester via Barnsley from 1 August 1870 until 30 April 1872. There was also keen competition for Irish sea traffic: for instance in 1887 the Isle of Man could be reached in $5\frac{3}{4}$ hours by the Midland via Barrow and $6\frac{1}{4}$ hours by the L & Y via Fleetwood. Again, in the 1900s both the Midland and the L & Y were running competitive Belfast Boat Trains for their respective night steamer sailings.

An interesting case was Harrogate, which from 1902 could be reached from any of the three Leeds termini. On 1 July of that year the Midland put on a through service from St Pancras, complemented with a number of its own local workings from Wellington, and this was suspended in 1917, re-introduced on 1 May 1922 and withdrawn by the LMS on 24 September 1928. In 1897 the existing NE services from New via both Arthington and Wetherby had been augmented by seasonal Liverpool–Harrogate expresses via Central. These operated all-the-year-round between 1899 and 1907, and from 1 October 1901 until withdrawal on 30 September 1915 were worked throughout by the L & Y. 'Foreign' workings were quite common at this time, particularly by the L & NW which ran its own trains from Liverpool through to York from 1 July 1893 to 31 December 1904 and to Hull from 2 October 1893 until 1 July 1915. Another company which made regular appearances at Leeds was the H & B on excursions from Hull to Wellington via Methley, and from 1904 to Central via Hemsworth.

Perhaps the most remarkable feature of all was the profusion of through coach workings, these reaching their climax in the Edwardian period. Scotland was particularly well served, and in the summer of 1903 the Midland was running to Aberdeen, Dundee and Perth by both day and night and Fort William, Inverness and Stranraer by night. The Lake District was also adequately accommodated, for during the same period through coaches served Barrow, Coniston Lake, Windermere, Lake Side and Whitehaven. Friendlier relations with the L & NW led to the introduction of the Lake District Express on 1 July 1910; this was a St Pancras–Scotland service running via Ingleton and Penrith so as to give connections for Keswick. Services from St Pancras to the new Heysham Harbour were put on from 1 September 1904, while London–Ilkley coaches were also well patronised. An excellent service was that to Bristol which was greatly accelerated in 1880 when also through coaches began to work over the Somerset & Dorset Joint to Bournemouth. In 1888 the opening of the GW/L & NW Severn Tunnel route created stiff competition, through Leeds–Torquay carriages being introduced on 1 June 1892. As an experiment the Midland had unsuccessfully attempted in 1890 to establish a working from Bradford and Leeds to Plymouth via Templecombe. Other through Midland workings connected Leeds with Folkestone, Dover and Deal via Herne Hill, and with Portsmouth and Southampton via Cricklewood, while in 1910 it was possible to travel without changing from Bristol to Glasgow, Harrogate to Bournemouth or Heysham to Torquay.

Many other resorts were similarly accommodated. Through services from Scarborough to Liverpool via the L & NW were running in the 1880s, as were the L & Y trains from Central to Blackpool, later to be augmented by Southport workings and to run in competition with an L & NW Leeds–Blackpool express from July 1892. In the summer of 1904 the 'Premier Line' was operating through coaches from Leeds to Aberystwyth, and in 1911 from Newcastle to both Llandudno via Harrogate and Cardiff via York. From Central a service was operated over the GC to Bristol and Ilfracombe. Many of these through workings continued after the Grouping, although on a slightly more limited scale, as did competition between the LMS and LNER for London passenger traffic. A noteworthy feature of the inter-war years was the variety of Pullman services running from Leeds; details of these are given in Volume 4.

SOUTH LEEDS

Detached from the main tide of events affecting the growth of railways in Leeds was the development of a minor network on the south side of the city. All the routes became freight-only lines, although in one case the promoters had much grander dreams. A glance at a pre-Grouping map shows a long spur merely connecting the GN with the Midland and yet having the grandiloquent title of the East & West Yorkshire Union Railways. This had its origins in the failure of the H & B to obtain the blanket running powers which it sought on formation in 1880. As a result two nominally independent lines were promoted with the intention of improving the company's access to the northern sector of the industrial West Riding. The Leeds, Church Fenton & Hull Junction Railway was thrown out in the session of 1883, but the E & WYU was successfully incorporated after its Bill had been rejected the previous year. It comprised a main line running from a junction with the H & B at Drax almost due west to cross the Midland at Woodlesford and terminate by a junction with the GN at Ardsley. Running powers sought over both the GN and the Midland to Leeds, and the GN to Bradford, were rejected in Parliament, but the company was to obtain its own access to Leeds by adapting the majority of the Middleton Railway and building a new passenger terminus near Leeds Bridge.

Lack of capital gradually led to the line becoming a purely local venture backed by the Charlesworth family so as to develop their collieries in the district, and extending from a connection with the GN at Lofthouse to Rothwell. Some coal traffic was coming off the E & WYU by November 1890, the opening for goods taking place in May 1891. Traffic from Lofthouse as far as Robin Hood was worked by the GN and the remainder by locomotives hired from Charlesworths. At this time there was a keen desire to provide rail access to the growing industrial area in south Leeds centred on Hunslet, and as the E & WYU pointed hopefully in this direction it became connected with a number of schemes. In 1892 the nominally independent South Leeds Junction Railway was formed to build an extension line from Rothwell to a terminus near Hunslet Lane. The Bill was thrown out, although a shortened SLJ running as far as the Midland at Stourton was incorporated in 1893 and opened in April 1895. It too was operated by Charlesworths until July when the E & WYU assumed responsibility for working both lines.

A 1901 Light Railway Order permitted the company to operate its main line as a light railway and build a new branch alongside the Pontefract–Leeds road as far as the then tramway terminus at Thwaite Gate, the idea being to operate a passenger service in connection with the trams. This scheme was abandoned when work started on a conventional street tramway linking Wakefield and Leeds via Stourton and having a branch to Robin Hood, but the E & WYU resolved to try and compete with the trams and in January 1904 introduced a passenger service between Robin Hood and Leeds Wellington. It was a disastrous failure, losing £200 per month until its withdrawal in September of the same year, only six weeks after the opening of the rival tram route.

Workmen's services were operated on a branch from Robin Hood to Royds Green Lower, sanctioned by what was only the second Order to be granted under the 1896 Light Railways Act and opened by 1898. By 1900 a waggonway had been reconstructed to provide an extension to Newmarket Silkstone colliery. All E & WYU lines, which at the Grouping became part of the LNER, had been closed by 1966.

The Hunslet Railway, incorporated in 1893 and transferred to the GN the following year, was a less ambitious south Leeds line. It was opened as a freight-only route in 1899, running from Beeston junction on the GN Leeds–Wakefield line and having to cross the Aire & Calder Navigation by a swing bridge because of proposals to transform the waterway into a ship canal. At the terminus on the east side of the river a connection was made with the NE Hunslet goods branch from Neville Hill, opened in the same year. In 1898 an extension from Beeston to the L & NW at Morley had been contemplated so that L & NW/NE through traffic could avoid the centre of Leeds, but the idea was dropped.

The GN branch closed in 1967 and the NE goods depot a year earlier, although a nearby rail oil terminal handles bulk loads of tank wagons from Teesside and keeps open the approach from Neville Hill.

CHAPTER II

Airedale and Wharfedale

LINKING LEEDS WITH BRADFORD

Airedale, or the Aire Valley as it has been more generally known since industrialisation, was an important routeway between the West Riding and Lancashire up to the end of the canal age. The more direct course which railways were to adopt, combined with changes in population and patterns of trade largely engendered by the growth of the textile industry, caused the Calder Valley route to be utilised for the first cross-Pennine rail link. The Aire Valley was thus initially regarded solely as a means of providing a level if indirect link between Leeds and Bradford: this route through Shipley used an approach which was low-lying but faced away from the main centres of population, helping to make Bradford's situation in a saucer-shaped depression most difficult from a railway engineering standpoint. The route was not universally favoured, and a split quickly developed among local interests between those committed to a railway along the valley and those agitating for a steeply-graded 'short line' running over the hills through Stanningley.

The 'short line' was selected for the initial proposal of 1830, a scheme having its origins in the successful incorporation of the Leeds & Selby Railway. Indeed, it was an attempt to link Bradford not so much with Leeds but with the navigable Ouse by means of a line running directly to a junction with the L & S at Neville Hill. The Bill was opposed and withdrawn, but two years later an atmospheric railway following approximately the same route as far as Leeds was projected and later merged with a scheme for a direct line from Leeds to Manchester. This fell through owing to lack of support, while an approach to the North Midland in 1835 brought nothing more than advice that the local interests should form their own company. Three years elapsed before a line was surveyed by George Stephenson, who naturally favoured the valley approach, as did Daniel Gooch when he came to the area in the same year. Nothing happened owing to lack of capital, and it was not until 1843 that a further approach was made to Stephenson. He consulted George Hudson, who persuaded the NM to build a Bradford branch only to see the scheme deferred as a result of the amalgamation proposals for the formation of the Midland. Not to be outwitted, the 'railway king' formed the independent Leeds & Bradford Railway which, as noted in the previous chapter, was incorporated in 1844 and opened two years later. The only important engineering work on the line was the 1,496yd (1,361m) Thackley tunnel, built in order to cut through a spur in the valley where the meanders of the Aire were too sharp for the railway to follow.

At this time the Aire Valley west of Shipley was already becoming partially industrialised. When Mrs Gaskell wrote her biography of the Brontës in the 1850s she noted that Keighley was in the process of being transformed from an old-fashioned village into a flourishing town. The convenient access by canal and river to Hull had been a fundamental factor behind the establishment here of cotton spinning, Yorkshire's first cotton mill being erected in the town in 1780. The same trend was evident at Bingley and at Skipton, which in 1792 had been referred to by John Byng as 'this nasty, filthily inhabited town' but by 1831 had a population of 4,181 with peripheral cotton mills providing employment.

There was thus a strong case for building an extension of the L & B up the valley, and indeed a promise to go at least as far as Keighley was given during the passage of the original Bill through Parliament in 1844. By September of the same year it had been decided to go even beyond Skipton to Colne, as this small Lancashire textile town had been chosen as the terminus of the proposed East Lancashire Railway. An end-on junction between the two lines would create a new and rival route to the M & L from Leeds to Manchester and Liverpool.

The extension ran from a double junction with the original line at Shipley, and was opened to Keighley in March 1847. In September a single line as far as Skipton came into use and was doubled by the end of the year, while opening through to Colne took place in 1848. The intermediate stations were at first only temporary, though that at Bingley certainly lasted over two years before being replaced by something more permanent. In November 1849 it was roundly condemned by the *Leeds Intelligencer*, which painted a magnificent word picture of its evils:

> A wooden station of the most wretched and disgraceful description. . . . It consists of a clerk's room, about three yards square, at one end, a small open shed in the middle, and at the other end a room similar to the clerk's, dignified with the name of the 'Ladies' waiting room'. During wet weather the clerks transact business with an umbrella over their heads, to protect themselves from the rain dropping through the roof. In the open shed are huddled together first, second and third class male and female passengers, sometimes for nearly an hour, exposed to all kinds of weather, as the trains are frequently this period behind time. 'The ladies' waiting room' is avoided from the dread of cholera, for the stench arising from the conveniences, only separated by thin boards, is dreadful. It is expected that the Improvement Commissioners intend to indict the station as a public nuisance, and that the inhabitants will take steps to compel the directors to provide them with proper and civilized accommodation.

In April 1849 completion of lines in Lancashire enabled two through expresses each way to be put on between Leeds and Liverpool via Colne. It was a roundabout route of $89\frac{1}{2}$ miles (143km), but so was that of the L & Y at $81\frac{1}{2}$ miles (130km), and the timings of $3\frac{1}{4}$ to $3\frac{1}{2}$ hours compared favourably with those of the older line. The service would have had little chance of survival after August and the opening of the L & NW trans-Pennine route, but it was even shorter-lived owing to changing allegiances brought about by Hudson's demise.

MIDLAND MAIN LINE

The reasons behind these changes lay in the infamous 1846 lease of the L & B by the Midland, an event which can be more clearly understood in the context of the next chapter.

But it should be remembered that Hudson took shares to the value of £30,000 in the company when they were already over-subscribed, and that John Waddingham, the deputy chairman, reputedly made the then quite colossal personal profit out of the lease of £62,500. These facts are of relevance in considering the Midland's financial assessment of the L & B after Hudson's departure for it found that the company's liabilities were £110,000 and its assets a mere £261. This was but one of many unpleasant revelations following the dethronement of the 'railway king' which led to a period of penny-pinching, and hence to less hostile relations with lines such as the L & Y.

Yet what was to be a gradual transformation began on 1 June 1850 when the 'little' North Western Railway was completed through from Skipton to Lancaster, thus creating a useful line of communication from the West Riding to Scotland. This fact was quickly noticed by the GN, then anxious to extend north of Yorkshire. It was partly to limit such aspirations that the Midland arranged to work the new line from 1 June 1852 and to purchase the L & B by an Act of 1851. The evolution of a branch into a section of a trunk route was aided by the lease of the 'little' North Western in 1859 and the completion in 1861 of a Midland/ L & NW cut-off from Clapham to Low Gill, an unsatisfactory arrangement which ultimately led to metamorphosis and the 1876 open:..ʒ of the Settle and Carlisle line. This had two immediate repercussions on the former L & B: a new station at Skipton, north of the original buildings, was opened on 30 April, while on the following day L & Y connecting services began to run through from Colne and were to last until the completion of the company's line to Hellifield in 1880.

Among other developments after the Midland take-over, perhaps the most interesting was the opening in 1859 of a station at Saltaire to serve Titus Salt's 'palace of Industry', a ten-acre alpaca and mohair mill providing employment for 2,500 people living in an adjoining village which was notable as an outstanding early attempt to provide adequate housing for the working classes. A disaster occurred at Apperley on 16 November 1866 when the viaduct over the

Aire was swept away by raging floodwaters and a goods train plunged into the gap. Perhaps more notable than the actual accident was the fact that John Crossley, the Midland's engineer, had the structure rebuilt by the following 1 January, and in recognition was given the very generous sum of 300 guineas by his directors.

Many improvements took place following the elevation of the route to Anglo-Scottish status, a major development being the gradual quadrupling of the line from Leeds to Shipley between 1896 and 1910. The work included the construction of a flyover at Kirkstall to take the Leeds–Bradford 'fast' lines over the 'slow' lines primarily carrying freight from Leeds and the south to Scotland. The valley settlements were greatly helped in their expansion when they found themselves on a main line. Frederick Williams in his history of the Midland Railway described the town of Keighley as 'one of the busiest and wealthiest in Yorkshire'. In 1882 it became a Borough with a population nine years later of 30,810, while that of Skipton increased from 6,078 to 9,091 between 1871 and 1881. The Aire Valley was in fact well on its way to becoming totally built-up, a fact lamented by Dr E. W. Benson, the then Archbishop of Canterbury, when he visited the area in 1892: 'The whole valley from end to end is spoiled, enslaved, dejected. It was the very home and spring of fresh air and water, and now it is a sewer of smoke, with a mantling ditch.'

One of the most interesting services through the dale was the evening residential express carrying wool magnates home from Bradford to Morecambe, its formation including two exclusive club cars in the 1920s. Noteworthy too was the introduction of workings by the NE, which ran a through Hull–Bradford train during 1903 and in the following year put on a summer-only working from Scarborough to Bradford. Local services were taken over by DMUs on 5 January 1959, but were withdrawn on 22 March 1965 when all intermediate stations between Leeds and Skipton except for Shipley, Bingley and Keighley were closed. Diversion of Leeds–Bradford passenger workings to the Stanningley route on 1 May 1967 caused closure of the fast lines from Armley to Thackley on the same date.

LINES TO ILKLEY

Lower Wharfedale long marked a transitional point between urban and rural West Riding. It differs from other major valleys featured in this volume in that lack of mineral resources and absence of any great routeway advantages meant there was no canal to establish a pre-railway pattern of industry. Yorkshire's first worsted spinning mill was built in 1787 at Addingham, which by 1821 had taken up cotton manufacture and had a population of 1,570. At this time many of the 1,200 people living in Burley-in-Wharfedale similarly worked in small cotton mills in the village, but these were isolated instances and the valley remained predominantly agricultural. Otley was a market centre for the distribution of corn to urban areas to the south and in 1831 numbered 3,161 inhabitants, but in the same year Ilkley was little more than a hamlet with a population of a mere 691.

This rather fragmented pattern of habitation meant that railways were late in coming to the area, although proposals put forward during the Railway Mania included the promotion in 1845 of the Lancashire & Yorkshire North Eastern Railway running from Skipton to Wetherby and York (incorporated in 1846 as the Wharfdale Railway, using the old and even then antiquated spelling for the valley). But the company failed to establish itself, even after the section east of Arthington had been abandoned by agreement with the Leeds & Thirsk Railway. It was left to the Leeds Northern to make an agreement with private operators for the running of 'good, safe and convenient omnibuses from Ilkley and Otley to connect with trains at Arthington'.

A number of other abortive schemes culminated in 1859 in an approach by local parties to both the Midland and the NE, which for once decided to sink their differences and henceforth adopted an attitude over Wharfedale deliciously summarised by Ahrons as 'a hostile courtesy'. It was agreed the NE should build a line from Arthington to Otley from where construction on to Ilkley would be undertaken jointly, while the Midland would form a steeply-graded connection from the former L & B near Apperley to a double junction near Burley. These arrangements were authorised in 1861, and in view of the never waning rivalry between Leeds and Bradford a clause in the Midland Act is of particular interest. It laid down that 'equal facilities and advantages as regards Trains and the conveyance and accommodation of passengers on the Railway shall be afforded to Passengers to or from Bradford as to those to or from Leeds', and if this was not done Bradford Town Council or Chamber of Trade were empowered to refer complaints to the Board of Trade. There were also difficulties with the aristocracy, one William Stansfield insisting that in the vicinity of his seat at Esholt Hall the line should be so laid as to minimise noise, and if necessary should be concealed in cut-and-cover tunnels. Further trouble came from Francis Hawkesworth Fawkes of Farnley Hall, resulting in angry correspondence and some lively pamphleteering.

In February 1865 NE passenger trains began running to Otley from Arthington Junction, the remaining lines being opened in August. The effect on Wharfedale was immediate: Otley had actually declined in population from 4,751 in 1851 to 4,714 ten years later, but now it suddenly increased to 5,855 in 1871. An even more dramatic change came over Ilkley, where the water had been found to contain sulphur suitable for the curing of certain skin diseases. The new transport facilities enabled the former village to become a health and holiday centre, soon considered second only to Malvern and described by a contemporary guide as 'abounding in hydropathic establishments, some of them of palatial character'. The first of these was at Ben Rhydding where the station was used by wealthy clients who from 1871 had their own waiting room provided at the hydro's expense. Ilkley's growth was also helped by it becoming a dormitory for Leeds and Bradford merchants, and the population rose from 1,043 in 1861 to 2,511 in 1871 and 4,736 in 1881.

DEVELOPMENTS IN WHARFEDALE

It appears that initially Midland trains from Leeds to Ilkley and Otley stopped at what was then termed Ilkley junction,

Apperley, to pick up coaches slipped from Bradford–Leeds services. Later complete trains were run from Bradford to be deposited in mid-country until 'rescued' by the service from Leeds. It was a far from ideal arrangement, and soon prompted the Midland to promote a cut-off from Shipley to Esholt junction, south of Guiseley, which was brought into use in 1876. Besides improving communications with Wharfedale it also opened up a direct route from Harrogate to Bradford via Otley, much more convenient than the former practice of changing at Holbeck. The NE was quick to obtain the necessary running powers over the Midland and on 1 August 1877 commenced to run a through service, at first consisting of three trains each way but by 1910 increasing to a total of nine. Another facet of early working was for Midland trains to divide into Ilkley and Otley portions at the short-lived station at Menston junction.

In her novel *Carr*, Phyllis Bentley described a Victorian picnic to Bolton Abbey and a party of young people who clubbed together to travel by reserved saloon coach to Ilkley and then by two wagonettes. Such outings were quite common among the Victorian upper classes, and the already considerable popularity of this part of mid-Wharfedale was one of the factors underlying attempts to build a link line from Ilkley to Skipton. Success did not come until 1883, when the Midland obtained the necessary Act. It was again essential to placate a large landowner, this time the Duke of Devonshire, who insisted that the embankments and cuttings through his estate should be neatly covered with sods of turf and that no trees liable to interfere with signals should be felled without his consent. During construction the extension was visited by Sir William Acworth, who made some interesting references to the work in his classic book *The Railways of England*, first published in 1889 a year after the opening. At Ilkley the new line had its own Midland through platforms, the original joint terminal arrangements being officially regarded as a separate station which was referred to in the LMS Appendix as Ilkley Old.

The railway brought an increasing number of tourists and holiday visitors to Bolton Abbey, and made the place one of the most popular in the West Riding. The station formed a destination for excursion trains of many companies, particularly the NE and L & Y, and indeed in the summers of 1894 and 1908–14 the NE worked a regular York–Bolton Abbey service, latterly by autocars. A more auspicious and almost annual event was when a double-headed royal train brought King George V for his stay with the Duke of Devonshire at Bolton Hall. Wharfedale in fact had a surprising number of interesting workings, these reaching their heyday during the Edwardian years. A Midland summer service from Ilkley to Manchester lasted from 1890 until World War I, while the same company operated through trains from Skipton to Harrogate during 1889 and 1890. A more startling innovation was the routing of a summer Saturday St Pancras to Edinburgh express via Ilkley from 1908 until 1914. The NE was equally enterprising in the summer of 1913 when it put on through carriages from Harrogate to Heysham in connection with the Isle of Man steamer, but the war caused this venture to be very short-lived. Other NE innovations included the running of autocars between Leeds and Pool from July 1906 to 1915, and the working of York–Morecambe and Bradford–Scarborough excursions over the Wharfedale lines. An interesting inter-war service ran from Bradford to Newcastle via Otley, and included a through coach to Berwick.

In the 1930s LNER Sentinel steam railcars ventured into the valley, while a notable post-war working was a summer Saturday Saltburn–Blackpool service via Harrogate, Ilkley and Colne. Freight traffic in latter years included tanker trains from Teesside to Heysham, and limestone from quarries at Embsay. An unusual event during this period concerned Baildon station, closed in 1953, which was reopened for passenger traffic during the Suez petrol crisis of 1957. Owing to greatly increased housing development it was again reopened, as an unstaffed halt, in 1973. Withdrawal took place on 25 February 1957 of the through Harrogate–Bradford service, which between the wars had included a club coach but finally shrank to just one train each way. DMUs, running from Bradford to Knaresborough on summer Sundays during 1960 followed the same route, and from 1957 also worked a similar seasonal service to Bolton Abbey from

Page 69 Railway companies in the West Riding—3: (above) a London & North Western express approaches Batley from Leeds. On the left of the train is the company's Birstall branch; on the right parallel to the main line is the Great Northern's Batley–Bradford route, and curving away is its line to Tingley; (below) a North Eastern train in Leeds (New) which the company jointly owned with the London & North Western

Page 70 Railway companies in the West Riding—4: (*above*) one of the Hull & Barnsley's domeless 0–6–0s pauses at Pickburn & Brodsworth on the South Yorkshire Junction Railway, worked by the company from the outset; (*below*) a Great Eastern T19 2–4–0 passes some Great Northern somersault signals on the approach to Doncaster

points as diverse as Leeds Central, Castleford and even Sheffield via Barnsley.

General dieselisation of the local passenger workings coincided with those of the Aire Valley on 5 January 1959, as did substantial withdrawals on 22 March 1965. In this case they included all services from Leeds to Ilkley via Otley and from Ilkley to Skipton, freight workings over these lines ceasing on 5 July when they were completely closed, except from Skipton to Embsay junction which was retained to serve the Grassington branch.

MINOR LINES

A well-known event in West Riding literary history occurred in 1848 when Charlotte and Anne Brontë walked through a thunderstorm from Haworth to Keighley station to travel overnight to London and reveal to their incredulous publishers the true identity of Currer and Acton Bell. At the time it was locally hoped such lengthy walks would soon become a thing of the past for the 1845 Leeds & Bradford Railway Act had authorised a branch to Haworth, which as every true Yorkshireman knows is pronounced 'How-ath'. Then in October of the same year the Manchester, Hebden Bridge & Keighley Junction Railway put forward a scheme following approximately the same route for its closing stages, proposing the atmospheric system as a possible form of traction and having as one of its promoters the Rev Patrick Brontë.

But both these schemes were unsuccessful and it was 1862 before incorporation took place of the Keighley & Worth Valley Railway, financed locally with the approval of the Midland. The branch was constructed to an average gradient of 1 in 70 up to the terminus at Oxenhope, a mile beyond Haworth, and was laid as a single line on earthworks formed to take double track should the need arise. The river Worth had to be diverted at several points. Opening took place in 1867 and provided a substantial fillip to local trade in spinning and worsted weaving as well as machinery manufacture. The line was vested in the Midland in 1881. During this decade foundation troubles developed with a timber viaduct

E

south of Oakworth, and so a deviation involving the construction of a brick viaduct as well as the 75yd (68·2m) Mytholmes tunnel was opened on 6 November 1892. On 18 May 1895 the running of a special train to Haworth for the opening of the Brontë Museum marked the beginning of a trend which was to bring considerable extra traffic on to the branch. By the turn of the century there were seventeen trains daily in each direction, but gradually traffic declined and the branch was closed in 1962.

Introduction of DMUs on 13 June 1960 had failed to bring in sufficient revenue, but local supporters remained confident that the branch could be made viable and formed the Keighley & Worth Valley Railway Preservation Society. Their enthusiasm was justified when 35,000 tickets were issued during the first six months after reopening, an event which did not take place until 1968 owing to legal complexities delaying the transfer of ownership and the granting of a Light Railway Order. One of the intermediate stopping points reopened, Damems, had been closed since 1949. With a platform just long enough for one coach, it was reputedly the smallest station on the Midland. According to legend the building was taken inside when it rained, and was once carried away by a farmer who had called to collect a hen hut! The branch is unusually rich in such lore, one of the favourite tales being that of the cow which ate the plans and caused delays in construction of the line. This and other incidents prior to the opening were well satirised by Bill o' th' Hoylus End (William Wright), a local dialect poet and historian, in *Th' History o' Haworth Railway*.

On the opposite side of the Aire Valley several proposals were made down the years for a branch to serve Yeadon, but it was not until 1885 that the Guiseley, Yeadon & Rawdon Railway was incorporated. The small company became surprisingly ambitious, the Leeds & Yeadon Railway Act of 1891 authorising a change of name to the Guiseley, Yeadon & Headingley Railway and an extension through Rawdon and Horsforth to a flying junction with the former Leeds Northern line. An almost inevitable shortage of finance led to purchase of the Guiseley–Yeadon section by the Midland, which agreed to open it on 1 June 1893. But it was February

1894 before goods traffic commenced to toil up the ruling gradient of 1 in 50, the section east of Yeadon having meantime been abandoned. No passenger service was ever introduced, and indeed there was little need for one after the trams reached Yeadon in 1906, but very occasional excursions were operated. The branch suffered a temporary wartime shut down in 1944, and was permanently closed in 1964.

Another off-shoot of the Midland Leeds–Ilkley line was a $\frac{1}{2}$ mile (804m) long private branch serving what is now Highroyds Hospital, Menston, but was originally known as the West Riding County Asylum. It was opened in 1883 to carry materials for construction of the hospital and was later used for the supply of stores and fuel. Prior to closure and dismantling in 1951, the types of motive power had included steam, battery and overhead electric. A larger internal system in the same area was built to serve Bradford Corporation sewage works at Esholt from 1909, and reached a maximum extent of 22 miles (35km) about 1931. Oil recovered from wool-combing effluent was used as a fuel for the locomotives, as well as being 'exported' as grease for wagon axleboxes. Completely different in concept was the 386yd (351m) long Shipley Glen tramway, opened on 18 May 1895, closed in 1966 and reopened on 12 June 1969. In its heyday the toastrack cars were thronged with crowds who had travelled as far as Saltaire station from Leeds or Bradford, while a more macabre use was to bring coffins and funeral parties from the top of the glen to hearses and carriages waiting on the road at the foot. Further west along the Aire Valley a Bill for the Lothersdale Railway, running south-west from Kildwick & Crosshills station, was promoted in 1871 but withdrawn.

Almost due north on the Ilkley–Skipton line is Embsay, divergence point of the picturesque Grassington branch. This was all that materialised out of a whole series of attempts to construct a main line through the Yorkshire Dales which would form part of a direct route between industrial Lancashire and the North East, shorter than that via York. The first attempt was the Liverpool, Manchester & Newcastle-upon-Tyne Junction Railway, incorporated in 1846. Starting from the Leeds & Bradford Railway extension at Elslack, it ran via Grassington and Bishopdale to Catterick on the Richmond branch and was backed by the Manchester & Leeds, then fondly imagining it was about to absorb the L & B. George Hudson's intervention at this point played a major part in the collapse of the trunk route scheme which would otherwise very probably have succeeded, a sad fact for the railway enthusiast but perhaps a blessing for a magnificent stretch of countryside now forming part of the Yorkshire Dales National Park.

Further attempts were made in the 1860s and 1880s, and again in 1895 when the Yorkshire Dales Railway running from Embsay and Hellifield to Darlington via Coverdale was put forward. This was too ambitious for so late a date, and so the promoters decided to seek powers for an initial stretch from Embsay to Grassington which was authorised in 1897, opened in 1902 and from the outset worked by the Midland. From 1910 until closure the normal branch line passenger service to and from Skipton was supplemented by a through coach working to Bradford via Ilkley. A corresponding return service in the form of a coach slipped off the evening Bradford–Morecambe residential express at Skipton was introduced at the same time but lasted only until 1917. The Yorkshire Dales Railway never got beyond Grassington, but the company did manage to remain nominally independent until the Grouping. Regular passenger services were an early casualty in 1930, although well-supported excursion traffic survived until the portion of the branch beyond a large limeworks at Swinden was completely closed in 1969.

At Skipton an Act of 10 May 1773 authorised the construction of the Springs Branch of the Leeds & Liverpool Canal to a wharf on the west side of the castle, from where a wooden waggonway to limestone quarries at Haw Bank, Embsay, was completed in 1797. Iron rails were substituted after 1808, while in 1846 a steam winding engine replaced horse haulage. The waggonway was converted to locomotive working in 1892, surviving in this form until about 1947.

CHAPTER III

The Aire and Calder Watershed

FIRST LINES TO BRADFORD

When contrasting the West Yorkshire railway network of today with that of sixty years ago the most noticeable difference is to be found on the dissected plateau between the Aire and Calder valleys. Out of seventy route miles (113km) of line which once criss-crossed this upland area less than a third are now in regular use. This was a region of suburban lines, and in their heyday it would have been hard to find another example of so concentrated a network over such rugged terrain with few stretches of track being either straight or level. These railways were built to serve the many separate urban communities lying within the area bounded by Leeds, Wakefield, Halifax and Keighley, but in spite of high population density there was no single town large enough to support a system of commuter lines in the motoring age.

At first sight a watershed is an extraordinary place to find intensive settlement, and hence a suburban railway system. Modern growth dates from 1774 when completion of the Bradford Canal opened up the mineral field to the south of the 'broad ford'. Wooden waggonways were laid down about 1780 to convey coal from pits at Wibsey, Little Horton and on the Royds Hall estate to Collier Gate, Bradford, where some was sold for domestic use but the majority sent out from the nearby canal basin. This form of working was soon overshadowed by technological developments which enabled high-quality iron to be produced from adjoining seams of Better Bed coal and iron ore. An iron foundry was built at Birkenshaw in 1782, and large ironworks established at

75

Bowling in 1788 and Low Moor in 1791. Both works sported an extensive system of waggonways, that of Low Moor eventually totalling some 30 route miles (48km) and stretching as far south as Kirklees at the confluence of the rivers Colne and Calder.

Establishment of ironworks to the south of Bradford coincided with migration of the worsted industry to the area. Bradford rapidly became a one-trade city, 'capital of the wool world' and a centre of the dyeing industry. A population explosion took place, so that in no decade between 1811 and 1851 did the rate of growth fall below 50 per cent. The town was described as 'one of the most striking phenomena in the history of the British Empire', even though by 1841 it was one of the few large centres in the country without a railway. It was costing more to bring wool from Leeds to Bradford than to transport it over the combined 58 mile (92km) length of the Leeds & Selby and Hull & Selby railways. The *Bradford Observer* protested in 1843: '. . . as long as there is no railway communication between this town and Manchester so long will the Leeds stuff merchants have the advantage over those of Bradford.'

The difficulties in promoting a line to Leeds have been described in the previous chapter. It was not until 1840 that Bradford was brought within $6\frac{1}{2}$ miles of a railway when the opening of the Manchester & Leeds line between Hebden Bridge and Normanton enabled coaches to connect with trains at Brighouse. They took an hour to rattle over the hilly road, but 40,000 passengers per annum were being conveyed this way by 1844. Hopes that something better might soon be provided were dispelled early in the same year when the M & L stated that it had no intention of extending its North Dean to Halifax branch as far as the wool capital. As a result the newly-formed Leeds & Bradford Railway undertook to make this link. In retaliation the M & L applied for powers to construct a line through the Spen Valley from Mirfield dropping into Bradford on ropeworked inclines as steep as 1 in 25 because tunnels were considered 'difficult and dangerous'. This proposal was successfully opposed by the L & B and the Leeds, Dewsbury & Manchester Railway.

In obtaining its Act of incorporation the L & B had overcome opposition only by promising to build a number of extension lines. To fulfil this promise it formed the West Yorkshire Railway with the intention of constructing lines from a junction with the L & B in Bradford to Sowerby Bridge via Halifax; Low Moor to Mirfield and Dewsbury; and from Low Moor to junctions with the L & B and LD & M at Wortley. The M & L, conscious of being edged out of Bradford in the same way it had already been nudged out of Leeds, promoted a separate scheme, the Leeds & West Riding Junction Railways, and was joined by the original 'short line' supporters who were aggrieved at the success of the L & B. The lines envisaged in this scheme closely paralleled those of the rival project, although atmospheric working of the inclines on either side of the summit was proposed. There was some acrimonious competition, hirelings being sent from all over the country to ensure that an 8,000-strong open-air meeting at Bradford came out in favour of the L & WRJ. But Robert Stephenson rightly prophesied that two similar Bills would stand little chance of success, and the parliamentary session of 1845 ended with both lines having been thrown out. The next move in November 1845 was for the M & L to propose amalgamation to the L & B in order to gain a through route to Leeds via Bradford; it was perhaps slightly surprised when George Hudson appeared to agree. In view of the apparent fusion of the parent companies, the West Yorkshire Railway and the L & WRJ heeded Stephenson's advice and pooled to form the West Riding Union Railways. The WRU was to have its own station at Bradford and the L & B was to build a cross-town link with its own system.

A dramatic development occurred in July 1846, when the L & B withdrew from the proposed amalgamation, accusing the M & L of altering clauses in the agreement. It immediately offered itself to the Midland Railway. Hudson, the chairman of both companies, not only took the chair at the meeting at which the lease was sanctioned but himself proposed that a then high rate of ten per cent interest should be guaranteed to the L & B. This rash action has been seen as the first step in the 'railway king's' downward path to ruin. The L & B had been opened to a terminus at Bradford

(Market Street) in July, but owing to the changed circumstances the link with the WRU was abandoned. The
squabble between the L & B and M & L had profound con-
sequences for Bradford, leaving a permanent legacy of
separate termini only 300yd (273m) apart, preventing the
town from being placed on a through railway route and helping to make Bradford something of a poor neighbour of
Leeds.

The WRU was incorporated in August 1846 at the second
attempt and under a clause in the Act was formally amalgamated with the M & L on 17 November. This compulsory
merger did not find much favour in Yorkshire where the
Manchester company was subjected to constant criticism. Part
of the antagonism was caused by county rivalry and a feeling
that cotton men could have little understanding of the West
Riding's wool interests, but there was also considerable truth
in allegations about the shocking services of the M & L. In
April 1848 its successor, the L & Y, had to apply to the Board
of Trade for a two year extension of time to construct the
WRU lines, a development which increased regret in Yorkshire that these had not been kept out of Lancashire hands.
The coach journey to Bradford from the south was shortened
when the section from Mirfield up the Spen Valley to Low
Moor was opened in 1848, but completion of the line north
of this point was delayed by difficulties in constructing the
1,648yd (1·49km) Bowling tunnel under the watershed. By
January 1849 only 300yd (273m) was finished but the sinking
of fifteen vertical shafts and use of six steam winding engines
enabled the entire work to be completed a year later. The
three mile extension to Bradford was opened in May 1850,
the *Bradford Observer* remarking of the town's second terminus: 'It is somewhat low and has a deficiency of glass.'
Another contemporary account referred to 'a platform
covered by a shed 120yds long and 63ft span'. It was
approached by a 133yd (121m) tunnel under Wakefield Road,
and the two mile (3·2km) climb out of the terminus was
mostly at 1 in 50. Passenger traffic into the station increased
from August 1850 with the opening of the Halifax to Low
Moor line, which put the wool capital in more direct contact
with Manchester.

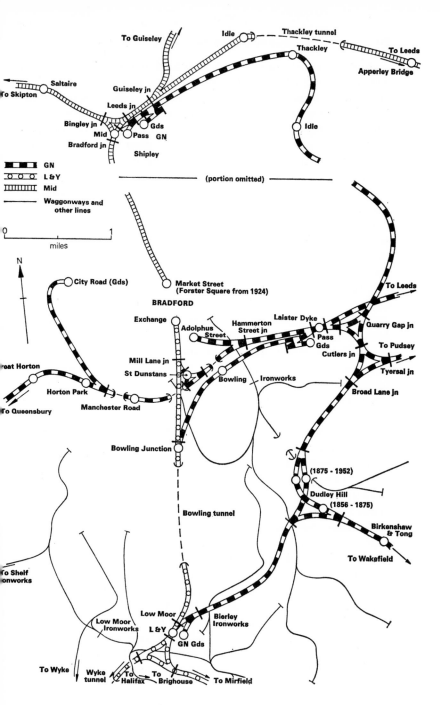

Map 2: Bradford

The arrival of railways in Bradford from both north and south boosted the town's expansion to still greater heights. It became a borough in 1847, adopting the official motto 'Work Conquers All', and the unofficial 'Where there's muck there's money'. The extension of boundaries took the population up to 103,778 in 1851, by which date half the worsted workers in England were resident in the immediate area and the town was responsible for 75 per cent of the West Riding's worsted merchandising compared with only 30 per cent in 1830.

One of the few retarding influences in an era of expansion was the L & Y, and in particular its announcement in 1850 that it would be unable to finance any further WRU lines. As outlined in chapter one, this snub to local pride eventually resulted in the incorporation in 1852 of the Leeds, Bradford & Halifax Junction Railway. A further Act of 1853 authorised the line to be worked by the GN and provided for the construction of a Bradford branch from the main line to Adolphus Street, away from the town centre but allowing an approach no steeper than 1 in 100. The branch was opened to a temporary terminus in 1854 at the same time as the main line which extended from Wortley to a connection with the L & Y at Bowling junction. A reporter of the *Leeds Mercury* noted: 'From the heights of Bowling, with its dingy unattractive aspect, the traveller looks down upon Bradford, with its canopy of smoke and its equally unattractive appearance.' The 455yd (414m) Hillfoot tunnel was the principal structural work on the main line, for west of Laister Dyke (later spelt as one word) heavy tunnelling to enter the Bradford basin was made unnecessary by 'engineering work' carried out during the Ice Age. The overflow channel of a glacial lake held back by the Airedale ice formed a deep cutting conveniently wide enough for two sets of rails.

Work on constructing Adolphus Street was delayed by the collapse of its 100ft (30m) wide Mansard-shaped roof in November 1854, and the station was not completed until the following 1 June. Only five months later several directors urged that some trains should run to the L & Y station, for the steep climb up to the existing terminus was making many passengers go to Leeds by the rival Midland line. The

LB & HJ had in fact captured only thirty per cent of the traffic between the two towns, despite its route being four miles (6·4km) shorter. The *Leeds Mercury* described Adolphus Street as 'a lofty, commodious structure, which though not over handsome, is well adapted for accommodating a large passenger traffic in every instance but one—it was built in the wrong place'. A Bill for a link line down to the L & Y terminus was rejected by the Lords in 1859, and an arrangement was then made with the Midland for a percentage division of Leeds–Bradford traffic. As a result, fares were increased and services reduced from 1 November 1859. The link line was finally sanctioned in 1864 and, although only $\frac{3}{4}$ mile (1·2km) long, took $2\frac{1}{2}$ years to build as it ran through almost continuous cutting up to 60ft (18·3m) deep. Most of the material excavated was fireclay and kept sixty men employed for fifteen years making drain pipes, chimney pots and bricks. The line descended on a gradient of 1 in 49 and was opened in 1867, two years after the LB & HJ had been absorbed by the GN. At the same time enlargements and improvements were completed at the L & Y terminus, which became known as Bradford Exchange but still remained pitifully inadequate. A decade later conditions had become so bad that major rebuilding was put in hand, the original four passenger roads being replaced by ten platforms under a distinctive double-arched roof with impressive fan-like glazing. The scheme, which also involved widening from Mill Lane junction to the terminus plus the opening out of the tunnel under Wakefield Road, was completed in 1888.

Most of the Leeds–Halifax trains were initially worked by the L & Y, although the GN handled those services conveying through carriages from King's Cross. Virtually all GN trains were diverted via Queensbury when this route was opened in 1879, and a further alteration occurred in 1882 when the GN began to enter Halifax via the Calder Valley. Prior to this date non-stop trains were run from Laister Dyke to Halifax in connection with London to Bradford expresses. Trains proceeding beyond Halifax to Manchester, Liverpool or the Lancashire coast were worked by the L & Y from Leeds and normally took on a Bradford portion at Low Moor.

This station grew into an important 'country' junction, well satirised by Ahrons, although it gradually became the practice for the faster trains to combine at Halifax and avoid the Low Moor stop. On the freight side, a specialised traffic was that to St James' wholesale produce market adjoining Adolphus Street. Block trains brought vegetables direct from Lincolnshire and Cambridgeshire growing centres and new potatoes from the Channel Islands through Hull. The GC worked goods traffic into the station under an 1892 agreement with the GN; the North Eastern also had running powers from Leeds but never exercised them.

On the Midland approach to Bradford, the original Market Street terminus was replaced by a new six-platform structure in 1890. Between Bradford and Shipley, railway surroundings remained pleasantly rural until the 1860s when Manningham began to be developed as a suburb, a station being opened in 1868. The new Manningham Mills, built in the 1870s to form Europe's largest silk mill, caused the former suburb to grow into what was virtually a self-contained town, its population increasing from 19,683 in 1871 to 37,304 in 1881. Manningham station's busiest period was at Whitsuntide when the Great West Riding Gala was held in nearby Peel Park, special trains arriving from a wide area until the gala was discontinued in 1936.

The Bradford area was badly hit by the McKinley tariff imposed on imports by the USA in 1890, and followed in the same decade by the Wilson and Dingley tariffs. Between 1891 and 1900 exports from the Bradford Consular District slumped from £4,100,000 to £1,600,000, while the population of Bradford has remained fairly static at just under 300,000 since the turn of the century. The suburban service between Leeds and Bradford, which was the most intensive in the West Riding, was badly hit by these trends. A further blow in 1909 was the introduction of through tramcars running between the two cities by using sliding wheels on splined axles to cope with the gauge difference. Standard ten coach train formations came down to five or six coaches, but the GN hit back by putting on a seventeen minute service, stopping only at Stanningley. Two decades later motor car competition caused electrification to be seriously considered, and on 14 June 1954 the line pioneered the use of DMUs in the North. On 1 January 1962 DMUs took over the Leeds–Manchester workings, reversing at Bradford Exchange and thus causing Low Moor to lose its status as a key country junction. It was closed in 1965, and the direct line between Laisterdyke and Bowling Junction ceased to carry passenger traffic in 1969.

A hopeful sign was the opening in March 1967 of New Pudsey, a 'park and ride' station sited to allow motorists to join long-distance trains without having to drive into Leeds or Bradford. Most expresses to King's Cross and the Manchester DMUs stop at the station, but no longer is it served by a through Harrogate–Leeds–Bradford–Liverpool service which was withdrawn in September 1967. The concentration of all Leeds–Bradford services on the former GN route the previous May greatly affected Forster Square (as the ex-Midland terminus had been known since 1924), which became primarily a parcels depot retaining just two passenger platforms for the Keighley and Ilkley local services. By this time Exchange was showing its age, and plans for a substitute four-platform station at a £7 million transport interchange 200yd (182m) to the south were announced in 1969. The original terminus was finally closed in 1973, when the new Exchange was partially opened, its facilities being likened to 'a football club changing room' at peak hours.

LINKS WITH WAKEFIELD

From 1850 passengers from Bradford could reach Wakefield by means of the L & Y Spen Valley branch, but this usually involved an inordinately long wait at Mirfield. The first stage of a more direct link started inauspiciously as the LB & HJ's Gildersome coal branch, promoted to supply fuel from this area to Bradford and Halifax and authorised in 1853. Just prior to the passing of the Act a meeting was held in Bradford to discuss a proposed connection from the branch to the projected Bradford, Wakefield & Leeds Railway, described in chapter one. It was pointed out that if the LB & HJ did not make a link the new company would almost certainly do so; as a result the Gildersome extension was authorised at the same time as the incorporation of the BW & L.

The national financial crisis of early 1855 nearly caused the abandonment of both the branch and the extension, a possibility heightened when the contractor had a disagreement with the company and relinquished his undertaking. But the situation gradually improved, and the branch was opened to passenger and mineral traffic in 1856. It was soon conveying about 1,000 tons of coal to Bradford per day. Work on constructing the extension was slowed down as there was little point in opening it before completion of the BW & L, which had been delayed by earth slips at Middleton Wood and Wrenthorpe. The extension was ready for traffic in August 1857, but it was 3 October before the BW & L was sufficiently complete to enable formal opening of both lines to take place. GN and L & Y local services began to work over the BW & L two days later, and the extension line was publicly opened on 10 October. GN expresses were diverted on to the BW & L on 1 November, and the first through workings from King's Cross to Bradford via Gildersome introduced on 1 December. By the following year the LB & HJ directors were dissatisfied with the GN handling of the line's coal traffic, and it was agreed that from 1 January 1859 the LB & HJ would itself operate the local passenger and mineral workings between Ardsley, Gildersome and Bradford. The company hastily acquired three tank engines from Kitsons, the working arrangement lasting until June 1863. There was a similar dispute over coal traffic between the BW & L and the GN which again resulted in a lightning purchase of engine power. As noted in chapter one, the BW & L was renamed the West Yorkshire Railway in 1863 and absorbed by the GN two years later. An interesting through passenger service provided over the route until the GN started to run along the Calder Valley was one between Wakefield and Halifax, stopping only at Ardsley, Laister Dyke and Bowling. Additional traffic came to the line under the GN/MS & L exchange of running powers agreement of 1892, the MS & L beginning to operate goods trains through to Adolphus Street from Wakefield.

The Gildersome branch curved through almost 180 degrees after leaving Laister Dyke in order to climb to a summit of nearly 700ft (213m) above sea level close to Dudley Hill, where the later station of 1875 had a remarkable hexagonal wooden booking hall topped by a louvred lantern and a weather vane! The extension continued along the crest of the watershed, the most important station being at Morley, a town producing distinctive mungo cloth with cotton warp and woollen weft and famed as a place which could 'mek wool from nowt'. Here the platforms stood directly over the tracks of the former LD & M running through their long tunnel 200ft (61m) below. The extension joined the BW & L at Ardsley, which during the second half of the nineteenth century developed into a junction in many ways similar to Low Moor but with more stress on the transfer of freight than passengers. East Ardsley Ironworks was erected in the 1860s and survived until 1929, the North Eastern obtaining running powers to the works over the Methley Joint in return for not opposing the GN absorption of the LB & HJ and the BW & L.

Tramcars caused a decline in receipts on both the Leeds–Wakefield and Bradford–Wakefield lines, and a further set-back occurred when Britain's first trolleybuses started operating between Laister Dyke and Dudley Hill in 1911. A fundamental change of more recent years took place on 25 February 1957 when local services between Bradford and Wakefield via Gildersome were withdrawn. The line was closed to all passenger traffic between Laister Dyke and Ardsley in 1966, after which freight services were gradually withdrawn until the route was whittled down to a short stub from Laister Dyke to Dudley Hill.

BATLEY

Since the mid-1960s synthetic fibres have caused a decline in the traditional industry of Batley, the making of shoddy by combing out reclaimed cloth. In the nineteenth century it was a staple trade which brought international fame to this town at the southern edge of the Aire and Calder watershed.

Batley was made a borough in 1868, and in the 1870s enjoyed a prodigious boom by supplying cheap uniform cloths to both sides in the Franco-Prussian war.

The opening of the Leeds, Dewsbury & Manchester Railway in 1848 gave the town its first station, this line's 1845 Act of incorporation also providing for a branch from Batley to Birstal. It was opened in 1852, and thus brought the L & NW within six miles of the centre of Bradford. In 1859 the company attempted to reach the woolopolis by putting forward a Bill for a link from Batley to the LB & HJ's Ardsley line at Drighlington & Adwalton, but this was rejected in favour of running powers over the L & Y Spen Valley route. The next move was for the L & NW to support an extension of the Birstal branch to Bradford, a Bill for this purpose being put forward in 1861 as the nominally independent Dewsbury, Batley, Gomersal & Bradford Railway. It was thrown out, but an LB & HJ branch from Adwalton junction to Batley successfully received the royal assent. It followed approximately the same course as the L & NW 1859 proposal and was authorised to approach Batley by using part of the Birstal branch.

By this time a project for a line from Wakefield to Batley via Ossett was well advanced. This scheme dated back to 1846 when the Wakefield, Ossett & Dewsbury Direct & Atmospheric Railway was promoted, the projectors being 'extremely anxious that the Atmospheric Principle of traction should be introduced into this district on account of the great engineering difficulties of Rocks and Hills presented to the formation of steam railways'. The scheme was unsuccessful, as was a branch from Dewsbury to Ossett put forward by the LD & M the following year. In 1859 the L & NW and the L & Y promoted lines from Thornhill through Dewsbury and Ossett to a junction with the BW & L, but both Bills were thrown out. A BW & L branch from Wrenthorpe, $\frac{1}{2}$ mile (0·8km) north of Wakefield, to Ossett met the same fate, but gained its Act the following year. An extension to Batley was authorised in 1861, the original intention being to have a joint L & NW/LB & HJ/BW & L station at this point. These arrangements were modified in 1862, the right of the LB & HJ to run over the Birstal branch being repealed

Page 87 Large stations: (*above*) a period study of Huddersfield, its 416ft long façade and classical styling forming the only railway architecture of any real merit in the whole of the region; (*below*) a 1963 interior view of the Great Northern's first Bradford terminus at Adolphus Street, closed to passengers in 1867 when services were transferred to Exchange and to freight in 1972

Page 88 Small stations: (*above*) the unique Queensbury, with the lines from Halifax to Keighley on the left and Bradford on the right. The Bradford–Keighley platforms are tiered out from the viaduct in the background, and the triangle is pierced by a colliery waggonway; (*below*) Pudsey Greenside, rich in ornamental ironwork and, as indicated by the buildings at an angle to the platform, originally a terminus

and provision made for a joint LB & HJ/BW & L station separate from the L & NW.

The BW & L Wrenthorpe junction–Batley line was constructed as a single-track branch but with earthworks sufficient for two lines of rails. It was opened in stages from 1862, finally reaching Batley in December 1864. The LB & HJ line from Drighlington & Adwalton was similarly brought into use piecemeal, but got to Batley a month earlier. Railway facilities encouraged manufacturers to build homes in Upper Batley, which became a 'room at the top' suburb with luxurious mansions occupied by the new rich. The station here stood on the notorious 400ft (122m) climb which northbound trains had to surmount in $2\frac{1}{4}$ miles (3·6km) on a continuous gradient of 1 in 43.

All these lines became part of the GN in 1865. The L & NW failed to gain its own route into Bradford and the Birstal (Birstall from 1907) branch was relegated to a single-line backwater. Another line into Batley was downgraded with the completion in 1880 of the GN Dewsbury loop, described in the next chapter. As part of this project the former BW & L branch was doubled from Wrenthorpe junction to Runtlings Lane junction, the east end of the loop, but the remainder was left as a single track line used mainly by coal trains from Shaw Cross to Pildacre collieries. All passenger workings were diverted to the Dewsbury loop except for a few trains still following the old route and a sparse service provided by the 'Chickenley Coddy', a GN rail-motor operating between Ossett and Chickenley Heath.

The GN decided to compete with the L & NW for traffic between the heavy woollen district and Leeds, and in 1881 obtained sanction for an interesting line which was in two sections. The first climbed from Batley at 1 in 50 through the curving 659yd (589m) Soothill tunnel, a nightmare to drivers in wet weather, and up to Woodkirk where standard gauge mineral lines with gradients as steep as 1 in 33 served stone quarries on the southern edge of Morley. It joined the Laister Dyke–Ardsley line at Tingley, from where the second section curved over the Leeds–Wakefield line by an imposing viaduct and then descended to connect with it at Beeston junction. The line was opened throughout in 1890.

F

A circular service was introduced on 1 November 1890 by extending the existing Leeds Central–Wrenthorpe junction–Dewsbury–Batley trains to return north over the new line, a routing which did not disappear from the timetables until October 1938. L & Y trains running over the Batley–Beeston section included a service from Barnsley to Leeds Central via Dewsbury, introduced in July 1903, while there were several GN workings from Wakefield to Leeds through Dewsbury and Tingley. The northern part of the line was used to compete with the L & NW for Morley–Leeds traffic, a service running from Bradford to Leeds via Morley and Tingley until World War II. The GN undercut the L & NW Dewsbury–Batley–Leeds fares, but had problems in attracting passengers from Morley. In 1896 the Morley Chamber of Commerce complained that it was 'quite ashamed' of the GN station, and pointed out that the company was not getting the benefit of its new route to Leeds 'due to wretched accommodation'.

An early casualty was the Ossett–Chickenley Heath rail-motor service which ceased in July 1909, less than a year after the inception of a parallel tram route with a fifteen minute interval service. Passenger trains were withdrawn from the Birstall branch in 1917, their numbers having previously been reduced on the opening in 1900 of the Leeds New Line with its station at Upper Birstal(l). The line between Batley and Beeston junction was closed to passenger traffic in 1951, through freight services being withdrawn two years later owing to the condition of Soothill tunnel. Services on the Bradford–Batley–Dewsbury–Wakefield route were taken over by DMUs on 25 February 1957, some of these workings being extended to Goole and Hull on 3 March 1958. Passenger trains over this line were withdrawn in 1964, complete closure taking place the following year between Drighlington & Adwalton and Wrenthorpe junction.

THE QUEENSBURY LINES

The Aire and Calder watershed east of the point where it is almost bifurcated by the Spen Valley and Bradford Dale is difficult enough territory for railways. West of this division the ridge quickly rises to over 1,000ft (305m) and broadens into a plateau broken by steep-sided valleys; it would seem to be an area to deter all but the most over-optimistic of engineers and yet paradoxically has had a long history of railway promotion. 'Bubble' schemes of the Railway Mania were followed by attempts to shorten the Aire Valley route between Bradford and Colne, towns with much closer trading ties than today. The East Lancashire Railway's Colne & Bradford Bill was withdrawn in the Commons in 1857, while the Bradford & Colne Railway was unsuccessful in the Parliamentary session of 1866. Several other schemes were promoted in the 1860s, many of them as an indirect result of the American Civil War which caused a sudden expansion in the wool trade as cotton prices soared. The Halifax, Huddersfield & Keighley Railway was rejected in 1864, and a branch to Thornton was included in a scheme for new railways in the Bradford area put forward in 1865. The Bill was withdrawn, but the Bradford & Thornton Railways were incorporated in 1871 and amalgamated with the GN the following year. The original Act provided for a line commencing by a triangular connection with the GN link between Hammerton Street and Mill Lane junctions, where an exchange station known as St Dunstan's was later opened. A branch was to leave the main line at Horton Park so as to serve the prosperous industrial district centred on Thornton Road.

One of the main objects of the B & T was to provide railway facilities for Queensbury, a town famous for its Black Dyke Mills and its altitude of no less than 1,150ft above sea level. It forms a classic example of upland coal supplies enabling a traditional weaving industry to resist the shift down to the valleys engendered by the Industrial Revolution. At this time moves were again being made for a rail link between Huddersfield, Halifax and Keighley. The Midland offered support but withdrew at the last moment, and the promoters therefore approached the GN. This company stated it was not interested in a line from Halifax to Huddersfield, but gave a pledge to extend the Halifax & Ovenden Junction Railway so as to join the B & T at Queensbury and then continue the lines to Keighley as one route.

The GN (Halifax, Thornton & Keighley Railway) Act was sanctioned in 1873.

The Queensbury lines were badly hit by the so-called 'great depression' which marked the end of a national boom in the mid-1870s and reached one of its lowest points in 1879. The B & T/GN amalgamation Act had optimistically stated that the GN 'will begin construction of works forthwith with a view to opening the line before August 1st, 1874', but it was not until February of that year that tenders for the line were accepted together with those for the Holmfield–Queensbury link. Contractors for both sections, and later the extension line to Keighley, were Messrs Benton & Woodiwiss. They were well qualified to build railways through difficult country as for four years they had been battling against the elements to construct the highest part of the Settle & Carlisle line. They started boring the 1 mile 741yd (2·28km) Queensbury tunnel on 21 May 1874 but it was 31 July 1878 before the work was finished; this was the longest tunnel on the GN until the opening of that at Ponsbourne near Hertford in 1910. Four streets of temporary houses were built in Queensbury for the navvies and, without over-stretching the imagination, were named Oakley, Great, Northern and Railway streets. Although 'temporary' the buildings were not condemned until 1957; at a public enquiry it was stated that the term Navvy Houses used in the clearance order was an attempt to belittle the objectors and their correct name was Great Northern Railway Cottages! Another major undertaking was the 1,057yd (963m) Clayton tunnel.

It was not until 1878 that the Bradford–Thornton line was opened to passengers, and even then celebrations were tempered by the depression. The GN was moved to suggest joint ownership of the Holmfield–Keighley section to the Midland, but its offer was declined. Between Queensbury and Holmfield the 1,033yd (940m) long and 59ft (18·2m) deep Strines cutting caused even greater difficulties with water-bearing strata than had the tunnel, and held up opening of this section until 1 December 1879.

A proposal to save costs by running into the Midland station at Keighley with passenger trains and making a separate terminus for goods only was approved by Parlia-

ment in 1880. By an agreement of 1 June 1881 the Midland
was to build a new station for the two companies and allow
the GN to enter it over part of the ex-Keighley & Worth
Valley Railway which would be widened. In return the
Midland received traffic concessions between Keighley and
Halifax. Work on the Thornton to Keighley section started
early in 1881, but severe earth slips in Doe Park cutting at
Denholme held up construction until inverted arches with
very strong side walls finally overcame the problem. The
line was opened in stages in 1884.

In penetrating unusually difficult country the Queensbury
lines provided perhaps the most spectacularly engineered
railways in the industrial West Riding. On the Bradford to
Holmfield section close on half the mileage was in tunnel,
the line being christened 'the Alpine route' by GN drivers
because of its gradients. A unique feature was Queensbury
station. At first it consisted of nothing more than bare
exchange platforms which were opened in 1879, the sole
approach from the town being a descent of 400ft (122m) by
'wretched footpaths with only one solitary lamp'. An inclined
tramway linking town and station was considered in October
1878 and again in 1887, when a two mile (3·2km) branch
with a 1 in 30 gradient and curves of ten chains (200m)
radius was also proposed. Eventually the GN provided a
road at a cost of over £3,000 and opened a vastly improved
station in 1890. Apart from Ambergate, it was the only
station in Britain with continuous platforms on three sides
of a triangular junction. The six platforms each had their
own buildings and were connected in three different ways:
by footbridge at the Bradford end; sleeper crossing at the
Keighley side; and a cave-like subway at the Halifax end.
Lack of level ground forced the station to be sited at a valley
head with the Bradford–Keighley platforms on a three-arch
viaduct and part of the layout filled in with rubble and
stone. Originally there was a signal box at each corner of
the triangle. Passing under the lines was an inclined waggonway conveying coal from pits near the station to the outskirts
of Queensbury. Features of the line to Keighley were massive
viaducts at Thornton, Hewenden and Cullingworth. Denholme station, 850ft (263m) above sea level and serving

another high-lying woollen township, preceded a descent averaging 1 in 50 for five miles (8km). There was no let-up for Bradford-bound trains through the unusually difficult Lees Moor tunnel turning through more than a right angle in its 1,533yd (1·39km).

Close on £1 million was spent on building the Queensbury lines, and it is doubtful if the expenditure was ever really justified. Advantages of the Bradford–Halifax section were to a considerable extent nullified by the 1882 GN/L & Y agreement, while the Bradford–Keighley route was too steeply graded to compete with the Midland's low-lying line along the Aire Valley. At first the GN provided the fastest service from Keighley to London in 4h 55m by a Keighley–Bradford train, stopping only at St Dunstan's to connect with a King's Cross express. A service from Halifax avoided St Dunstan's by using the Leeds curve to connect with London trains at Laister Dyke. After a brief heyday the routes settled down to concentrate on purely local traffic, and even this diminished when trams started running from both Bradford and Halifax to Queensbury in 1901. Buses caused a further reduction in traffic in the late 1920s and Sunday trains were withdrawn in December 1938, but by 1946 the service was still surprisingly lavish with one through coach working to King's Cross, running from Halifax to Bradford in 22 minutes. It was only after a survey showed the line was losing £48,000 a year that regular passenger trains were withdrawn in 1955. All lines west of Great Horton were completely closed by 1965, and those east of this point followed suit in 1972. Queensbury and Lees Moor tunnels were abandoned in 1956 owing to their poor state of repair, but both were subsequently put to unexpected uses. In January 1958 highly secretive tests, believed to have been on the effects of fumes from DMUs, were carried out in Lees Moor. At Queensbury, scientists from Cambridge University's Department of Geophysics had by 1969 adopted the tunnel for undertaking investigations into movements of the Earth's crust.

LATER DEVELOPMENTS

During the second half of the nineteenth century many

former textile villages, sited above the smoke of the valley towns, expanded into dormitory suburbs. The GN met and accentuated this development by building a number of short suburban lines, none of which was in the long term really successful. They were constructed in two phases: during the flush of national prosperity of the early 1870s, and in the brief respite in the 'great depression' a decade later. All of them took an inordinately long time to complete owing to the period's financial instability.

The first of the lines was promoted by two independent concerns, the Bradford, Eccleshill & Idle Railway incorporated in 1866 and the Idle & Shipley Railway of 1867. In both cases the GN agreed to subscribe most of the capital, but as even the balance could not be raised locally it took over the two companies in 1871 and opened the line to passengers in 1875. The route climbed gradually from a triangular junction with the Ardsley line near Laister Dyke and then descended at 1 in 60 into the Aire Valley from Thackley to Shipley. A number of spectacular runaways took place on this stretch, more than one locomotive hurtling through the bufferstops and on to the road at the Shipley terminus, which was built after negotiations for use of the Midland station had broken down. Although constructed as a suburban line, the branch also carried a heavy freight traffic. Limestone from Ingleton and Skipton bound for Bowling and Low Moor ironworks came this way, while until the turn of the century world-famous Idle Moor stone was dispatched to widely-scattered destinations.

Another end-product of the prosperous early 1870s was a GN branch from Stanningley to Pudsey Greenside, authorised in 1871. Deputations from Pudsey had been protesting since 1856 to the LB & HJ and later the GN about having to walk a mile to Stanningley station, a situation brought about by the 'short line' avoiding the town for reasons of engineering convenience. By the 1870s Pudsey, with a population of almost 15,000 and a thriving centre for woollen manufacture, stone quarrying and coal working, could no longer be ignored. The branch was opened to passengers in 1878.

The single line was built with earthworks for double track which were utilised in an interesting project of the 1880s.

Several proposals had already been made for better links between the GN lines in this area and the Spen Valley. The L & Y promoted a Low Moor–Pudsey connection in 1871, freely admitting it had made a mistake in not extending to Leeds when the opportunity arose, but the Bill was withdrawn. Earlier unsuccessful Bills were for a Gildersome–Low Moor link in 1866 and a BW & L branch to Low Moor in 1863. Success came as a result of the 1882 GN/L & Y agreement, more fully described in chapter four, which provided for better connections of this nature. These materialised in the form of a direct curve from Bramley to the Pudsey branch, an extension from Pudsey Greenside to a double junction with the Ardsley line north of Dudley Hill, and a link from Dudley Hill to Low Moor, thus placing Pudsey on both a direct line to the Spen Valley and a Leeds–Bradford loop.

Lack of capital again delayed construction. The Pudsey loop line became operative in November 1893 with the opening of the curve at Bramley and the extension to Cutlers junction through the 616yd (560m) Greenside tunnel and across what was claimed to be the highest embankment in the country. The connection at the Pudsey end of the original branch from Stanningley was taken out and the curve made into a siding. Opening through to Low Moor took place on 1 December when an unusual circular service was introduced. From Leeds Central trains ran through Pudsey, Low Moor, the L & Y Spen Valley stations, Thornhill and over the Headfield junction spur to Dewsbury Central and Batley. From here the starting point was regained by means of the line to Beeston junction via Tingley. The service started with six trains in one direction and seven in the other, the GN working nine of them and the L & Y the other four. They took up to 1½ hours to cover the 30 miles (48km) and ceased to provide the fastest times between Leeds and the Spen Valley when the L & NW Leeds 'New Line' was opened in 1900.

At this time a grandiose attempt was being made to transform the rail facilities of Bradford. After the L & B had abandoned its junction line with the WRU in 1846, there were several unsuccessful bids to complete this important cross-town link. In 1865 the L & Y put forward a Bill to unite the railways in Bradford at a cost of £260,000 which was to be shared with the GN, Midland and LB & HJ, but these companies withdrew and the scheme lapsed. The Bradford Central Railway of 1884, which envisaged a new central station, was also abortive. Then in 1898 the Midland obtained its West Riding Lines Act with an authorised capital of £2,100,000. A new main line was to run from Royston to Thornhill and then up the Spen Valley before plunging under the watershed in a tunnel over two miles (3·2km) long to join the Bradford–Shipley line just north of Market Street. A second Act of 1899 authorised the company to build junction lines at Low Moor in order to serve Halifax by means of running powers over the L & Y.

Extensions of time for the West Riding Lines were authorised in 1901, 1904 and 1907, but as noted in the next chapter the only section constructed was that from Royston to Thornhill. Running powers north of this point through the Spen Valley opened up the Midland's new approach to Bradford, eleven miles shorter than that via Leeds, while the wool city was in a sense placed on an Anglo-Scottish route in 1908 when certain up expresses began slipping Bradford portions at Saltaire. These events did not put an end to a more competitive line to the North, despite the pact of friendship made in 1909 between the Midland, L & Y and L & NW. The Low Moor junction lines were abandoned in 1910 and the unbuilt West Riding Lines in 1911, but in the same year sanction was obtained for the Bradford Through Lines running from Low Moor to Manningham and crossing Forster Square on a viaduct. Their cost, including a new high level station, was estimated at over £800,000, but Bradford Corporation agreed to deduct £8,000 per annum from the Midland rates for twenty years. Construction was postponed on the outbreak of war in 1914, and the categorical assurance of the Midland in 1918 that the line would be built was never fulfilled. A few years before nationalisation the LMS and the LNER decided that a link across the town could not conceivably be justified, and thus Bradford became one of the few major inland cities in Britain without a through railway route.

Another casualty of war was the GN/L & Y circular service

which was withdrawn on 31 August 1914. The Dudley Hill to Low Moor line, which had carried relatively little traffic, was closed as a wartime economy measure in 1916 and largely lifted two years later. Passenger services on the Pudsey loop were taken over by DMUs at the same time as those on the 'short line', but were withdrawn in 1964. On the Laister Dyke–Shipley line all intermediate stations had a direct tram service to Bradford by 1910; closure to passengers took place in 1931. A replacement bus service was introduced between Laister Dyke and Idle, one of the earliest examples of a practice that was later to become commonplace. Complete closure of the line took place in 1968.

MAIN LINE SERVICES

Trains between Bradford and London have followed a variety of routes. Through coaches from Bradford Exchange joining Leeds–King's Cross expresses at Wakefield at first travelled via Gildersome, but from the opening of the Dewsbury loop were diverted through the heavy woollen district until the Midland accelerations of the 1880s forced the GN to be more competitive and revert to the original route. A fast service from Batley, Dewsbury and Ossett then connected at Wakefield with London trains. The dawn of the twentieth century saw the start of the trend to serve Bradford by through expresses reversing at Leeds Central. A through dining car service running up in 4hr 10min was introduced following pressure from Bradford businessmen, who had demanded restaurant facilities throughout the journey and not just from Wakefield. The fastest timings continued to be via Gildersome until the introduction on 27 September 1937 of the 'West Riding Limited' which drastically cut the journey time to London to 3hr 5min. On 11 September 1961 a major acceleration of services to the capital saw the 'West Riding' again routed via Leeds. The pre-war time was equalled from 1966 when the express, by this time unnamed, began taking the Wortley curve.

Midland trains to London from Market Street did not normally compete directly with those of the GN. An exception was the inauguration on 1 June 1874 of the first Pullman

service in Britain, offering luxury travel between Bradford
and St Pancras until 30 April 1876 when it was withdrawn
to enable the Pullman cars to be used on the new Settle &
Carlisle line. London services over the L & Y via Huddersfield and Penistone to King's Cross and Marylebone are
described in chapter five; the normal routing was by the
Pickle Bridge branch, although some trains served Halifax.
Another route to the capital was opened up by the Midland
from 1 July 1909 via the Spen Valley, Thornhill and Royston.
The 'Yorkshireman', introduced in March 1925, came this
way and following the LMS accelerations of 1937 reached
Bradford from London in 4hr 5min, stopping only at Sheffield. A flash in the pan was the first and only L & NW
sleeping car service to Yorkshire, introduced in January 1906
and travelling from Euston to Bradford via Huddersfield and
Halifax. It lasted only until June of the same year.

Some noteworthy cross-country services were also operated
from Bradford. Another use by the L & NW of its running
powers into the city (see next chapter) was to work specials
to the wool sales at Bristol. They covered the 221 miles
(353km) of the Shrewsbury and Severn Tunnel route in a
very creditable time of 5hr 2min, running in competition
with specials put on by the Midland. A second competitive
service to the south prior to 1914 was that to Bournemouth.
Through coaches over the L & Y/GC route via Huddersfield
and Sheffield Victoria, introduced in July 1902, reached the
resort in 7hr 54min, a time nineteen minutes slower than the
Midland's service which took a route $27\frac{3}{4}$ miles (44km) longer
over the Somerset & Dorset Joint. Post-Grouping summer
Saturday workings via Gildersome or Batley had as their
destinations such East Coast resorts as Cleethorpes, Skegness
and Yarmouth.

CHAPTER IV

The Calder Valley

The Calder Valley will figure prominently in any historical or geographical account of West Yorkshire, for it is of supreme importance in terms of both settlement and communications. At its western end it links up with the Walsden gorge, a glacial spillway across the watershed, and thus forms part of a trans-Pennine route which nowhere exceeds 600ft (183m) above sea level. This is the lowest crossing south of the Aire Gap; it thus became an important routeway from very early times for it formed the easiest, if not the most direct, line of communication from Manchester to Halifax, Bradford and Leeds. The number of travellers passing this way was increased by the fact that the many tributary streams rushing down the valley slopes were ideal for fulling cloth, and a textile industry was thriving by the seventeenth century. These factors meant the valley was an obvious choice for the first trans-Pennine waterway, created in 1804 with the opening throughout of the Rochdale Canal, which joined the earlier Calder & Hebble Navigation of 1770.

Collieries were developed around and below Wakefield from 1700, and up the valley close to the Navigation from 1775. They led to the creation of an extensive waggonway network, and indeed perhaps the earliest printed reference to a Yorkshire railway concerns this area. It appeared in the *York Courant* of 22 October 1745:

To Be Sold: On the Low End of Wakefield Out-Wood—The Bottom Coal, called Warren-House Coal, where a Waggon Way is made from the said Pitts, to Bottom Boat Staith, situate on the River Chalder, which Coal makes a large sweet Cinder, and are to be delivered by Robert and William Wood. P.S. A sufficient Number of Waggons is made to convey the said Coals and Cinders down to the said River.

This line, and some later wooden waggonways in the same area, were the precursors of the unusually interesting Lake Lock Rail Road, built under the Wakefield Inclosure Act of 1793 which provided for the construction of a railway that could be used by anyone possessing waggons with suitable wheels. It is therefore arguable that it was the first public railway in the world, pre-dating the Surrey Iron Railway which traditionally enjoys this honour. The line, built to a gauge of 3ft 4in (1·02m), was opened to Lofthouse Gate about 1796 and probably continued to East Ardsley in the following year. Its eastern terminus was originally some distance from the Calder, but had been extended to Lake Lock by 1800 and was moved to Bottom Boat in 1804. Traffic was primarily coal, although lime for the land and stone for road repairs was also conveyed. A 4ft 5in (1·35m) gauge tramroad running on an almost parallel course was opened by William Fenton in 1824, after an understandable dispute between the two lines which went as far as York Assizes. Both systems had largely been abandoned by 1840. On the opposite bank of the Navigation at Stanley a line extended for 1½ miles (2·4km) to St John's Colliery, Normanton, and provided the only instance of rail transport of the famous 'Tom Puddings', iron compartment boats which were normally coupled together in 'trains' and hauled by a barge. At Stanley they were hoisted out of the water on to specially built twelve-wheel double bogie trucks for the return journey to the colliery, the system being in use from 1891 until the autumn of 1949.

Another instance of duplication of lines occurred between Wakefield Bridge and New Park collieries, near Alverthorpe, both William Fenton and Robert Smithson opening parallel routes in 1800. Fenton, an eccentric who died in 1837, reputedly worth £1½ million, used bullocks as motive power. Probably the first line to take advantage of the Calder & Hebble Navigation was a wooden waggonway extending from Flockton to Horbury Bridge. It was brought into use between

1772 and 1775, its 300ft (91m) long Dial Wood tunnel being among the earliest in England.

THE MANCHESTER & LEEDS RAILWAY

It was the Rochdale Canal proprietors who successfully opposed the second attempt to build a railway from Manchester to Leeds. The first, in 1824, has already been mentioned in chapter one. This was followed by a scheme, surveyed in 1830 by George Stephenson and James Walker, to follow the Calder Valley as far as Brighouse and then turn north through Low Moor to link up near Pudsey with the concurrently proposed direct line from Bradford to Leeds. It lapsed the following year when the canal interests twice caused a Bill for the portion from Manchester to Sowerby Bridge to be thrown out. Other schemes followed, such as that of 1831 which proposed a Leeds to Liverpool four-track line lit by gas so as to facilitate travel at night, but it was not until 1836 and the incorporation of the Manchester & Leeds Railway that any real progress was made.

The general route of this line, and the reasons for its use of North Midland metals from Normanton to Leeds, have been referred to in chapter one. In laying out the first trans-Pennine railway, George Stephenson was forced to abandon his ideal of 1 in 330 as a maximum gradient, but he did manage to keep the steepest incline on the Yorkshire side at a respectable 1 in 160 by tunnelling through the watershed at Summit, north of Littleborough. From here the line paralleled the Rochdale Canal down the extremely constricted Calder Valley to Todmorden, a cotton town more closely linked with Lancashire than Yorkshire, and then on to Hebden Bridge, another cotton centre. The route continued through what was already almost a continuous chain of settlement, serving Sowerby Bridge, Elland, Brighouse, Mirfield, Horbury and Wakefield, but missing the centres of Halifax and Dewsbury in their tributary valleys.

Opening of the portion from Normanton to Hebden Bridge took place in 1840. It was altogether a riotous affair, with passengers casually riding on the carriage roofs and ducking as they passed under the many bridges and short tunnels west of Sowerby Bridge. So crowded in fact did the roofs become that the train dare not stop, and as a result there ensued the spectacle of several barristers angrily chasing their lost luggage! When normal services began this isolated stretch of the M & L was temporarily worked by the North Midland, passengers travelling from Hebden Bridge by road coaches to Littleborough where the section of line from Manchester had been opened in 1839.

The remaining gap in the system was to be closed by the great Summit tunnel, which took three years to build and cost nine lives and £251,000 compared with an estimated £156,800. Completion was delayed by a treacherous belt of shale, and it was not until March 1841 that the first trains ran through this 1 mile 1,125yd (2·63km) masterpiece of early engineering. Summit was then the longest railway tunnel in the world, although it lost this honour only three months later when Brunel completed his work at Box on the Great Western Railway.

Opening of the line throughout meant that the time to travel from Manchester to Leeds dropped dramatically from $6\frac{1}{2}$ to $2\frac{3}{4}$ hours, but the coaches running between the two cities did not immediately succumb as the first class rail fare was 15s compared with 12s inside a coach and 8s outside. More immediate sufferers were the canal proprietors; according to Acworth the shares of the Calder & Hebble Navigation had dropped from £525 to £180 by 1843 when the M & L took an unauthorised lease of the waterway. Between 1839 and 1842 toll receipts fell from £62,712 to £27,266 on the Rochdale Canal which was to be jointly leased by the L & Y, L & NW, MS & L and NE in November 1855. The M & L quickly achieved a high profit level, owing to the density of population along the route and the fact that in the early years much southbound traffic from Manchester was routed this way owing to disputes affecting the Grand Junction Railway.

But not everything ran smoothly. The chairman of the board and two directors resigned owing to the introduction of Sunday trains, while Francis Whishaw castigated the company for building stations like 'so many Elizabethan villas'. Some of them did indeed verge on the extravagant, but others such as Walsden and Eastwood were quaint and cramped owing to the lack of space in the narrow valley of the upper Calder. Dismissal of an assistant clerk at Ludden-den Foot in January 1842 for improper keeping of accounts and drinking while on duty may not appear to be significant, but this clerk was Branwell Brontë, who began his short-lived railway service at Sowerby Bridge in August 1840. More serious was inter-company friction: for instance, in July 1844 the M & L seized all the Midland goods wagons on its system in order to run a cheap excursion from Dewsbury to Liverpool. In reprise for this piece of pirating the Midland commandeered all M & L wagons on which it could lay its hands and hauled them away in triumph to Derby! The result was a complete stoppage of commercial traffic between Leeds, Manchester and Liverpool. There was nothing abnormal in this mode of conveying passengers, as is shown in an icy reference to the M & L in the *Leeds Intelligencer* of 17 August 1844: 'They must put seats in their third class carriages and not stow human beings away in them like so many pigs and sheep.' By virtue of its treatment of passengers, disregard for punctuality and a generally restrictive policy, the company became extremely unpopular in Yorkshire and this reputation persisted until long after the formation of the L & Y in 1847.

At the western end, a line was built giving access from the L & Y east of Todmorden to Burnley, and hence Preston and Blackpool. It made use of another glacial spillway, the Cliviger gorge, to cross the watershed at Copy Pit 750ft (233m) above sea level, but this time the gradients were severe with a climb of two miles (3·2km) at 1 in 65 and another mile at 1 in 80 through three tunnels and over Nott Wood viaduct. The route was opened as a single line in 1849, doubling being completed in 1860. At this time all trains from Yorkshire to Burnley and beyond had to reverse at Todmorden, a drawback overcome by opening a spur in 1862. The development was welcomed everywhere except in Todmorden which lost a substantial part of its train service; its complaints were answered when a station was opened on the north-west side of the new triangle at Stansfield Hall in 1869.

Quadrupling of the L & Y main line from Hebden Bridge

Page 105 Viaducts: (*above*) Canadian-style trestles at Denby Dale on the Huddersfield–Penistone line. This 1884 view shows dismantling in progress following completion of the adjacent stone viaduct; (*below*) Oaks viaduct on the Midland's Cudworth–Barnsley branch was over a thousand feet long and spanned two railways, two canals, a river and a main road

Page 106 Tunnels: (*above*) Thackley, between Leeds and Shipley, photographed soon after the quadrupling of this section of the Midland main line in 1901; (*below*) a contractor's special at the eastern portal of Totley tunnel, at 3 miles 950yd the longest in Britain after the Severn

to Luddenden Foot and from Brighouse to Wakefield took place in stages between 1884 and 1906. Interesting features of this work included the removal of the 128yd (116m) Horbury tunnel, and the filling in of a sixteen-arch viaduct west of Wakefield Kirkgate. An earlier improvement at Mirfield, the exchange point for L & Y and L & NW services, was the opening in 1866 of a new station with a large overall roof. A billiard saloon helped to occupy passengers 'becalmed' by the company's desultory connections, while frequent accidents provided a more morbid source of entertainment. These were in part caused by the shocking congestion which continued to prevail at the station until the opening of the Leeds New Line; a typical year was 1895 when three L & NW goods trains were involved in a collision on 28 March, and a Newcastle–Liverpool express ran sidelong into a GN train in November.

GN trains were seen at Mirfield as a result of the 1882 agreement between the company and the L & Y, more fully described under Dewsbury. Through King's Cross–Halifax services began on 1 July 1882; by 1890 they had been extended to Burnley, the GN being irritated that the L & Y took two hours to work the trains over the $38\frac{1}{4}$ miles (61·2km) from Wakefield. Later developments brought GN through coaches to Huddersfield and as deep into Lancashire as Blackburn. Similarly, L & NW trains were not just confined between Heaton Lodge and Dewsbury junctions, the portion of the Calder Valley route which in effect formed part of that company's Manchester–Huddersfield–Leeds line. In 1859 the L & NW received running powers to Halifax in one direction and Normanton in the other, introducing passenger services from Huddersfield to Wakefield on 2 January 1860 and extending them to Normanton on 1 April 1863. The arrangement ceased on 1 October 1889, but the company continued to run livestock trains as far as Wakefield. Another foreign user was the NE, which on 1 July 1903 began a service of three trains each way between Hull and Halifax. Summer workings from Leicester and Nottingham to Blackpool and Fleetwood via Penistone, Huddersfield and the Calder Valley route were introduced by the GC in 1900.

Holiday workings of this nature began to build up from

G

the 1850s. In July 1855 the L & Y and NE agreed to a special third class return trip from Manchester to Scarborough for a fare of ten shillings, and four years later excursions were frequently being run from Lancashire to this resort as well as to Bridlington and Hull. A regular service between Liverpool and Hull via Goole commenced on 1 September 1870. By the 1880s there was keen rivalry for Scarborough traffic between the through service from Liverpool operated by the L & NW and that from Manchester run by the L & Y, the respective times from Manchester in August 1887 being 3hr 25min and 3hr 35min. There were several through Blackpool workings at this date, while a later development was the introduction of a service from Bradford to Bridlington in the summer of 1901. Towards the close of the nineteenth century the L & Y and L & NW also began to compete with through trains from Liverpool to York and Newcastle; the L & Y had the more difficult route, but according to Ahrons was achieving a five minutes faster timing to York in 1888. Later the company further accelerated these workings by introducing the longest non-stop run on its system, covering the 47 miles (75km) from Manchester to Wakefield in 58 minutes. Perhaps the most interesting working over the main line was the afternoon Continental Boat Train from Liverpool, which divided into three portions at Wakefield. One was taken on to York, a second to Hull Riverside Quay in connection with the joint L & Y/NE steamer to Zeebrugge, and a third to Doncaster where it was attached to the York–Harwich boat train.

In July 1932 the most radical signalling innovation in this country during the inter-war years was introduced between Heaton Lodge and Thornhill junctions. Known as speed signalling and based on American practice, it indicated both the speed and the route to be taken at a junction. As shown in the diagram, a driver could be presented with red, yellow and green lights at the same time on some of the signals! The system ended when re-signalling took place in 1969–70. A major development was the opening of a hump marshalling yard at Healey Mills, between Dewsbury and Wakefield, on 23 July 1963. Replacing thirteen separate yards, it was designed to handle up to 4,000 wagons a day passing from the

South Yorkshire coalfield to West Yorkshire factories and Lancashire. It cost £3¾ million and involved diverting both the main line and the river Calder, but local railwaymen claimed it was redundant before completion and were critical of the fact that traffic was worked from Leeds, shunted at Healey

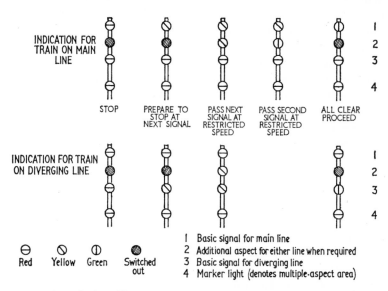

Speed signalling at Mirfield; junction signal aspects

Mills and then worked back again. At the other end of the valley regular passenger services on the Todmorden–Burnley line ceased in 1965, and local trains between Manchester and Todmorden in 1966. Main line services were worked by DMUs from 1 January 1962, but one of the West Riding's pioneer railway routes has been without a regular passenger service from end to end since 1970 when the through York-Manchester trains were withdrawn to be replaced by a service from Wakefield to Huddersfield in connection with expresses on the ex-L & NW route.

A RAILWAY CROSS-ROADS

In the motorway age Normanton has styled itself 'the cross-

roads of England'. It is a rather ambitious claim, but one
that could have been applied without much exaggeration in
the early railway age from 1840 to 1850. For then the town
was 'the Crewe of the coalfields' and the focal point for
traffic which converged from Lancashire, London and the
Midlands for Leeds, York and points north, and Hull. George
Hudson's paramount influence in making Normanton the
radial point for early northern lines has been outlined in
chapter one; it should also be stressed that the two trunk
routes approaching from the south-west merged here rather
than at Wakefield owing partly to opposition from what
became the county town and additionally because of the need
to minimise gradients.

Looking at the local railway geography in more detail, the
position on 1 July 1840 was that the York & North Midland
joined the North Midland at Altofts junction. This was
a mile (1·6km) north of a temporary Normanton station,
where paused the first day expresses from London (Euston
Square) to York. These took 11¾ hours for their 219 mile
(350km) journey via Rugby, although by the following year
this timing had been cut by 45 minutes. On 27 July 1840
the Y & NM opened a spur from Methley junction on the
North Midland to Whitwood junction; it was used by passenger traffic on Hudson's enforced and indirect route from
Leeds to York and Hull as well as by goods trains carrying
woollens and linens for export to the Baltic. The first workings over the M & L in October joined the North Midland
at Goose Hill junction, almost half a mile (0·8km) to the
south-west of Normanton which increased in importance
with the introduction of through Manchester–Leeds services
in 1841. In November 1840 it had been agreed that a permanent station in the 'Italian villa' style be erected at the
joint expense of the three users but managed solely by the
North Midland, which was empowered to sell any part of
the site to the other two companies. Construction work to
designs attributed to G. T. Andrews was finished by September 1841, and control passed to a joint committee of
management in 1843. The famous 'Normanton Hotel and
Refreshment Rooms' opened in 1842, the hotel being connected directly to the station by a covered footbridge. For

decades the population of Normanton had stood close to the
280 mark, but with the sudden rise in importance it almost
doubled to 481 in 1841.

By 1844 the junction's glories were already becoming a
little tainted. The *Railway Times* complained that the
porters at Normanton were rude on principle to all passengers and especially to those arriving from the M & L, while
unattended single ladies were frequently put in a state of
near hysteria at the thought of using the station. At least
the standard of train services was steadily improving; in
1847 day expresses from Euston were pausing only at Rugby,
Derby and Masborough prior to Normanton and then reaching Newcastle in 8hr 35min at an average speed of well over
30mph. The volume of traffic in the area also greatly
increased, causing the Midland to resolve in 1849 to proceed
with the enlargement of Normanton station.

The first blow to the near monopoly of Normanton came
in the same year when the completion of the L & NW trans-
Pennine line and the Leeds & Thirsk created an alternative
route from Lancashire to the North East. Much more serious
was the opening throughout of the GN in 1850, for it commandeered the majority of traffic from London to York,
Newcastle and Scotland which now passed no nearer than
Knottingley. GN trains to Leeds did however join Midland
metals at Methley junction, less than $2\frac{1}{2}$ miles (4km) north
of Normanton, reaching this point by travelling over a
branch foreshadowed by the Wakefield, Pontefract & Goole
Railway incorporation Act of 1845. This was vehemently
opposed by Hudson, who in the same session had put forward
a line that would form part of a shorter route from Leeds to
Goole. Parliament preferred the WP & G because it would
serve an important coal-producing area, but did insist that
within a year the company should apply for powers to make
a more direct Leeds–Goole link. Hence the Methley branch
was authorised in 1846.

Its opening was intended to coincide with that of the GN
Retford–Doncaster section, but was delayed because of a
dispute concerning running powers into Leeds. The existence
of Hudson's agreement of 1847 giving the GN access to this
key centre was by now regretted by the Midland, which tried

To Garforth
To York
Old Station in
Moss Street
(1840 - 1871)
(1871)
NE
CASTLEFORD
L & Y
Cutsyke Jn
To Pontefract
Tanshelf
Featherstone
Featherstone Main Col
Don Pedro Pit
Methley
L & Y
MJ
Lofthouse Jn
Methley Joint Jn
2
Mid
Methley Jn
Altofts & Whitwood
Altofts Jn
Normanton
Goose Hill Jn
To Leeds
Bottom Boat
Sharlston
Newmarket Silkstone Col
New Sharlston Col
Snydale Jn
Royds Green Lower
Stanley
Crofton
Dearne Valley Junction Railway
To Doncaster
To Robin Hood
Wrenthorpe jns
Turners Lane Jn
Calder Bridge Jn
Oakenshaw
LMS
10
6
9
8
7
5
Gds (GC & Mid Jt)
Pass (GC & GN Jt)
Kirkgate (L&Y & GN Jt)
Sandal & Walton
Hare Park & Crofton
To Derby
To Leeds
GN
Lofthouse
MJ
1
N
S
W
Westgate
3
4
WAKEFIELD
West Riding Jn
Sandal
To Batley
Alverthorpe
To Manchester
Horbury Junction

1 Lofthouse North Jn
2 Whitwood Jn
3 Westgate South Jn
4 Ings Road Jn
5 Oakenshaw Jn
6 Oakenshaw North Jn
7 Oakenshaw South Jn
8 Crofton Jn
9 Crofton West Jn
10 Crofton East Jn

GN
L&Y
Mid
NE
E &WYU
MJ
WR &G Jt
Waggonways and other lines

N

0   1   2
miles

Map at Wakefield and Normanton

to force the new company to give an undertaking that it would never construct its own line into the town. If the GN refused to give such an assurance, then all its trains would be stopped at Methley and the maximum tolls extracted from every passenger. On the evening before the scheduled opening day of 4 September 1849, the dispute culminated in the so-called 'Methley incident', one of the most famous events of early railway history. It was described by the *Doncaster Chronicle* under the heading 'Atrocious Conduct in a Railway Company':

> The Superintendent at Doncaster, having heard it whispered that something was going on at the junction of the Doncaster line with the Midland Railway at Methley, sent over a special engine before the trains and found the servants of the Midland Company had removed the points at the junction, so that had the train proceeded thither it would have inevitably run off the road.

Both the GN and the L & Y, which had now absorbed the WP & G, made forceful protests but to no immediate avail. The GN made arrangements to circumvent the Midland by working its St Leger traffic of 11–14 September between Doncaster and Leeds via Wakefield and Dewsbury, although it is doubtful if this plan was put into practice. The GN timetable for September 1849 indicates that the company's approach to Leeds was via Wakefield and Normanton, but as the L & Y put on additional Wakefield–Leeds trains on 10 September it would seem that these formed a connecting service and that the the GN made Kirkgate its enforced terminus. It was 1 October before the Methley branch was first used and the GN entered Leeds in its own right; official opening of the line took place on 1 December, and L & Y through services from Goole to Leeds via this route commenced on 1 April 1850.

The return of the railway 'cross-roads' to trunk importance lasted only until 1857 when GN expresses and most L & Y Goole–Leeds trains were diverted over the newly completed Bradford, Wakefield & Leeds Railway. It was 1860 before the L & Y instituted a separate service from Knottingley to Leeds via Methley and at the same time opened a station to serve Castleford. In 1854 further decline had been created by the completion of the Leeds, Bradford & Halifax Junction Railway, which caused some Calder Valley traffic to be re-routed through Low Moor. A particularly ominous year was 1869, for April saw the opening of the link from Leeds New to Marsh Lane and the end of most Leeds–York via Methley workings. Some coke traffic continued to come this way until 1904, while for many years the NE main line was regarded as beginning at Altofts junction rather than Shaftholme junction. Then in October 1869 the opening of the NE Thorne–Staddlethorpe line created a new route through Wakefield and Goole for L & Y Manchester–Hull traffic. Hitherto it had travelled via Normanton and Selby under the aegis of an agreement signed by Hudson in 1846. The final blow came ten years later when completion of the Swinton & Knottingley Joint in 1879 took trains from Sheffield and the Midlands on a more direct route to York and the North than that through Normanton and Castleford.

Yet not all was negative. The Bradford, Wakefield & Leeds Railway changed its name to the West Yorkshire Railway in 1863 (as noted in chapter one), and at the same time obtained powers for a branch from a double junction at Lofthouse to Methley, where connections were to be made with both the NE spur from Methley junction to Whitwood junction and the L & Y line from Pontefract. Representations from these two companies led to agreement that they could be admitted as joint owners, and under the Methley Railway Act of 1864 a joint committee was established. Construction was largely undertaken by the GN, which following its absorption of the West Yorkshire became the main user of the line. Goods traffic was running over the Methley Joint by June 1865, the GN soon obtaining running powers over the NE as far as Milford junction and instituting a freight service to this point from Bradford on 8 June 1866.

A skeleton passenger service over the line was begun by the GN on 1 May 1869, and from 13 May trains started to work through to the NE station at Castleford from both Wakefield and Leeds. In reply the Midland commenced a Leeds–Castleford service on 1 August, but despite the more direct route it was soon taken off. An even shorter-lived experiment was a through GN service from Bradford to York via the MJ, which was operated only in the summers of 1876 and 1877. The MJ station at Methley was the third in this locality, its nearest namesake being Methley Junction on the L & Y Pontefract line. At its eastern end the MJ crossed the floodplain of the Calder and inundation of the tracks was a perpetual hazard; in 1892 it was recommended that the line be lifted by as much as four feet (1·22m) for a length of 500yd (455m). Another difficulty which became severe in later years was mining subsidence.

Positive development returned to Normanton when it was selected as the refreshment stop for Anglo–Scottish expresses following the completion of the Settle–Carlisle line in 1876. The station, originally consisting of two island plat-forms, had been rebuilt in 1871 as a single island, at almost a quarter of a mile (0·4km) the fourth longest in the country. The refreshment rooms were now extended to accommodate passengers gobbling food which had been ordered in advance by electric telegraph. The Midland's summer timetable of 1887 stated that 'a dinner of five courses, with dessert, and no fees to waiters, is prepared at Normanton and half an hour is allowed for the discussion and disposal of the good things so liberally provided'. Yet once again the days of glory were abruptly terminated, for the introduction of dining cars on Midland expresses caused the greater part of the main refreshment rooms to be closed in 1895 and turned the station into what Ahrons succinctly described as 'a sight something of the nature of the Sahara desert furnished with a beer pump'. It did manage to remain an important point for the interchange of mails, a joint Midland and NE service from Bristol to Newcastle conveying TPOs from St Pancras which were attached at Derby and then taken off at Normanton for Leeds. Another mail train approached from Carnforth, but much more famous was the 'Bangor Mail', introduced in June 1855. It travelled via Crewe, Stockport and Stalybridge to terminate at Normanton until 1 July 1902 when it was diverted to Leeds New. Other developments affecting the station included the granting of running powers as far as York to the L & Y, passenger work-ings commencing on 1 May 1884 and cattle traffic from Liverpool and Fleetwood on 6 October 1886.

At Castleford the main development was the incorporation in 1873 of the Leeds, Castleford & Pontefract Junction Railway, designed to open up the coalfield in the Kippax and Ledston areas. The NE agreed to subscribe three-quarters of the capital and absorbed the company in 1876. The main portion of the line, extending to Castleford from a junction with the former Leeds & Selby Railway at Garforth, was opened in 1878. Thus four companies provided Leeds–Castleford services: the GN and Midland as already mentioned; the L & Y by means of the station on its Methley branch; and now the NE. This last was extended to Pontefract S & K on 1 April 1880, when a spur was opened at Castleford giving access to the Methley branch. Originally put forward by the Pontefract & Castleford Railway in 1860, it was heavily used by traffic from collieries on the former LC & PJ which was worked as far as Pontefract (L & Y) by the NE and then taken on to Goole. On 1 June 1899 this arrangement was changed, the L & Y hauling the trains right through from the collieries to the port.

Many changes have occurred at the 'cross-roads' in recent years. On 1 November 1926 the former NE service from Leeds to Pontefract was cut back to Castleford, and then eliminated altogether in 1951 with the closure to passengers of the line from Garforth. But on 5 May 1958 DMUs began working from Leeds Central over the MJ into Castleford Central (as the NE station had been renamed), and then followed the same route on to Pontefract. This service succumbed to the Beeching axe in 1964, when the MJ was closed to all passenger traffic. It was survived by infrequent Leeds City–Knottingley trains which called at Castleford Cutsyke (the name given to the former L & Y station), although from 2 January 1967 these were augmented and extended to Goole to compensate for the withdrawal of the Wakefield–Goole service. Then in 1968 the direct line from Methley junction to Cutsyke junction was closed to passengers, and trains diverted via the Methley curve into the more convenient Central station where they reversed in order to rejoin the Methley branch. The once vast and bustling marshalling yards at Normanton were out of use by the end of 1968. A similar comment could almost be applied to the passenger station, for in the same year the ex-Midland main line was closed to passenger traffic between Wath Road and Goose Hill junctions because of subsidence and trains diverted via the S & K, WR & G and Wakefield Westgate. In 1970 came the withdrawal of the York–Wakefield Kirkgate–Manchester services, meaning that 'the Crewe of the coalfields' was left with just Leeds–Barnsley–Sheffield locals. Passenger trains returned to the closed portion of the Midland main line in 1973, but merely emphasised the downfall of Normanton by rushing contemptuously past this once key junction.

WAKEFIELD

Until the middle of the eighteenth century Wakefield was the capital of the Yorkshire clothing trade, a pre-eminence achieved largely as a result of its position at the then navigable limit of the Calder. But the restrictive practices of its merchants and the extension of inland navigation further up the valley soon caused the trade to diminish. Wakefield escaped the worst problems of rapid expansion in the Industrial Revolution and became an important agricultural centre; at the beginning of the railway age it had one of the largest corn markets in the country handling 15,000 quarters of grain a week, while its malt market was almost equally as extensive.

The first Wakefield station was on the North Midland Railway, two miles (3·2km) south of Normanton and 1½ miles (2·4km) from the town centre. It was renamed Oakenshaw in 1841 to avoid confusion with the M & L station at Kirkgate once through Manchester–Leeds services were operating. The Railway Mania's contribution to the town was the Wakefield, Pontefract & Goole Railway, the only successful contender out of four similar schemes put forward in this period. This line, which has already been referred to in connection with the Methley branch, enabled the L & Y to achieve its ambition of becoming a port to port system. The necessary amalgamation was approved on 15 December 1845 and legalised in 1847, the opening of the WP & G main line taking place in April 1848. Five months later the L & Y had gained access to Doncaster by means of the ex-WP & G

Askern branch, and introduced a service from this town to Wakefield. Some of the trains reversed here to continue to Leeds, at once stage providing the only direct link to this city from Wakefield owing to the re-routing of L & Y main line expresses through Morley. As a result the Midland put on a special service from Oakenshaw to Leeds, but it was discontinued when the L & Y started to run additional trains from Wakefield in September 1849.

The GN had originally planned to build its own branch to Wakefield, but when this intention was thwarted by Parliament an agreement was made with the WP & G for running powers. After completion of the Retford–Doncaster portion of its main line in 1849, the GN's traffic to Wakefield quickly became established and in 1851 the company was authorised to provide additional facilities at Kirkgate. At this time it was described as nothing more than 'a small wooden hut with a platform in front, with miserable waiting room accommodation'. In August 1853 the GN agreed with the L & Y to appoint a joint committee for the management of the station and its complete rebuilding, the work being finished in 1857. Ironically, in the same year Kirkgate ceased to be a terminus for the company, when it began to work its Leeds traffic over the newly opened Bradford, Wakefield & Leeds Railway. This line left the L & Y at Ings Road junction and climbed over a 22-arch viaduct to a new Wakefield station at Westgate, which was adapted from a private house.

Kirkgate remained a joint station until nationalisation, but its use by the GN was reduced after 1866 when the opening of the West Riding & Grimsby Joint provided a more direct route from Doncaster. This system, fully described in chapter eight, had a complex evolution at its Wakefield end which created much inter-company wrangling. When incorporated as a nominally independent railway in 1862 it was provided that the WR & G and users of the line should run over the BW & L into the existing Westgate station. However, in 1864 the company obtained powers to build its own station at Wakefield, agreeing to provide the West Yorkshire Railway (the former BW & L) with substitute accommodation in the new structure and also to allow the Midland to use it. Construction was in hand by the following year when the GN acquired the WY and reached agreement with the MS & L for a joint take-over of the WR & G. It thus had a key interest in the development of the new Westgate, and opposed efforts by the MS & L and Midland to reduce its cost by £3,000, even to the extent of seeing the matter taken to arbitration. The station was notable for its rich Italianate façade and a clock tower extending to no less than 97ft (30·1m) above street level, but owing to the fratching was not ready for the WR & G opening and trains used the former WY buildings on the opposite side of Westgate until 1 May 1867. A fortnight later the GN claimed that the old station had been demolished and the staff moved to the new buildings without its consent! There was further wrangling over the neighbouring goods depot, opened in 1868, which was owned by the WR & G but rented in perpetuity to the MS & L and Midland. These two companies and the GN ultimately agreed to share the cost of both the passenger and goods stations, which had been placed under the control of a tripartite joint committee by an Act of 1867. The same Act confirmed the right of the L & Y to continue to use Westgate under the terms of an 1854 agreement by which it had secured running powers over the then BW & L.

The main engineering feature at the Wakefield end of the WR & G was the '99-arch' viaduct, reputedly consuming 800 million bricks in carrying the line across the Calder and above the town for almost three-quarters of a mile (1·2km). It was preceded by a west to south spur, connecting with the Midland which began to work passenger trains over it and into Westgate on 1 August 1868. An L & Y spur half a mile (0·8km) to the north was opened in 1861 and had an almost parallel curvature, providing a link between Kirkgate and the Midland. L & Y connecting trains reversed at the junction with the main line and then terminated at Oakenshaw, but in order to eliminate this practice and make the best use of both spurs the station was closed to passengers in 1870. It was replaced by a new structure near the south end of the WR & G curve at Sandal & Walton. At the same time the Midland opened its branch to Barnsley and put on a through service from this town to Westgate, while MS & L coal traffic also came this way until the completion of the Barnsley Coal

Railway in 1882. Competition for Wakefield connections ended in May 1887 when the L & Y withdrew its service. Among the other inter-company connections in this area was one between Hare Park and Crofton junctions, built as a result of the GN and L & Y pact of 1882. Its opening in 1886 meant that King's Cross–Calder Valley trains no longer had to reverse on to the L & Y by means of the Westgate–Kirkgate connection.

A minor development in the area dated from 1 January 1859 when the NE began to work livestock trains through to Wakefield, but most other changes stemmed from the growth of coal mining alongside the former WP & G. The surprising instigator of this trend was Samuel Cunliffe Lister who, having fulfilled most of his ambitions at Manningham Mills, bought a comparatively small colliery at Featherstone. With his customary zeal he quickly developed it into one of the most important mines in the county, and from 1870 a town which was to have a population of 20,000 began to evolve from the former village. Similar if less spectacular growth followed the commencement of large-scale working at New Sharlston Colliery in 1865; here a specially constructed settlement formed the first purpose-built mine village in the West Riding, apart from the much smaller Waterloo, and received its own station in 1869. The NE began to work coal traffic from the colliery via both Castleford and Pontefract S & K, while the GN hauled 'black diamonds' from Sharlston and Featherstone over L & Y tracks as far as the link with its own system at Ings Road junction, Wakefield. The Midland decided to make a bid for this lucrative traffic, and in 1885 opened branches from Snydale junction, almost a mile (1·6km) north of Oakenshaw, to Don Pedro Pit near Loscoe and Featherstone Main Colliery. A request that the branches be opened for passenger traffic was made without success in 1897.

Widening of the North Midland main line south from Snydale junction was begun in 1898, one of the last works being the removal in 1923–5 of the 684yd (622m) Chevet tunnel to create what at almost 100ft (30·5m) was claimed to be the deepest railway cutting in the country. As already indicated, one of the major post-nationalisation changes in the area was the withdrawal of the Wakefield–Goole passenger services in 1967. This was partly motivated by the need to increase line capacity for the frequent 'merry-go-round' trains travelling from the South Yorkshire coalfield to Ferrybridge, Drax and Eggborough power stations.

DEWSBURY

At the beginning of the seventeenth century Dewsbury was a mere hamlet of 33 houses and three mills. It grew gradually after the completion of the Calder & Hebble Navigation in 1770 to reach a population of 4,566 in 1801, and then more rapidly following the invention of shoddy in 1813. This material was ultimately to be influential in turning the town into the capital of the heavy woollen district, although initially progress was checked by the lack of an adequate rail link with Leeds. The direct distance between the two settlements was eight miles (12·8km), but a journey over the M & L involved travelling for 21 miles (33·6km) from a station which was itself more than a mile from the town centre. It rather optimistically took the name of the township until 1851, when it became Thornhill.

The change recognised that since 1848 the L & NW had provided Dewsbury with both a central station and a direct line to Leeds through the 1 mile 1,609yd (3·07km) Morley tunnel which pierced the Aire and Calder watershed at an altitude of about 300ft (93m) above sea level. The foundation stone of the first shaft of this tunnel had been laid on 23 February 1846, but disputes soon arose with the contractor and the tenders had to be re-let in August. Large amounts of water encountered in the workings and several earth slips caused further delays, although these were reduced by sinking as many as eighteen shafts so that at one stage tunnelling was being undertaken at the rate of 300yd (273m) per month. Dewsbury's two most prosperous decades of the nineteenth century followed the opening of the new route.

An M & L branch into the centre of Dewsbury was authorised in 1846, but the powers were allowed to lapse. In the same year the Act for the West Riding Union Railways included a branch which left the company's main line at

Low Moor and then proceeded down the Spen Valley to Heckmondwike, where it diverged for Mirfield and Dewsbury, as Thornhill was still known. Production of shoddy had spread up the Spen Valley from 1820, and by 1844 there were populations of 3,500 at Heckmondwike, almost 4,000 at Cleckheaton and 6,000 at Liversedge. The line from Low Moor to Mirfield thus carried a heavy traffic from its opening in 1848, and particularly so in the early days for it formed the nearest rail approach to Bradford from the south until the completion of the link from Halifax to the woolopolis in August 1850. Further traffic came in 1859 when the L & NW gained running powers up the Spen Valley to Bradford. A passenger service from Huddersfield was inaugurated on 2 January 1860, but the trains were not permitted to stop at the intermediate stations until 1884. Two years earlier one of the most spectacular runaways in railway history had occurred when some coaches being shunted at Low Moor broke loose and careered down the whole length of the valley line before coming to a stop near Cooper Bridge, a total distance of over ten miles (16km).

The spur from Heckmondwike to Thornhill was one of the many WRU lines abandoned in 1852, and all L & Y Bradford–Wakefield trains had either to reverse at Mirfield or travel via Halifax. Thus by the early 1860s many passengers journeying between these two centres were using the link provided by the Leeds, Bradford & Halifax Junction and Bradford, Wakefield & Leeds railways, while at the same time schemes for a more direct line from Dewsbury to Bradford were being put forward. The L & Y was thus virtually forced into reviving its 1846 proposal for a branch into the centre of Dewsbury and coupling this with the construction of the Heckmondwike–Thornhill line. The branch with its passenger terminus at Market Place was opened in 1867, but the connection from Heckmondwike was not completed until two years later.

The 1860s and '70s were a boom period for Dewsbury, the population reaching 18,148 in 1861 and 24,764 ten years later. Much of this expansion stemmed from the growth of the shoddy industry. By 1842 the number of rag merchants in the town totalled seventeen; soon afterwards Dewsbury

Page 123 Freight facilities—old and new: (*above*) the cramped yard at Sheffield (Wicker), filled with a fascinating variety of traffic in its pre-Grouping heyday; (*below*) Tinsley marshalling yard, opened in 1965 and designed to handle 275 freight trains every 24 hours

Page 124 Locomotive facilities: (*above*) the Midland's Sheffield (Millhouses) depot, shortly after its opening in 1901; (*below*) a 1961 interior view of Doncaster locomotive works, familiarly known as the Plant, which with the nearby carriage and wagon works once provided employment for 4,500 men. Appropriately, the locomotive undergoing overhaul is A3 no 60048 *Doncaster*

became the only place in the world in which woollen rags were sold by public auction, the earliest sales taking place from railway wagons at the L & NW station. In 1871 the number of rag merchants had increased to seventy, and the following year 30,000 tons of rags were imported, more than ten times the figure of fourteen years previously. Completion of the link from Bradford to Wakefield through Batley, described in the previous chapter, led to this rival shoddy centre providing the GN with considerable additional traffic. The company was keen to repeat the experience with Dewsbury, and at the same time counteract the influence of the L & Y's new lines. A branch from Runtlings Lane junction, west of Ossett, to a temporary terminus in the town was opened in 1874, but owing to the slump of the mid-seventies it was 1880 before a permanent through station on an extension to Batley was brought into use.

These developments did not improve relations with the L & Y, and matters seemed likely to become worse when the GN projected a line running from Batley Carr, just north of Dewsbury, to Cleckheaton. Its genesis was stimulated by the poor quality of the Spen Valley services provided by the L & Y, which were such as to cause the local residents and businessmen to be incessantly pressing for improvements. Henry Oakley, the GN general manager, stated that a deputation from the district had been 'an annual festival at King's Cross since 1876'. The Bill for the branch was thrown out when it came before Parliament in 1882, but only after the L & Y had given a number of important pledges which culminated in a key agreement for better relations between the two companies. The resulting connecting lines and exchanges of running powers are noted elsewhere in this chapter as well as in chapters three and eight. At Dewsbury an inter-company link known as the Headfield spur was opened to freight in 1887, and from 1893 was used by the GN/L & Y Leeds–Pudsey–Cleckheaton–Batley–Leeds circular service. Among other developments of this period the most important were the opening of the Thornhill wagon works on 1 January 1878 and an enlarged L & NW station at Dewsbury on 24 March 1889. In 1891 the L & Y brought into use a station at Northorpe, on the Heckmondwike–

H

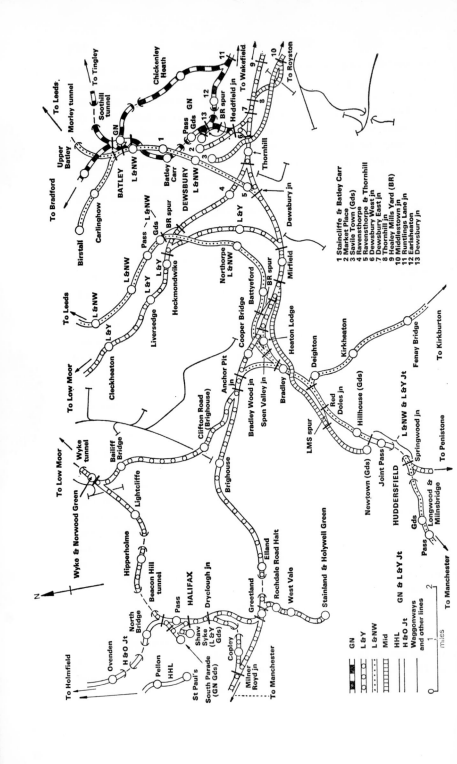

Key:
1 Staincliffe & Batley Carr
2 Market Place
3 Savile Town (Gds)
4 Ravensthorpe
5 Ravensthorpe & Thornhill
6 Dewsbury West Jn
7 Dewsbury East Jn
8 Thornhill Jn
9 Healey Mills Yard (BR)
10 Middlestown Jn
11 Runtlings Lane Jn
12 Earlsheaton
13 Dewsbury Jn

To Leeds.
To Tingley
Chickenley Heath
To Wakefield
Morley tunnel
Soothill tunnel
To Leeds
To Royston
GN
Upper Batley
BR spur
Heddfield Jn
Pass GN
Gds
BATLEY
13
12
L&NW
Batley Carr
2
Thornhill
To Bradford
DEWSBURY
3
L&NW
Carlinghow
4
Dewsbury Jn
Birstall
5
Pass
L&NW
Gds
BR spur
L&NW
L&Y
Northorpe
To Leeds
Heckmondwike
L&NW
Mirfield
BR spur
Liversedge
Battyeford
L&NW
L&Y
Cooper Bridge
Heaton Lodge
Cleckheaton
To Low Moor
Anchor Pit Jn
Bradley
Deighton
Kirkheaton
Clifton Road (Brighouse)
Bradley Wood Jn
Spen Valley Jn
Red Doles Jn
Fenay Bridge
To Kirkburton
Wyke & Norwood Green
Wyke tunnel
Bailiff Bridge
Brighouse
LMS spur
Hillhouse (Gds)
L&NW & L&Y Jt
Springwood Jn
To Low Moor
Lightcliffe
Newtown (Gds)
Joint Pass
To Penistone
Hipperholme
HUDDERSFIELD
Beacon Hill tunnel
Elland
Longwood & Milnsbridge
Gds
North Bridge
HALIFAX
Pass
Drycough Jn
Greetland
Rochdale Road Halt
West Vale
Pass
To Manchester
To Holmfield
Ovenden
H&O Jt
Shaw Syke (L&Y) Gds
Stainland & Holywell Green
Pellon
HHL
St Paul's
South Parade (GN Gds)
Copley
Milner Royd Jn
To Manchester

GN
L&Y
L&NW
Mid
HHL
H&O Jt
GN & L&Y Jt
Waggonways and other lines

N

miles
0   1   2

Mirfield line, reputedly spending £10,000 on it at a time when the company's shares were below par and provoking Thomas Normington to write that the architecture was more fitted to a Bishop's palace than a railway building.

Dewsbury nearly got a fourth passenger station when the Midland proposed to build the cut-off from Royston to Bradford, already outlined in the previous chapter. The original scheme was truncated when the L & Y offered the company running powers along its Spen Valley line in return for abandonment of a proposed Huddersfield and Halifax branch. A connection was made with the L & Y main line at Thornhill, while a branch followed the route of the cut-off for about a mile (1·6km) and then descended steeply at 1 in 40 through a 188yd (171m) tunnel into a goods depot at Dewsbury Savile Town. Opening to here took place in 1906, passenger workings over the Royston–Thornhill section beginning in 1909. They comprised a basic service between Sheffield and Halifax which was worked throughout in both directions by the L & Y, as were certain goods trains from 6 March 1911. There were also through coaches or trains from Bradford, Halifax and Huddersfield to St Pancras and Bristol but, apart from a brief revival in 1960, all-the-year-round workings over the route ceased in 1946. An ignominious end to what was envisaged as a superb main line came with complete closure in 1968. Engineering works on the line included a 21-arch viaduct between Crigglestone and Middlestown.

Other long overdue rationalisation has taken place at Dewsbury. Market Place handled its last passengers as early as 1930 and complete closure took place in 1961. A curious revival has been the Headfield spur, which saw only a daily Leeds–Barnsley train after the withdrawal of the circular service in 1914 and was lifted in 1933. Fortunately the formation and the fine girder bridge over the Calder were allowed to remain, and under the Healey Mills scheme provided a direct route from the new yard to the former GN goods depot at Dewsbury (Railway Street), enabling the Wakefield–Dewsbury–Bradford route to be completely closed in 1965. On the Spen Valley line DMUs began running from Bradford to Huddersfield on 2 November 1959, but this service was withdrawn on 14 June 1965 and the section from Heckmond-wike to Mirfield completely closed. Passenger trains over the spur to Thornhill dwindled after World War II, Bradford–Thornhill services being terminated in 1957 and the last regular working withdrawn in 1962. Much has vanished, but the memories which remain include the moment in October 1954 when the Queen and the Duke of Edinburgh arrived at Dewsbury Central. With a true Yorkshire approach, the station had been specially repainted—on one side only!

HALIFAX

On the completion of the Calder Valley main line in 1841, a Halifax worthy remarked that 'he did not know whether he was more struck by the atrocity of the Manchester & Leeds company's first project in daring to pass by such towns as Halifax, or the audacity with which they had performed their abominable promise'. This Victorian reproval tended to overlook the fundamental difficulties caused by the town's position in a narrow and steep-sided tributary valley; these were such that the Halifax branch of the Calder & Hebble Navigation was not completed until the dawn of the railway age in 1828. Three years later the population of the town had reached 15,382, and cotton manufacture had begun to erode the local monopoly of wool which had existed for at least 600 years. By the 1840s industrialisation was proceeding apace, reducing the average life expectancy of the inhabitants to a mere 26 years and causing Charles Dickens to remark of the community: 'It is as horrible a place as I ever saw.'

The M & L somewhat reluctantly agreed to build a branch from its main line at North Dean (later Greetland) to Shaw Syke, Halifax, and obtained the necessary Act on 1 July 1839. Its provision that the line should be constructed 'as speedily as possible' and completed within three years went unheeded, for it was not until 1844 that it began to carry traffic. Even then there was intense discontent over the poor connections to Manchester, and the difficulties in working trains over a single line which climbed for three-quarters of a mile (1·2km) at 1 in 44½ and a further quarter of a mile (0·4km) at 1 in 53. Many drivers set back into the tunnel at Elland in order to get a run at the bank. The first real hope of an improvement came with the 1846 West Riding Union Railways and their proposed Sowerby Bridge–Halifax–Low Moor–Leeds main line. Engineering works north of Halifax were extremely heavy, including two high viaducts and tunnels of 1,105yd (1·01km) at Beacon Hill and 1,365yd (1·24km) at Wyke. These meant that opening to Low Moor did not take place until 1850, a temporary through station at Halifax replacing the former M & L terminus which became a goods depot. Another result was that little money was available for the section from Sowerby Bridge to Dryclough junction, on the original M & L branch, and the doubling of the earlier line through difficult rock cuttings north of this point. Loose rock caused a tunnel to be substituted for planned cutting, while a further factor which delayed the opening to passengers until 1852 was the 66ft (20·4m) high 23-arch viaduct over the Calder. In 1856 an intermediate station was opened at Copley to serve the then utopian factory village of Copley Mills, the forerunner of Saltaire, which had been completed three years earlier by Col Edward Akroyd, founder of the Yorkshire Penny Bank.

The GN began to work into Halifax following the opening of the Leeds, Bradford & Halifax Junction Railway in 1854, this additional traffic being handled by a permanent through station which came into use on 23 June 1855. In rejoicing at the passing of the 'miserable, dirty and disagreeable' temporary station, the *Halifax Courier* commented: 'We are sure there is not a town from Caithness to Cornwall which could exhibit a more filthy doghole of a place than that in which all the railway traffic of Halifax has so long been transacted.' A through service from Halifax to London (Euston Square) via Huddersfield, Sheffield and Derby was introduced on 1 April 1856 but owing to the break up of the Euston Square Confederacy lasted only until 1 August 1857; a lesser substitute was provided by L & NW trains which worked through from Huddersfield to Halifax from 2 January 1860 until 1864. Long-overdue improvements included the establishment of through services to Manchester in 1863, and the widening of the North Dean–Dryclough junction section in 1869.

Two L & Y branches in the Halifax area were authorised in 1865, but both took a long time to materialise. That from North Dean to Stainland was opened in 1875, and like many minor L & Y extremities was rather extravagantly provided with double track. Its main engineering features were two viaducts, respectively 179yd (163m) and 230yd (209m) in length. A branch from Sowerby Bridge to Rishworth was built to main line standards, as it was foreseen as the initial part of a cut-off which would pass under Blackstone Edge by a four mile (6·4km) tunnel to Littleborough, thus shortening the Calder Valley route by about five miles (8km). As part of the scheme a new Sowerby Bridge station, almost half a mile (0·8km) east of the original buildings, was opened in 1876, although the two platforms intended to serve the new main line were never constructed. Opening as far as Ripponden took place in 1878, the delay being caused by landslips near Triangle and quite extraordinary difficulties in boring the 593yd (540m) Ripponden tunnel which ultimately cost some £40,000. Workings were extended to Rishworth in 1881, but at this point the grand plan came to an abrupt halt. The decision not to proceed with the extension to Littleborough has been described by John Marshall as 'perhaps the most regrettable in the history of the L & Y'.

A more successful cut-off, although one inordinately long in gestation, ran from south of Low Moor to join the Calder Valley main line east of Brighouse, and enabled expresses from Bradford to Huddersfield and beyond to avoid the detour through Halifax. It was first sanctioned in this form in the West Riding Union Railways Act of 1846; an L & Y Act of 1866 provided for a similar scheme but extending only as far as a terminus at Clifton Road on the north side of Brighouse. This relegation to branch status was a result of the L & Y promoting a direct line to Huddersfield from Halifax, as explained in the next chapter. Another seven years went by, and then a further Act was obtained in 1873 because an obstructive landowner was insisting that the western end of the line be diverted to the opposite side of the valley. This piece of autocracy was ultimately to lead to the erection of an otherwise unnecessary 22-arch viaduct, but by this time the project must also have been overburdened with legal expenses as a fourth Act was procured in 1875. It authorised an extension to Anchor Pit junction on the main line, for by now the Halifax–Huddersfield proposal was dormant. The cut-off was finally opened in 1881, and was termed the Pickle Bridge branch after the station which was actually on the Halifax–Low Moor line but close to the junction with the new route. The description stuck, even though the station was renamed Wyke in 1882.

By 1861 the population of Halifax had soared to 37,014, while ten years later considerable boundary extensions helped to bring the total to 65,510. Crossleys' Dean Clough Mills had grown from employing 300 men in 1837 to 5,000 in 1870, and were known as 'the largest carpet factory in the world'. John Crossley was one of the leading promoters of a line from Halifax to Keighley rejected by Parliament in 1864. An alternative scheme for the first $2\frac{3}{4}$ miles (4·4km) as far as Holmfield was however sanctioned as the Halifax & Ovenden Junction Railway. This project was supported by the L & Y, which expected substantial traffic from the mills and dye works in the valley, and the GN which rightly foresaw the scheme as the first stage of an independent route to Halifax from Bradford. Construction started soon after the incorporation, but was later stopped for over three years owing to lack of capital and did not resume until the company was vested jointly in the GN and L & Y in 1870. A further delay of almost a year was caused by a massive landslip at Wade Street, Halifax, and it was 1874 before through freight traffic commenced. Passenger workings, which were provided by the GN, did not begin until completion of that company's route through Queensbury tunnel in 1879. The line climbed almost continuously at 1 in 45 from North Bridge to Holmfield.

The additional traffic from the H & OJ was augmented by the 1882 agreement which brought GN trains into Halifax over both the Calder Valley main line and the Spen Valley route via a south curve at Low Moor opened in 1886. In the mid-1890s this curve was used for a short-lived L & Y Halifax–Wyke–Cleckheaton–Mirfield–Halifax circular service. Prior to this period it had become obvious that the existing Halifax station was inadequate, and accordingly it was rebuilt in two stages, the first being opened on 25 October 1885 and the second on 30 May 1886. The west side of the new buildings was allocated to the GN and the east to the L & Y, and the station was named Halifax Old in 1890.

The 'Old' was added partly to avoid confusion with North Bridge but also because a new station was about to be opened at St Paul's, $1\frac{1}{4}$ miles (2km) to the west but no less than 325ft (100m) higher in altitude. Halifax had by this time extended in the only possible direction, up these western slopes of the Hebble valley, and 80,000 tons of coal were annually being dragged up the steep roads to supply 130 mills. This was partly the reason for the incorporation in 1884 of the Halifax High Level & North & South Junction Railway, more of a description than a title. Its rosy-eyed promoters saw the line as a vital link in a new route for Midland Anglo-Scottish expresses, which would reach a high-level station in George Street, Halifax, via the projected extension of the Hull & Barnsley Railway through Huddersfield (see next chapter) and then continue over the GN to Keighley. When this dream collapsed the works were limited to a branch from Holmfield to St Paul's, costing some £300,000, a substantial sum representing an average expenditure of over £100,000 per mile. The main engineering works were an 810yd (737m) tunnel through solid rock and a ten-arch viaduct, while the steep gradients included a short stretch of 1 in 35 at Holmfield and a longer pull at 1 in 50 up to Pellon. The line was opened throughout in 1890 and from the outset was worked jointly by the GN and L & Y, the former normally operating all the passenger services. It was vested in the two companies in 1894.

L & NW and NE workings into Halifax were outlined at the beginning of this chapter. As also already mentioned, the Midland proposed to serve the town by means of a line passing through Huddersfield, but this was dropped in return for running powers over the L & Y. The company then sought to build its own Halifax terminus under an Act of 1899, although the proposal was abandoned and running powers exercised into the L & Y station via the Spen Valley and the Low Moor curve. The effect of tramcar competition was particularly noticeable in the hilly area around Halifax, and to combat this the L & Y introduced steam rail-motors on both its Stainland and Rishworth branches on 1 March 1907, opening new halts on the former at Rochdale Road and on the latter by the tunnel at Sowerby Bridge and at Watson's Crossing. The railcars, like many DMU services of more recent times, merely staved off the inevitable, for trams were extended from West Vale to Stainland in 1921 and the branch termini were in direct competition with bus services by 1927. Passenger traffic on both branches managed to survive for only another two years. The Halifax High Level Railway also proved vulnerable, as a rail journey from St Paul's to say Sowerby Bridge, little more than a mile (1·6km) away, involved two changes and took at least 35 minutes. Passenger services, which from the outset had brought in disappointingly low receipts, ceased as early as 1917.

Stopping trains on the Pickle Bridge branch ended on 14 September 1931, but in other respects Halifax was still well served by rail. One of the most remarkable examples of variety in West Riding services is shown in the choice of through trains to London immediately before World War II. A Halifax businessman wanting an early arrival in the capital could leave at 7.12 am and travel via Brighouse and the Thornhill–Royston line to reach St Pancras at 11.50 am. A more leisurely train was the 7.45 am departure which was routed through Huddersfield, Penistone and over the GC main line to enter Marylebone at 1.10 p.m. A careful perusal of the timetables would however reveal the folly of this move, for a now forgotten service left at 8.12 am and journeyed by way of Huddersfield and Stockport to be in Euston at 1.0 pm. Faster still was the 9.20 am, travelling along the Calder Valley to Wakefield so as to reach King's Cross at 1.47 pm, but even this was eclipsed by the 9.50 am departure which was routed via the Low Moor curve, Cleckheaton and Thornhill to Sheffield Midland. Here through coaches were attached on Mondays to Fridays to an express arriving at St Pancras at 2.5 pm; on Saturdays they formed part of a through working to Yarmouth via Nottingham and the Midland & Great Northern Joint line. Services in the reverse direction provided two further routes. The 5.50 pm from King's Cross approached Halifax along the

Spen Valley and over the Low Moor curve, but perhaps a more interesting train was the 4.45 pm Yorkshire Pullman which detached a Bradford and Halifax portion at Wakefield. This was worked forward from Bradford via Queensbury, reputedly because the LMS would not allow Pullman cars on the direct line through Low Moor, and covered the difficult 9½ miles (15·2km) in 22 minutes inclusive of a stop at North Bridge. Another noteworthy service at this time, although running only on Friday nights in the summer, was a through train from Halifax to Glasgow and Edinburgh via the Todmorden–Burnley line, Blackburn, Preston and the West Coast route.

Post-war changes began in June 1948, when passenger trains using the Pickle Bridge branch were re-routed via Halifax or the Spen Valley owing to the deterioration of the 'unnecessary' Wyke viaduct. This carried a 5mph speed restriction for twenty years prior to official closure in 1952. The Rishworth branch was closed completely in 1958, a fate which also befell the Stainland branch a year later. Halifax Old was renamed Halifax Town in 1951, but reverted to plain Halifax ten years later. Differentiation from other stations was no longer necessary, as North Bridge had been closed in 1955 on the withdrawal of passenger services over the Halifax & Ovenden Junction route. This line, along with the Halifax High Level Railway, was completely closed in 1960. DMUs took over the Bradford to Huddersfield via Halifax services on 2 November 1959, but most of these were withdrawn on 14 June 1965 to leave only scant passenger workings between Dryclough junction and Greetland.

CHAPTER V

Huddersfield

MAIN LINE THROUGH THE PENNINES

The façade of Huddersfield station has the only railway architecture of real merit in the whole of South and West Yorkshire. Dominating the town's St George's Square, it boasts a magnificent frontage no less than 416ft (129m) long with a central projecting portico of eight Corinthian columns 68ft (21m) high. On either side colonnades connect with identical smaller buildings each incorporating a further four columns. John Betjeman has described the structure as 'the most splendid station façade in England' and as being 'like an enormous classical country house', while Nikolaus Pevsner sees it as 'one of the best early railway stations'. It is the presence of a carved coat of arms surmounting each of the end-buildings which gives a clue as to why Huddersfield, by no means the largest of West Yorkshire settlements, was favoured with such architectural grandeur. At the southern end is the L & Y crest, while its confrere is that of the less familiar Huddersfield & Manchester Railway & Canal Company with its possibly unique beehive alluding to general industry. These two companies were originally hostile to one another, but eventually came to a local agreement and decided to celebrate the fact by building a common station to the highest possible standards.

The genesis of this agreement was protracted for, like so many other towns in the region, Huddersfield was bypassed by the first wave of railway promotion. The Huddersfield & Wakefield Railway was a stillborn child of 1824–5, while the Huddersfield & Leeds Railway of 1835 met with no more success. It was projected to join the North Midland near Methley, but the fear of Parliamentary opposition from the

Manchester & Leeds company caused the scheme to be abandoned. The town was brought within $1\frac{1}{2}$ hours of Leeds in 1840 when coaches began running to Cooper Bridge in connection with M & L trains, and in 1843 this company surveyed a $3\frac{1}{4}$ mile (5·2km) branch from the same station into the centre of Huddersfield. The route selected was so close to the bottom of the valley that it would have been impossible to extend the line beyond the town, and therefore the scheme was received with decided coolness. The M & L was described as 'the most brutal line in the whole kingdom', while another local citizen remarked: 'They have clapped us in a hole and want to keep us there.' A public meeting ended in uproar when the company's general manager stated that the Huddersfield traffic 'was not worth stopping the engine for'.

One result of the opening of the M & L was to cause a decline in the receipts of the Huddersfield Canal, which after seventeen years under construction had been completed in 1811 to provide a link with Ashton-under-Lyne. It cost over £400,000, largely as a result of the then prodigious difficulties in boring a 3 miles 176yd (5·00km) tunnel through the Pennine watershed at Standedge (a nineteenth century corruption of the more accurate Stanedge (stoneedge). As early as 1825 it had been suggested that the canal be filled in and the tunnel used for a railway, while the M & L later attempted to purchase the waterway so as to gain a monopoly of the local carrying trade. The canal company rejected this offer, and decided in May 1844 to sell out to the Huddersfield & Manchester Railway which had been locally promoted earlier the same year to build a line from Cooper Bridge to a junction at Stalybridge with the Sheffield, Ashton-under-Lyne & Manchester Railway. The combined interests took the title of the Huddersfield & Manchester Railway & Canal Company, it being agreed that the proposed line should be built on a course approximately parallel to that of the canal. This would save construction costs, particularly in passing under Standedge where the existing tunnel would enable estimates to be more accurate, allow for the old shafts to be re-used and permit the removal of earth by barge. It was in fact later estimated that the presence of the earlier tunnel saved as much as £70,000.

When the preamble of the Bill for the formation of the H & M was proved, the *Railway Times* commented that 'a great blow has been struck against the grasping monopoly of the Manchester & Leeds'. This company had at the same time put forward its own scheme for a low-level branch to Huddersfield, but it was rejected by a Commons committee. The H & M was looked on with more favour and was incorporated in 1845; it not only absorbed the Huddersfield Canal but was able to purchase for £46,560 Sir John Ramsden's Canal which connected the town with the Calder & Hebble Navigation and had been completed in 1776.

The H & M formed a part of one of several schemes put forward during the Railway Mania to provide a more direct route from Leeds to Manchester. It was promoted contemporaneously with the Leeds, Dewsbury & Manchester Railway, which was initially planned to run through Morley and Dewsbury to Thornhill and then parallel the M & L almost as far as Cooper Bridge. The section on to Huddersfield was included in both the H & M and LD & M Bills, but under its 1845 incorporation Act the Leeds company was only permitted to build this stretch if work on it was not begun by the H & M within eighteen months. A similar clause was included in the Act of another company which was incorporated in the same year. This was the Huddersfield & Sheffield Junction Railway, more fully described in the next section, which was to join the H & M at Paddock or Springwood junction as it was later known. The company was to have running powers from Paddock as far as Huddersfield station, but could build this section of line itself if six months elapsed without construction work beginning on the H & M.

This rather confusing situation was resolved by a series of negotiations which could easily have given Huddersfield a totally different pattern of railway ownership. Amalgamation of the H & M, LD & M and the Leeds & Thirsk Railway to form a trunk line connecting industrial Lancashire with the North East was an ideal which only just failed to materialise. The Sheffield, Ashton-under-Lyne & Manchester Railway, which had itself projected a line through Standedge to Huddersfield in 1843, now sought to acquire a monopoly of the area's rail network. Its plan was to use Huddersfield as a springboard from which to reach Leeds, and it was nearly successful for in February 1846, the H & M shareholders rejected an amalgamation by a narrow 4,088 votes to 3,475. The SA & M also managed to have no less than five directors on the provisional committee of the Huddersfield & Sheffield Junction, but again there was disagreement and the M & L seized its opportunity to get into Huddersfield. Despite the most intense Parliamentary opposition from the SA & M, it absorbed the H & SJ under an Act of 1846. At the same time the LD & M obtained sanction to abandon its line from Thornhill to Cooper Bridge, the M & L having granted running powers over this section of its main line. The final development occurred in February 1847 when the M & L obtained the running powers from Cooper Bridge to Paddock which were essential to reach its isolated H & SJ metals; in return it agreed not to oppose the amalgamation of the H & M and LD & M with the London & North Western which was authorised in 1847.

The agreement in fact went further for under it Huddersfield station and the section of line from here to Paddock were to be made at the joint expense of the H & M and M & L (it was formally made L & NW and L & Y joint in 1862). This was a complete change from the acrimonies of three years earlier, and hence plans were drawn up for a common station which would suitably commemorate the new-found harmony. J. P. Pritchett the elder of York was commissioned to carry out the designs, for which the tenders totalled just over £20,000. When the foundation stone had been laid on 9 October 1846 by Lord Fitzwilliam a public holiday was declared, the church bells in the town being rung from dawn to dusk. One wing of the station was completed for the opening in August 1847 of the most-needed section of line, running from Huddersfield to join the L & Y at Heaton Lodge junction, while a second line of rails on this stretch was brought into use in November when goods traffic began. The major constructional work was the 663yd (603m) Huddersfield viaduct, which had to be raised to a higher level at an additional cost of £1,000 owing to errors in laying out the gradients. It was October 1850 before the station was finally finished, the central portion housing elaborate refreshment rooms which functioned until at least 1883.

The L & NW trans-Pennine route was noted for its remarkable engineering, almost $5\frac{1}{2}$ miles (8·8km) of the line being in tunnel. On the LD & M section the main work was Morley tunnel, described in the previous chapter. On the H & M portion it was not Standedge but the comparatively minor 685yd (623m) Huddersfield tunnel which caused delays. The difficulties were primarily due to poor setting out, although the labourers claimed they were divine retribution on the directors for having reduced their wages! Completion of this key trans-Pennine link did not therefore take place until 1849, when the L & NW took over the existing H & M locomotive stock which had been operating the isolated Huddersfield to Heaton Lodge junction section for very nearly two years. Through traffic from Huddersfield to Leeds had however been included in the 1848 agreement by which the L & Y temporarily worked the LD & M.

From Huddersfield the H & M climbed up the Colne Valley on a ruling gradient of 1 in 105 to enter the 3 miles 66yd (4·89km) Nicholson tunnel at Standedge almost on the 700ft (217m) contour. Like both Summit and Woodhead this work was the longest in Britain when opened, but it managed to go one better than its predecessors by retaining the distinction for nearly forty years. It was the Great Western which once again removed the underground 'blue ribbon' from Yorkshire, this time with the completion of the Severn tunnel in 1886. The Nicholson tunnel was named after its contractor, Thomas Nicholson, who worked on the original Woodhead tunnel. It cost £201,608 compared with an estimate of £147,240, provided employment for almost two thousand men at the height of constructional operations, and used over 150,000lb (67,500kg) of candles at a cost of £3,618. All trains were at first preceded through the single-line bore by a pilot engine, one of its drivers appearing in court in 1850 for 'being found drunk and incapable at his engine but nevertheless had taken his engine through the tunnel and back again piloting trains'. As traffic increased this system caused substantial delays and, according to G. P. Neale in

Railway Reminiscences, led to the first introduction of staff working in this country.

The opening of the H & M caused expansion of industry in the Colne Valley all the way up to Marsden, transforming the factory pattern which had originally been established by the Huddersfield Canal. The area led the West Riding in the introduction of the Jacquard loom, specialising in tweeds and woollens for the popular market and supplying much of the material for the traditional cloth caps of the northern working man. Huddersfield itself had been less than half the size of Halifax in the mid-eighteenth century, and John Wesley had said of the inhabitants: 'A wilder people I never saw in England.' But from 1811 it began to pull ahead, largely as a result of being placed on a through waterway, and this trend continued when the town was served by a trunk railway route. Its population increased from 13,284 in 1821 to 30,880 in 1851. Huddersfield established a name throughout the world for fine worsteds, and was well laid out by the Ramsden family who were virtually the sole proprietors. In 1844 Friedrich Engels described the community as 'the handsomest by far of all the factory towns of Yorkshire and Lancashire, by reason of its charming situation and modern architecture'.

It was not until 1868 that Huddersfield was incorporated as a Borough, the boundaries being extended at the same time so that the number of inhabitants jumped from 34,877 in 1861 to 70,253 ten years later. A chemical industry was also by now becoming established as a result of the success of the local dyeing trade. Main line traffic into the town was thus increasing prodigiously; on a Saturday in August 1869 over 160 trains used the solitary platform which still formed a functional anti-climax to the station's grandiose façade. The tunnel at one end accentuated the bottleneck and, with one major accident occurring on average every two years, the existing layout was condemned by the Board of Trade. Yet it was not until 1878 that it was agreed to enlarge the station and at the same time erect joint L & NW/L & Y goods depots both here and at Hillhouse, $\frac{3}{4}$ mile (1·2km) to the north. Work on the station was delayed when the new overall roof collapsed on 10 August 1885, killing four men; it was finally

Page 141   Handling the traffic: (*above*) gas lighting and coal heating add little warmth to the grim interior of a pre-electronic Rotherham control office; (*below*) the computer-controlled train describer panel in the new Leeds (City) signal box, opened in 1967 and superseding seventeen manual boxes

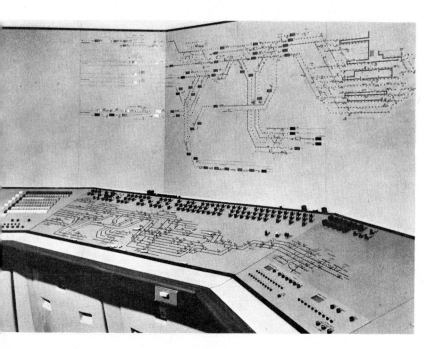

Page 142 Minor lines: (*above*) inaugural train at Kirkburton on the opening in 1867 of the $4\frac{1}{4}$ mile branch from Deighton, near Huddersfield. The locomotive is London & North Western 2–4–0T no 37 *Hawk*; (*below*) track-laying train at Royds Green Lower, on the East & West Yorkshire Union Railways' branch from Robin Hood

completed in October 1886, the extensions including a new
island platform.

At Standedge work on making a second single line bore,
the Nelson tunnel, was started in 1868 and completed on 12
February 1871. The unique water troughs inside the twin
bores were in use by 1878, the tunnels providing the only
suitable level stretch of line on this steeply graded route.
Between 1883 and 1894 the L & NW quadrupled the whole
of the Colne Valley main line, providing a third railway
tunnel at Standedge, this time a double line bore, which
was opened on 5 August 1894. At this time most of the main
line services comprised expresses between Newcastle, Hull
or Leeds and Manchester or Liverpool. The L & NW did
not seriously compete for London traffic from Huddersfield;
in 1896, for instance, there was only one through train from
the town to Euston.

The next three decades brought few changes. In 1930
George Bernard Shaw claimed that Huddersfield was 'in a
dark and pagan condition', a statement which some critics
might also apply to its post-war rail facilities. Traffic through
the town fell to the extent that the two single-line Standedge
tunnels were closed on 31 October 1966, just after being
used for tests in connection with the Channel Tunnel project.
Yet there have been some positive improvements, as
instanced on 2 January 1961 when 'Trans Pennine' DMUs
took over the Hull–Leeds–Manchester–Liverpool express services. In the first week they brought about a thirty per cent
rise in the number of passengers travelling over this route
from Huddersfield. Easily the most important development
was the decision to save the town's finest building from
threatened demolition, the station façade and platform 1
being purchased by Huddersfield Corporation for £52,400
to mark the centenary of the Borough in 1968. This splendid
gesture was followed by extensive restoration, involving a
complete cleaning of the stonework.

SOUTH TO SHEFFIELD

The Huddersfield & Sheffield Junction Railway cut across
the grain of the country, burrowing through minor water-

I

To London for five shillings. An undated excursion bill of the London & North Western Railway, probably about 1860

sheds and striding over tributary valleys of the rivers Colne,
Dearne and Don before joining the Manchester, Sheffield &
Lincolnshire line at Huddersfield junction, Penistone, $\frac{1}{2}$ mile
(0·8km) east of the original passenger station. Some costly
engineering works were therefore involved, there being in
all over $2\frac{1}{4}$ miles (3·6km) of tunnels, four major viaducts and
57 bridges. The line parted from the H & M in a short cutting between the Huddersfield and Springwood tunnels.
Within the first mile were Paddock viaduct, fifteen arches
and four iron spans curving 70ft (22m) above the Colne; the
short Yew Green tunnel; and then Lockwood viaduct, one
of the largest in Britain with its 34 arches towering 136ft
(41·5m) over the river Holme. The valley of the Holme was
then followed as far as the longest tunnel on the line, the
1,631yd (1·48km) Thurstonland in which severe flooding
occurred during construction. Further engineering works
were Cumberworth tunnel, 906yd (824m); Denby Dale
viaduct, 112ft (34·7m) high; Wellhouse Hill tunnel, 415yd
(378m); and Penistone viaduct, only 98ft (29·8m) high but
330yd (300m) long. There were no settlements of any
importance along the route, the prime purpose of the line
being to shorten the rail journey from Huddersfield to
Sheffield from $43\frac{3}{4}$ miles (70km) to $26\frac{1}{2}$ miles (42·4km).

Opening of the H & SJ in 1850 was a rather inauspicious
occasion for the first train stalled in Thurstonland tunnel and
had to be divided. The line was initially worked by the
MS & L, which in 1857 retimed the trains to connect with
the new King's Cross–Manchester expresses introduced on
1 August. In 1859 this company and the GN inaugurated
through coach workings from King's Cross to Huddersfield.
An Act of 1859 laid down that the L & Y must provide 'all
reasonable facilities' for the transmission of such traffic,
although the L & NW had opposed the move as the new
trains used a route which was 21 miles (33km) shorter than
that from Euston via Stockport. On 30 July 1866 the Midland
was authorised to run into Huddersfield from Beighton on
the former North Midland line via Sheffield Victoria and
Penistone, while a further Act of 1872 sanctioned the provision of additional accommodation at Huddersfield station.
But the company made little if any use of these powers owing

to the large number of restrictive clauses. Change came on
1 July 1870 when the L & Y began to work the Sheffield–
Huddersfield trains forward from Penistone; precisely twelve
years later it collaborated with the MS & L in introducing a
new service of through coaches to King's Cross from Huddersfield (later Bradford) in conjunction with the lightweight
expresses then being put on by the GN to and from Manchester. MS & L trains reappeared at Huddersfield on 1
December 1882, when the L & Y also began to work trains
throughout between Huddersfield and Sheffield. The final
stage in the progress of the Penistone route towards main line
status came on 1 May 1900 when a through service was put
on between Bradford Exchange and Marylebone over the
Great Central's new London extension. It was worked as far
as Sheffield Victoria by the L & Y, which made great play
of the fine scenery to be enjoyed from the carriage window.
The Huddersfield–King's Cross workings were then diverted
by Wakefield Kirkgate and Doncaster.

   The accident prone nature of the Huddersfield station area
tended to seep southwards towards Penistone. Owing to a
strike of stone masons, Denby Dale viaduct was originally
built as a timber trestle which perhaps erred on the spidery
side for during construction it partially collapsed in a gale
on 27 January 1847. In 1851 Robert Stephenson examined
this structure as well as a number of other L & Y timber
viaducts and reported an 'entire conviction of their perfect
safety', but by 1874 the timbers at Denby Dale were decaying
and a speed restriction was recommended. A stone viaduct
was opened on 16 May 1880; in November 1881 it was
reported unsafe owing to the effects of coal workings, and it
was not until 1884 that underpinning was completed and
the original timber trestle dismantled. Another disaster
occurred on 2 February 1916, this time at Penistone viaduct
when two arches disintegrated and plunged a 2–4–2T into
the wreckage. Its chimney was accorded the doubtful accolade
of becoming a plant pot on Brockholes station platform, but
the rest of the engine was cut up on the spot. The collapse
was diagnosed as being due to heavy rain scouring the
foundations. The viaduct was reopened on 14 August, trains
terminating at a temporary Barnsley Road Halt at the north

end of the structure prior to this date. There was also a large number of accidents caused by runaways; one of the more spectacular occurred on 20 August 1865 when the breakage of a coupling at Lockwood caused some coaches to run free for almost two miles (3·2km) before coming to grief over the edge of Huddersfield viaduct.

Unique and famous features of the line were the carvings in sandstone at Berry Brow station. One depicted a train of four-wheeled coaches leaving a tunnel and was made about 1866 by Thomas Stocks, while the other was executed by his son, J. C. Stocks, in 1886. It represented a Barton Wright 0–4–4T and train surmounted by a facial study of Thomas Swinburn who worked as an engineer on the H & SJ. The earlier carving has been damaged beyond recognition by vandalism, but the later work was moved to York Railway Museum in 1963. By this time the route had lost its main line status with the withdrawal of the Bradford–Marylebone workings on 4 January 1960 as a result of the run-down of the former GC London extension. On 24 February 1958 the 'South Yorkshireman' had been temporarily embedded in a large snowdrift just south of Denby Dale viaduct, while another noteworthy date was 2 November 1959 when DMUs took over the local services. Single line working between Clayton West junction and Penistone was introduced on 24 November 1969.

MORE TALK THAN ACTION

Neighbouring urban centres of any size were often connected by rail at the first attempt, although sometimes a Bill had to be reintroduced before success was achieved. Occasionally, as with the main line between Doncaster and Wakefield, repeated efforts had to be made in order to obtain Parliamentary sanction. But a most unusual case was that of Huddersfield and Halifax, towns with a combined population of over 135,000 by 1871, for despite more than a dozen attempts they never acquired a direct rail link. All the schemes fell through owing to conflict between rival companies, shortage of finance or engineering problems presented by the 750ft (232m) high watershed between the Colne and Calder valleys.

The indirect link was provided by a curve from Bradley on the H & M to Bradley Wood junction on the L & Y, which was opened for passenger services in 1852. Most of these were worked by the L & Y, taking an average of about 25 minutes to traverse the 10¾ route miles (17·2km) between the two towns. The direct distance was only 5¾ miles (9·2km), and in fact a short line was sanctioned in the same year as the H & M curve. It formed part of the ill-fated West Riding Union Railways, described in chapter three. There were no further developments until 1864 when the independent Halifax, Huddersfield & Keighley Railway was rejected in preference for the shorter Halifax & Ovenden Junction scheme. The following year the Midland came up with the first of its projects to gain access to the two towns, promoting a line from Barnsley to join the L & NW Kirkburton branch which is described in the last section of this chapter. It was to have running powers into Huddersfield, from where the two companies intended jointly to construct an extension to Halifax. The Barnsley–Kirkburton scheme was withdrawn when the L & Y offered running powers via Penistone, while the extension was rejected on standing orders. It was jointly put forward once more in 1866 and rejected, and then again the following year only to be withdrawn. The L & Y had also promoted a Bill for a Huddersfield–Elland line in 1866, but this too was unsuccessful. There matters rested until 1872 when the Midland decided to postpone a line between the two centres for a year, by which time the Huddersfield–Halifax–Keighley scheme had reappeared. The company hence supported this project only to withdraw at the last moment and, as related in chapter three, the GN then stepped in to build the section north of Halifax. There was renewed hope in 1874 when the Midland put forward a Huddersfield–Halifax–Bradford line, in effect forming a new route to the north, while the L & NW and L & Y countered with a joint Huddersfield–Elland link. Yet once again rival schemes proved to have a rather negative value for both Bills were rejected.

This sad saga seemed at last to be coming to an end when in 1882 the Hull & Barnsley Railway (to use its abbreviated title) was authorised to build an extension to Huddersfield and Halifax from a double junction with its main line near Hemsworth. Two years earlier the company had unsuccessfully sought running powers to the two towns, while the GN had backed the abortive Huddersfield South & East Junction Railway running along approximately the same course from a junction with the West Riding & Grimsby Joint. Now at last success seemed at hand, and the Midland obtained running powers over the extension in 1883. Yet disappointment was to follow as a result of the chronic insolvency of the H & B. In 1887 the powers as far as Huddersfield were transferred to a new local company, the Hull & North-Western Junction Railway, while the section to Halifax was abandoned. But the new venture was no more successful than its predecessor, and it too was abandoned in 1894.

Four years later came the final attempt on the grand scale in the form of the Midland's West Riding Lines Bill. As already outlined in earlier chapters, it originally envisaged a main line from Royston to Bradford with an off-shoot to Huddersfield and Halifax. Just over fifty years after the first attempt, this last bid for a cut-off between the two towns was abandoned when the L & Y provided running powers up the Spen Valley to Halifax. The Midland hence obtained sanction in 1899 for a branch from the Calder Valley main line at Mirfield to a terminus at Huddersfield Newtown. Here there were to be extensive passenger facilities and a station hotel, while the company intended to have independent access by building a connection to the east end of the branch from the Royston–Thornhill section of the West Riding Lines scheme. It promoted a Bill for this purpose in 1907, but instead accepted running powers over the parallel Calder Valley route when these were offered by the L & Y.

The single track branch was opened for goods traffic in 1910. It had some substantial engineering works built to accommodate two lines of rails, including a 15-arch viaduct over the Colne at Bradley, but fundamentally they represented money wasted for at no point was the branch more than a quarter of a mile (0·4km) from the existing L & Y/ L & NW approach to the town. The Midland's dreams of rosy independence at Huddersfield quickly faded, the passenger station plans being shelved on the outbreak of World War I. A quick move following the Grouping was the construction of a connecting link where the Newtown branch ran alongside the Colne Valley main line. This was Red Doles junction, opened in October 1923 and making the section from here to Mirfield largely superfluous. It managed to survive until 1937, latterly for wagon storage, while the remainder of the branch into Newtown was closed in 1968.

NEW LINE TO LEEDS

During the attempts to obtain the Halifax direct line, counsel frequently made play of the fact that Huddersfield was suffering through being one of the few towns in Britain to have had no successful railway promotions since 1846. There was some truth in this claim, and indeed after 1850 only one new line of any real importance was opened in the area. It was authorised at the second attempt in 1892 and had a threefold purpose. The L & NW, having by now largely completed the widening of the former H & M, was anxious to eliminate the bottleneck formed by the section of the L & Y from Heaton Lodge junction to Dewsbury junction at Thornhill. It was also keen to widen the former LD & M on to Leeds, but was deterred by the vast number of old mine workings in the vicinity of Morley tunnel and the fact that at Staincliffe it was wedged between the GN and a steep scarp. A third influence was a campaign by the Spen Valley towns for a better service than that provided by the L & Y, a particularly sore point being the poor connections to Leeds. The L & NW therefore conceived a route which left the H & M between Bradley and Heaton Lodge junction, dived under the Calder Valley main line and then paralleled the L & Y's Spen Valley line from Mirfield as far as Cleckheaton. Curving through more than a half-circle and then back through a quarter-circle, it crossed two minor tributary valleys before piercing the Aire and Calder watershed by the 1 mile 571yd (2·13km) Gildersome tunnel to join the LD & M route at Farnley by an impressive flying junction. Other engineering works included the 819yd (745m) Gomersal tunnel.

The Leeds New Line, as it was always known, was opened for passenger traffic in 1900. Stopping services were withdrawn on 5 October 1953, but the route remained popular as an avoiding line despite being $1\frac{1}{2}$ miles (2·4km) longer than the ex-LD & M and having a total of five miles (8km) at 1 in 70. Many expresses not booked to stop at Dewsbury, including the 'Trans-Pennine' DMUs, were routed this way, the last remaining working being diverted via Mirfield in 1965 and the New Line closed completely in the following year.

BRANCH LINES

The Huddersfield area made up for its lack of through railway routes by having more branch lines than any other region in the industrial West Riding. They were all on the south side of the town, serving settlements which grew up at the heads of tributary valleys as a result of early textile or mining activities. Yet none of these operations achieved a sufficiently large scale to result in blanket industrialisation, and thus for the most part the branches ran through attractive rural surroundings.

Three of them were off-shoots of the H & SJ which, as already described, left the Holme Valley by means of Thurstonland tunnel. The promoters decided to serve the upper part of this valley by a double track branch terminating at Holmfirth which was opened at the same time as the parent line in 1850. There were other less fortunate similarities with regard to viaducts, the branch initially crossing the New Mill Dyke valley at Mytholmbridge by a timber trestle. Like that at Denby Dale, it was blown down during construction, in this case on 19 February 1849. Work on a replacement stone viaduct started in 1864; it had been brought into use and the timber structure partially demolished when inadequate foundations caused a total collapse on 3 December 1865. The incident occurred just prior to the approach of an early morning train, but fortunately this was stopped in time. Passengers were conveyed by road to and from Honley station until a new viaduct was opened in 1867. The branch was closed to passengers in 1959.

Troubles also beset the Meltham branch, which left the

H & SJ at the north end of Lockwood viaduct and climbed at
1 in 60 through pretty woodland surroundings. Opening for
goods traffic was delayed by the collapse of the 33yd (30m)
Netherton tunnel, and then had some false starts owing to a
severe slip in a cutting ¾ mile (1·2km) from Lockwood and
the subsidence of an embankment to such an extent that
several nearby cottages and a toll bar had to be demolished.
Passenger traffic finally commenced in 1869; as soon as the
branch was established the price of coal at Meltham fell by
3s 6d a ton. One of the shortest lived of stations was that at
Woodfield, about ½ mile (0·8km) from the junction, which
was open for only a month in 1874, it being locally estimated
that receipts averaged little more than a shilling a day.
Another unusual station was Meltham Mills Halt, erected
solely for the employees of Jonas Brooke's Thread Mills in
return for the sale of land for building the railway. Tickets
were issued at the mill office until the halt closed in September 1934, passenger traffic over the branch as a whole
ceasing in 1949. Like the other two branches to be described,
it was built as a single line.

The third off-shoot from the H & SJ was constructed not
only to tap traffic from collieries and mills but also to honour
a pledge made by the Midland Railway. When this company had sought powers for a Barnsley–Kirkburton link in
1865 it had agreed to serve the small town of Clayton West
en route. As already mentioned, the scheme was abandoned
by agreement with the L & Y which therefore undertook to
obtain powers for a line to this point from a junction between
Shepley and Denby Dale. The Act was procured in 1866, but
there then seemed to be some reluctance to fulfil obligations
for it was not until 1879 that the branch was opened. The
line fell at 1 in 70 and had the 511yd (465m) Shelley Woodhouse tunnel and all bridges built to accommodate double
track. An extension to the company's Barnsley branch, only
three miles (4·8km) from Clayton West, was authorised in
1893. It was envisaged in conjunction with the Retford,
Rotherham & Barnsley Railway of 1893, which would have
provided the GN with a direct route to Huddersfield as well
as giving the L & Y access to the developing South Yorkshire
coalfield. When this ambitious project collapsed the extension

became of dubious value, particularly as the Horbury fork (chapter seven) was then being constructed and would provide an equally good route between Huddersfield and Barnsley. It was accordingly abandoned in 1899. The Clayton West branch has followed the same pattern as its parent line, the passenger workings being taken over by DMUs on 2 November 1959. It is in some ways a remarkable survival for as long ago as 1881 receipts per annum were put at £1,811 and the working costs at £2,500.

The fourth and longest branch in the Huddersfield area had a rather different flavour in that it was built by the L & NW. It curved sharply away from the Colne Valley main line between Hillhouse and Bradley to climb at 1 in 66 through the outer suburbs of Huddersfield and then terminate amid more rural surroundings at Kirkburton. By a most remarkable co-incidence there was again trouble with a viaduct, this time at Whit'acre Mill where one of the seven arches fell into the Ramsden Canal on 15 February 1866 and delayed the opening of the branch to passengers until 1867. Trains were motor-fitted from 1916 onwards, but the 'Kirkburton Dick'—as the service was nicknamed— survived only until 1930. A major drawback had been that the stations were in the valley bottom whereas the settlements were well up the hill slopes. The branch completely closed except for traffic to private sidings at Deighton in 1965, the remaining short stub being abandoned in 1971.

An interesting industrial line, opened in February 1922, was the Huddersfield Gas Works Railway, which started at Newtown Yard and for a quarter of a mile (0·4km) ran down the centre of Beaumont Street and through the town's market. Flagmen preceded each train, and the wheels and motion of the locomotives were protected by wooden guards.

Huddersfield's tramways were laid to a gauge of 4ft 7¾in (1·41m) with the intention of allowing standard gauge wagons to be worked over the system by running them on their flanges. No connection with the main line network was ever made, although in September 1904 two specially built electric coal trams began running to local mills from a spur laid into Hillhouse goods yard. This service, which was unique in Britain, lasted until September 1934.

CHAPTER VI

Sheffield and Rotherham

CITY OF STEEL

Sheffield, the principal settlement of South Yorkshire, must inevitably be compared with Leeds, the dominant centre of West Yorkshire. The two communities have several similarities, and also some significant differences. Sheffield, from a communications standpoint, is less favourably situated. It has grown up around a source of abundant water supply, provided by small rivers flowing steeply down from the Derbyshire hills which form a barrier to the south and west. The only level exit is along the Don Valley to the north, and thus Sheffield has shared with Bradford the handicap of having its sole natural routeway facing in the wrong direction. Leeds had all the advantages of a navigable river by 1700, but it was not until 1751 that the Don Navigation was completed to Tinsley. It was 1819 before the waterway was further extended by the opening of the three mile (4·8km) Sheffield Canal.

Yet it has been aptly said of Sheffield that 'no other city has grown to such a size in a situation so unfavourable to greatness'. The growth, like that of Leeds, had its origins in the later Middle Ages, but instead of cloth-making the industry responsible was cutlery. The reference of Chaucer's miller to 'a Sheffield thwitel' (a table knife) is well known, and by the 15th century the town had numerous water grinding mills along the banks of the several rivers. Subsequent landmarks were the invention of crucible steel in 1740 by Benjamin Huntsman, a Doncaster clockmaker, and Thomas Boulsover's discovery of a means of plating copper with silver. Steel manufacturing was established in the town by 1780.

These developments were not at first sufficient to overcome the drawbacks posed by physical situation. In 1831 at the start of the railway age Sheffield's population was 91,692, markedly less than the 123,393 of Leeds. By 1849 the town was served by only two railway companies; in the same year Leeds accommodated the tracks of four companies and the trains of two more. But steel-making soon proved more compatible with railways than the lighter industries of Leeds, and the two engendered mutual growth. Railways proved ideal for distributing the steel: the steelworks expanded and hence more railways were needed. By 1851 the town was producing 86 per cent of Britain's cast steel. This chain reaction brought about a remarkable if delayed expansion, and L. Faucher was able to remark: 'Sheffield is the only city in England which presents as gloomy an appearance as Leeds.' The population of the town trebled between 1843 and 1893, the number of employees in the heavy trades increasing fourfold in the period from 1843 to 1873. Sheffield became a city in 1893, and in the 1911 census its population for the first time exceeded that of Leeds.

THE FIRST RAILWAYS

Sheffield shares with Leeds the distinction of having important links with the first primitive railways. In this case it provides the first documentary evidence of the spread of wooden waggonways southwards from Tyneside. A waggonway was probably built at the Duke of Norfolk's Sheffield Park Colliery in 1722–3, and was certainly in existence by 1729. A series of accounts include references to one Robert Littlewood being paid 'his Expences in going to Newcastle about the Wagen Way', and to expenditure 'Pd for the Woman that was killed with the Waggon 0.10.6'. The line, which ran to a yard in the town, was out of use by the 1770s.

About 1772 John Curr, later author of *The Coal Viewer and the Engine Builder's Practical Companion* (1797), was appointed viewer to the colliery, and in 1774 laid out a two mile (3·2km) wooden waggonway into the centre of Sheffield at a cost of £3,000. It reduced the cost of carriage from 2s 8d to 1s 2d per ton, but meant that the colliery proprietors were no longer willing to sell low-priced coal direct from the pit-head to the public. This, according to a contemporary letter to *The Universal Magazine of Knowledge and Pleasure*, was

> so disagreeable to the populace, that they assembled in a prodigious number, and destroyed several of their [the proprietors'] carriages, totally pulled down a watch-house and compting-house in their new coal-yard, and set fire to all the timber machinery erected for discharging their loading, brought one carriage through the town, afterwards kindled a fire in, and sent it flaming into the river.

Curr's son refers to the event in his book *Railway Locomotion and Steam Navigation* (1847), stating that 'a riot ensued —the railway was torn up—the coal staith burnt, and the inventor, my father, reduced to the necessity of concealment in a wood, for three days and nights, to escape the fury of the populace'. The waggonway was rebuilt with wooden materials, and was closed before the end of the century.

The spirit of discontent in Sheffield towards the monopoly enjoyed by the Duke of Norfolk and his colliery proprietors continued to smoulder for another sixty years, and was directly responsible for the promotion of the first locomotive-hauled railway in South Yorkshire. An alternative source of coal became feasible from the 1770s with the construction of the short Greasbrough Canal which, with its associated waggonways, tapped the coal deposits to the north-west of Rotherham. Bills for a rail link between Sheffield and Rotherham were unsuccessfully promoted in both 1834 and 1835. An ingenious proposal was that tubs of coal would be loaded on to barges at Greasbrough, transferred by crane to the railway at Rotherham, and then at Sheffield off-loaded on to road carts for distribution round the town. Not surprisingly, the proposals provoked intense opposition from the Duke of Norfolk, as well as from the Don Navigation and the Sheffield Canal. In addition, 120 inhabitants of Rotherham petitioned against the line because they dreaded 'an incursion of the idle, drunken and dissolute portion of the Sheffield people'.

In the meantime, the minor Railway Mania of 1835–6 had brought the promotion of the North Midland Railway from Derby to Leeds. Sheffield was by far the largest of the

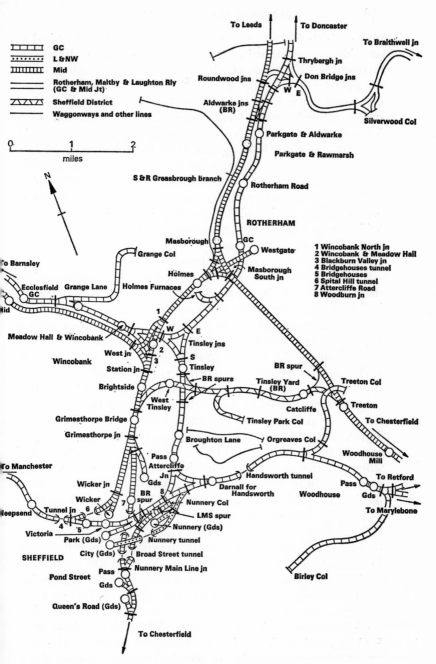

Legend:
- GC
- L &NW
- Mid
- Rotherham, Maltby & Laughton Rly (GC & Mid Jt)
- Sheffield District
- Waggonways and other lines

0   1   2
miles

N

To Leeds
To Doncaster
To Braithwell jn
Thrybergh jn
Roundwood jns
Don Bridge jns
W E
Aldwarke jns (BR)
Silverwood Col
Parkgate & Aldwarke
Parkgate & Rawmarsh
S & R Greasbrough branch
Rotherham Road
ROTHERHAM
Masborough
GC
Westgate
Grange Col
Hölmes
Masborough South jn
To Barnsley
Ecclesfield GC
Grange Lane
Holmes Furnaces
Mid
1
Meadow Hall & Wincobank
W
E
Tinsley jns
West jn
2
S
Wincobank
3
Tinsley
Station jn
BR spur
BR spurs
Tinsley Yard (BR)
Treeton Col
Brightside
West Tinsley
Catcliffe
Treeton
Grimesthorpe Bridge
Tinsley Park Col
To Chesterfield
Grimesthorpe jn
Broughton Lane
Orgreaves Col
Woodhouse Mill
To Manchester
Pass
Attercliffe Jn
Handsworth tunnel
Pass
To Retford
Wicker jn
Gds
Darnall for Handsworth
Woodhouse
Gds
Wicker
BR spur
8
Nunnery Col
To Marylebone
Deepsend
Tunnel jn
6
7
LMS spur
4
Nunnery (Gds)
5
Victoria
Nunnery tunnel
Park (Gds)
City (Gds)
Broad Street tunnel
SHEFFIELD
Nunnery Main Line jn
Pond Street
Pass
Birley Col
Gds
Queen's Road (Gds)
To Chesterfield

1 Wincobank North jn
2 Wincobank & Meadow Hall
3 Blackburn Valley jn
4 Bridgehouses tunnel
5 Bridgehouses
6 Spital Hill tunnel
7 Attercliffe Road
8 Woodburn jn

Map 5: Sheffield and Rotherham

towns which George Stephenson contemptuously brushed to one side as a result of his insistence on minimal gradients. He favoured a due south–north route along the Rother valley via Eckington, arguing that a deviation through the Drone and Sheaf valleys to serve Sheffield would be indirect, too steeply graded for the locomotives of the day and too costly because of the 100ft (30·5m) deep cuttings which would be necessary. Instead, he suggested that the town would be best connected to the North Midland by resurrecting the Sheffield & Rotherham scheme. Understandably, the idea of such an indirect route southwards was not well received in the town, and a shorter Sheffield Union Railway to join the North Midland at Woodhouse Mill was put forward. But after a great deal of controversy a local committee ultimately accepted Stephenson's suggestions.

The Sheffield & Rotherham Railway was incorporated at the same time as the North Midland in 1836. It was authorised to extend from the Wicker, in the centre of Sheffield, to a terminus at Westgate in Rotherham, a town with a population of 4,083 in 1831 and already famous for its ironworks founded by Samuel Walker in 1746. Frederick Swanwick, one of Stephenson's pupils, was the engineer. The main line of the S & R opened in glorious isolation in 1838, a 'very elegant' train of yellow-painted carriages leaving the 'handsome and spacious shed' at Wicker. In the first nine weeks 82,175 passengers were carried, the number growing to 455,375 in the first year. The coal situation was greatly eased when a single track branch alongside the North Midland main line from Holmes to the Greasbrough Canal was built by the NM and leased to the S & R. It was opened in 1839, making an end-on junction with Earl Fitzwilliam's private railways and enabling coal to be transported from the Greasbrough area to Sheffield without dependence on other canal interests. Opening of the NM from Derby to the Rotherham station at Masborough, and a connecting spur with the Greasbrough branch, took place simultaneously in May 1840. From this date North Midland trains commenced to work into Wicker station, and it became possible to travel from Sheffield to London via Derby and Hampton in about $9\frac{1}{2}$ hours. By October there were 24 North Midland and 20 S & R

Page 159 Special motive power: (*above*) steam rail-motor at Sowerby Bridge on the Rishworth branch service. These vehicles were introduced by the Lancashire & Yorkshire Railway in 1907 in an attempt to combat tramcar competition; (*below*) the one-off Beyer-Garratt no 9999 (originally no 2395), built by the LNER in 1925 for assisting heavy coal trains up the 1 in 40 Wentworth bank, near Barnsley. The most powerful steam locomotive in Britain here takes a breather on the Wentworth Silkstone Colliery branch at the foot of the bank

Page 160 Modernisation: (*above*) Co-Co electric no 27005 *Minerva* pauses at Penistone in 1966 with a Manchester–Sheffield train. Through passenger services on this route were electrified in 1954 but withdrawn in 1970 when the line west of Penistone became freight-only; (*below*) rebuilding of Leeds (City) in 1964 in readiness for the closure of Leeds (Central). The river Aire flows underneath the station to be joined by the Leeds & Liverpool canal.

trains in and out of the terminus each weekday, the latter operating to and from Rotherham on an even interval basis. The previous month special trains had been run to Swinton for the Doncaster races.

At first the S & R passed through comparatively rural countryside, but its presence quickly stimulated the outward movement of steel-making firms from both Sheffield and Rotherham. As early as 1845 five major companies had transferred their works to sites alongside the line, and this once picturesque stretch of the Don Valley was rapidly succumbing to all-embracing industrialisation. The successful growth of the S & R culminated in it being worked by the Midland Railway from 10 October 1844, and absorbed into the larger company in 1845.

LINKS EAST AND WEST

Sheffield's railway position in the early 1840s was unenviable. The S & R, despite its success, was only a glorified branch line, and all traffic for the south had to reverse at Masborough. The town was impatiently looking forward to the day when it would have rail links not only up the Sheaf valley but also to the east coast and westwards into Lancashire. Manchester, only 35 miles (56km) away in a direct line, had attracted many early schemes, but between the two communities was the major barrier of the Pennine chain with a watershed which at no point dropped below the 1,300ft (403m) contour.

In 1813 William Chapman proposed to build a railway surmounting the ridge by six inclined planes and a $2\frac{3}{4}$ mile (4.4km) water tunnel to link up with projected extensions of the Peak Forest Canal in Derbyshire. It was clumsy, but it would have been an improvement on the 90 mile (144km) canal journey via Huddersfield which frequently took eight days. A proposal of the late 1820s for a Grand Commercial Canal linking South Yorkshire with Lancashire collapsed, as did an 1826 scheme for a 21 mile railway from the Sheffield Canal basin to the Peak Forest Railway at Chapel Milton. At this time there was increasing European competition in the American market for edge tools and cutlery, and Sheffield

K

was losing ground because of the lengthy journey time to Liverpool.

The difficulties seemed to be approaching an end with the incorporation in 1831 of the Sheffield & Manchester Railway. It was a most ambitious scheme for so early a date, ascending the Sheaf Valley by means of a 1 in 32 self-acting incline, plunging through a three-mile (4·8km) tunnel into the Hope Valley, and then conquering the main barrier of Rushup Edge with the aid of four inclined planes. The engineers were George and Robert Stephenson and it is perhaps surprising that they, as leading advocates of locomotive haulage, should have put forward a scheme relying on rope working. It has been suggested by George Dow that the Stephensons, owing to pressure of work, simply put their names to the survey.

Despite the optimism, the Sheffield & Manchester project proved to be hamstrung by the engineering obstacles and controversy over capital estimates. It faded away in 1833, but all the while the need for a line between the two centres was increasing. Remarkable industrial expansion was taking place in Lancashire, and thus a good market for South Yorkshire coal seemed assured. Further surveys were undertaken by Charles Vignoles in 1836, the result being the incorporation in 1837 of the Sheffield, Ashton-under-Lyne & Manchester Railway. It followed a more northerly route via the Don and Etherow valleys, passing under the Pennine ridge by what was to become the infamous Woodhead tunnel. This was in a bleak and windswept location remote from any large settlement, and four miles (6·4km) of cart roads had to be constructed across the moors for the conveyance of materials for the works and the building of houses and stables. After a dispute over shares, Vignoles resigned as engineer in December 1839 and was replaced by Joseph Locke.

By 1841 the economic depression was creating great difficulties, it even being suggested that the project should be abandoned as it formed a duplicate east-west route to the Manchester & Leeds Railway. Passengers from Sheffield could, it was argued, now travel via Normanton and the M & L. The company was critically short of money, and it was only after a struggle that it agreed to provide tents for

400 men who were working on the tunnel's west shaft and had been sleeping in the open. When money was available work went on day and night, and by 1842 the labour force had grown to a thousand men who were living almost like savages in stone shelters. In the following year atmospheric traction was seriously considered so that capital could be saved by reducing the dimensions of the tunnel.

Momentous changes could have stemmed from a Bill deposited in 1844 under which the SA & M would have been jointly leased by the Midland and Manchester & Birmingham railways. It would have provided the Midland with a direct route to Manchester, but at the last moment was repudiated by the SA & M shareholders. The line had reached Woodhead at the western end of the tunnel by 1844, and opening of the eastern section, from Dunford Bridge at the opposite end to a temporary terminus at Bridgehouses in Sheffield, took place in July 1845. Its 19 miles (30km) were on a virtually continuous gradient of 1 in 120 to 1 in 135, steepening to 1 in 100 to the east of Penistone and having some severe curvature.

Coaches plied over the moorland between Dunford Bridge and Woodhead until the opening of the great tunnel, and hence the complete route, in December 1845. At 3 miles 22yd (4·85km) the tunnel was then the longest in the country, and was described by the *Sheffield Iris* as a 'a wondrous triumph of art over nature'. It was a single bore built on a gradient of 1 in 201, rising to a summit level of 1,010ft (313m) at the eastern portal; it was thus exceptionally difficult to work, all trains at first being taken through by a pilot engine. The tunnel cost some £200,000 compared with the initial estimate of £60,000, and consumed about 157 tons of gunpowder.

More sadly, 26 lives were lost during its construction and 140 navvies injured. These figures caused considerable public outcry which was inflamed by three papers read before the Statistical Society of Manchester. John Roberton, the Society's president, alleged that as many as fifteen men had been living in a small and filthy hut with only a roof of thatch, and added: 'It is difficult to conceive a set of people more thoroughly depraved, degraded and reckless.' He claimed many accidents were caused by intoxication. Thomas

Nicholson, the contractor for the eastern portion of the tunnel, denied most of the allegations in a pamphlet, but the controversy was instrumental in leading to a Select Committee of the House of Commons on Railway Labourers being established in 1846. This in turn brought about a gradual improvement in working conditions for railway navvies.

The tunnel had been opened for less than a year when it was realised that a single bore was inadequate. The contract for a second tunnel for the up line was let in February 1847, and this time more attention was paid to welfare, a school for the children of the workpeople being established at Woodhead in September 1848. During May 1849 there was a serious outbreak of cholera, many of the navvies on the site taking flight when they saw an extra supply of coffins being brought up to Woodhead to meet the need. Only 100 out of 750 men remained four days after the outbreak which claimed 28 victims. The new tunnel came into use on 2 February 1852.

Schemes for a line providing a sea link east from Sheffield date back to 1830 when the Sheffield & Goole Railway was surveyed by George Stephenson. This was unsuccessful as was a larger project, the Sheffield, Rotherham & Humber Railway of 1836, which would have extended to Hull. It was not until the Railway Mania that the desired link eventually materialised out of many conflicting proposals. The Sheffield & Lincolnshire Junction Railway, in effect an extension of the SA & M from Sheffield to Gainsborough and Lincoln, was incorporated in 1846, while the Great Grimsby & Sheffield Junction Railway, a further extension from Gainsborough to Grimsby, had come into being the previous year. The SA & M, S & LJ and GG & SJ now reached agreement to amalgamate as the Manchester, Sheffield & Lincolnshire Railway, thus forming a continuous route from Manchester to the North Sea, and this took effect from 1 January 1847.

A minor development at this time was the construction of a connecting spur from the Midland at Wicker junction to the MS & L at Tunnel junction to the west of Bridgehouses. It opened in 1847, but because of its 1 in 36 gradient was only used for the exchange of relatively small amounts of freight traffic. The spur passed through the 300yd (273m) Spital Hill tunnel, an early example of cut and cover work whose roof collapsed in February 1861, killing six men who were working in the tunnel.

More important was the opening in February 1849 of a portion of the S & LJ section of the MS & L from Sheffield to a junction with the Midland at Beighton. A major engineering work immediately outside Bridgehouses station was the Wicker viaduct, 660ft (205m) long with a magnificent arch of 72ft (21·9m) span across the Wicker road. When completed on 12 December 1848 it was claimed to contain a greater amount of masonry than any similar work in the country. Four men were killed during its construction, one more than on the Rother viaduct where disaster occurred when 21 of the 36 arches collapsed. The MS & L completed its main line with the opening in 1849 of the section from Woodhouse junction, just north of Beighton, to Gainsborough.

The third main line company to work into Sheffield was the GN which had been granted running powers from Retford as a consolation for twice failing to gain Parliamentary approval for its own branch to the town. In 1850 it advised the MS & L that it was to run passenger trains from Lincoln commencing on 7 August. This date coincided with completion of the southern end of the GN into London, the competition presumably stimulating a desire to improve the existing Midland service from Sheffield to the capital which involved changing at Masborough. In July 1851 through coaches were introduced between London (Euston Square) and Sheffield via Eckington and Beighton, being worked into Bridgehouses station by Midland locomotives. Their presence here was short lived, for the permanent MS & L Sheffield station of Victoria was opened in September 1851 when Bridgehouses was relegated to a goods depot. The new station attracted mixed comments. The *Sheffield & Rotherham Independent* noted that 'its front is destitute of ornament', but another contemporary description commented on 'this costly station covered with a light glass roof like that of the Crystal Palace'. More recently Nikolaus Pevsner has referred to the latterday building as making 'a singularly unpromising entry to Sheffield'.

The opening of Victoria marked something of a watershed in the development of Sheffield's railways. Apart from a direct exit to the south, the trunk routes had now been established and for almost the next twenty years no really key additions were to be made to the local network.

The MS & L was part of the Euston Square Confederacy, and thus the GN was only admitted to Sheffield under sufferance, there being no connections forward to Manchester. The collapse of the Confederacy in 1856 brought rapid changes, the most important being the introduction on 1 August 1857 of the GN 'Manchester fliers'. They were worked by GN locomotives as far as Sheffield, and covered the 203 miles (325km) from King's Cross to London Road in 5hr 20min, soon to be cut to an even five hours. Their success quickly put an end to the through coach workings from Euston Square to Sheffield which were withdrawn on 1 February 1858. Until February 1859 the GN paid £1,500 per annum for the use of Victoria, but then made an outright payment of £25,000 to secure permanent half-rights to the station. In 1851 the company had obtained powers to make its own goods depot at Navigation Hill, near Victoria, but never exercised them.

In November 1849 the Midland introduced a service of through trains between Wicker and Doncaster on the opening of the first portion of the South Yorkshire Railway. An agreement of 3 July 1854 provided for SY trains to run into Wicker in their own right, this taking effect in September with the opening of the SY line from Aldam junction, east of Barnsley, through the Blackburn Valley to Blackburn junction on the former S & R between Brightside and Holmes. At this time the unfortunately named Brightside was passing through a period of rapid growth owing to the expansion of heavy industries, the famous Atlas Works being established in 1856 by John Brown, father of the South Yorkshire iron trade. From small beginnings in Sheffield in 1844 his firm had grown through perfecting a conical spring buffer adopted by the L & NW, and at the Atlas Works he pioneered the making of rails by the Bessemer process in 1861. By 1873 the Sheffield district had an annual capacity of some 250,000 tons of rail a year, or one-third of the national total, and remained prominent in this field until the 1930s.

As is more fully related in the next two chapters, the SY was a highly individual railway which, among other things, tended to regard Acts of Parliament as unnecessary evils. In 1860 it placed contracts for its own line into Sheffield from a junction with its Blackburn Valley route at Meadow Hall. The original intention was for the terminus to be at the Sheffield Canal basin, but the opening in 1861 of lease negotiations with the MS & L enabled a junction to be agreed with the parent system at Woodburn, a mile (1·6km) east of Victoria. The new venture got off to a bad start when the SY, without the blessing of Parliamentary authority, utilised an existing underbridge to lay rails beneath the former S & R near Wincobank. The Midland promptly tore them up, the SY relaid them and the Midland once more carried out a removal operation! These farcical proceedings were finally terminated when the SY managed to prove that it had a right of way at this point, and warned the Midland not to trespass on its property. But it may have been this fracas which persuaded the SY to obtain an authorising Act for the extension in 1862. What must by this time have been uneasy relations with the Midland at Wicker were ended when the new line was opened two years later and all Blackburn Valley services diverted to Victoria.

The SY had now been formally leased but its policies survived into the new regime for one of the first steps by the MS & L was to start construction without an authorising Act of a line from Tinsley through Rotherham to Mexborough. This would provide the company with a direct link between Sheffield and Doncaster, although as it paralleled the Midland it would clearly attract intense opposition. The SY, by virtue of its absorption of the Don Navigation in 1850, already owned most of the land on the route, and therefore it was decided to go ahead without the blessing of either the Midland or Parliament. This created a number of difficulties, one of the most acute being the problem of passing under the S & R line into Rotherham as the Midland was under no legal compulsion to provide a new under-bridge. The only possible way was by the existing canal bridge, and so for ½ mile (0·8km) the Navigation was diverted from its Jordan Cut back to the original course in the river Don. The level of the cut was then raised by sinking old barges filled with stone, the water drained and the rails laid. Until recently deep incisions on the bridge abutments made by the tow-ropes of barges remained to indicate the strange origins of this stretch of railway.

In the autumn of 1867 the MS & L became increasingly concerned about the spiralling construction costs of the new line, and ordered all work to stop when it discovered that total expenditure was likely to be in the region of £250,000 compared with an estimate of £80,000. At this juncture help seemed likely to materialise from a most unexpected source. Earlier in the summer the MS & L had been greatly alarmed when a L & NW Bill for a line from Chapel-en-le-Frith to Sheffield via the Hope Valley passed the Commons, and in return for its abandonment hurriedly arranged for the 'Premier Line' to take up running powers right through from Ardwick junction, Manchester, to Sheffield Victoria as provided for in an Act of 1861. Having achieved its objective and at the same time saved the expense of construction, the L & NW now sought to spread its net still further and indicated that it would be willing to become joint owner of the new line as far as Rotherham. In view of the financial position the MS & L quickly agreed, providing the L & NW would meet half the construction costs and also abandon plans to build its own station at Sheffield. In the event Parliament frustrated this forced marriage, throwing out the Bill promoted by the L & NW in the session of 1868. The new line was opened to a temporary terminus at Rotherham in the same year, but further north much work still remained to be done. A swing bridge had to be constructed over the Greasbrough Canal at Park Gate, while it was necessary to rebuild the existing single track potteries branch from Kiln-hurst to Mexborough in order to complete the last stretch of the route. Opening throughout took place in 1871.

THE SOUTHERN EXIT

The Midland long remained content to let Sheffield be served by a branch of its main system. It was not in fact until the company's renaissance of the 1860s that moves were made to end the by-passing of a town of 200,000 inhabitants by what was about to become an Anglo–Scottish trunk route. In December 1862 the Midland promised a Sheffield public meeting that, provided sufficient support was received from the town, it would in the session of 1864 seek powers for a direct line from Chesterfield.

It might be thought that after thirty years of waiting support would be a foregone conclusion, but this was far from the case. In August 1863 the Midland discovered that local parties were promoting a Sheffield, Chesterfield & Staffordshire Railway to extend through Baslow, Bakewell and Ashbourne to Stafford with a branch to the second town of its title. The Sheffield town council even went so far as to ask the Midland to withdraw its own proposals and seek running powers over the new line. It seems that an influential element in Sheffield opposed the Midland because it had for so many years ignored the town; it was, as the *Sheffield Independent* succinctly remarked, 'a matter of hope deferred making the heart sick'.

In 1864 both Bills came before Parliament, which rejected the local company's scheme in favour of the Midland proposals. The Act provided for a line which would leave the former North Midland at Tapton junction, just north of Chesterfield, and then follow the contentious route of 1836 by climbing up the Drone Valley to a tunnel at Bradway before descending the Sheaf Valley at 1 in 110 to reach a new through Sheffield station at Pond Street. After passing beneath the MS & L, the line would join the former S & R at Grimesthorpe junction, $1\frac{1}{4}$ miles (2km) north of the Wicker terminus. In those days there was no town planning to prevent development on possible future lines of communication, and an unfortunate feature of the new route was that it involved the demolition of large numbers of newly erected houses on the south side of Sheffield. The Midland had to expend no less than £500,000, more than four times the original estimate, on the purchase of property for the line, and was authorised to acquire compulsorily '1,061 houses occupied by 5,035 people of the labouring class'. Further difficulties occurred in central Sheffield where the Ponds had to be drained and the new station built over the confluence of the Porter and Sheaf rivers, while to the north a long cutting with a large number of bridges had to be made instead of a lengthy tunnel because of previous sandstone quarrying and coal working. Additional expense was also created by the Duke of Norfolk who obtained a clause in the Act compelling the Midland to cover the line and construct an ornamental terrace at the point where it passed through his property known as 'The Farm'. In all the total cost of the $13\frac{1}{2}$ route miles (21·6km) came to £1,180,000 compared with an original estimate of £430,000.

The new line was eventually opened in 1870 when the Wicker terminus was closed and a goods depot erected on the site. In a memorable obituary the *Railway News* referred to it as 'a miserable station, small in size, hideous in aspect, dirty, dilapidated, and situated in one of the least inviting districts of the town, which, even in its best parts, is quite sufficiently unattractive'. The *Sheffield Independent* welcomed the end of another evil, 'the inconvenience and annoyance of having to change at Masbro' and there wait under the exposed sheds until the through trains arrived', and flamboyantly described the new Sheffield station at Pond Street as 'Grecian with Gothic headings'. A new and improved service of main line trains was inaugurated to coincide with the opening, although even now certain expresses continued to follow the old main line and avoid Sheffield. The railway brought considerable development in the Sheaf Valley, with small houses being erected at the foot and villa-type residences in the higher reaches. Some property values increased tenfold in the ten years to 1870.

The southern exit from Sheffield became even more important when it formed the initial stretch of a competitive Midland route to Manchester via the Hope Valley and Chinley, a distance of 45 miles (72km) compared with the more mountainous $41\frac{1}{4}$ miles (66km) of the MS & L. The various schemes for a Hope Valley line which culminated in the L & NW's far-reaching Bill of 1867 were followed in 1872 by an interesting proposal for a narrow gauge Sheffield & Buxton Railway. This was jointly extinguished by the Midland and MS & L, and at about the same time the former withdrew its Bill for a Hassop & Dore line. Matters rested until 1884 when the nominally independent Dore & Chinley Railway was authorised to build a 20½ mile (33km) link, a quarter of which would be underground, between the Sheffield–Chesterfield and Ambergate–Manchester lines. It failed to raise sufficient capital and sought an abandonment Bill, but at the eleventh hour was taken over by the Midland which started construction work forthwith. The major undertaking was the great Totley tunnel, at 3 miles 950yd (5.69km) the longest in Britain after the Severn. Engineering techniques had by this time greatly improved, but the work ran into almost insuperable difficulties through encountering vast amounts of water. At one stage over five million gallons a day were being pumped from the headings, excavations often having to be stopped altogether for weeks at a time. It was not until 1894 that the route was opened for passenger traffic, express services being put on from the former S & R terminus at Rotherham to Manchester Central. A large summer traffic was quickly established between Sheffield and Hope Valley stations, giving ready access to the Derbyshire moors.

CONSOLIDATION

With the exception of the Dore & Chinley line, railway growth in and around Sheffield in the last part of the nineteenth century was largely confined to the development of existing facilities rather than wholesale new construction. Most of the work involved the building of short connecting spurs, quadrupling of main lines and improvements to stations. One of the most interesting of the spurs was that built under the Midland's 1864 Chesterfield to Sheffield Act, which provided for this company and the MS & L to have mutual running powers between the stations at Pond Street and Victoria. In order to exercise these powers the Midland in 1870 opened a connection which climbed eastwards at

1 in 45 from Nunnery Main Line junction to join the MS & L main line east of Victoria station by a back-shunt. The spur had gone out of use for interchange purposes prior to 1898, although it had been extended to give access to Nunnery Colliery in 1886.

At Rotherham the original buildings at the S & R terminus were used as a post office from about 1872 to 1906 and then a labour exchange from 1918 to 1938 until they were again taken over by the railway to become the district operating manager's offices. They were demolished in 1970. A 'temporary structure', which was to remain in use for eighty years, was built to provide replacement terminal facilities on the town's Main Street and was known locally as 'the rabbit hutch'.

Another town in the Sheffield area which received railway prominence in this period was Penistone, where a Bessemer steelworks specialising in rail manufacture was built in 1862. A new station at the divergence point of the former Huddersfield & Sheffield Junction Railway (see chapter five) was opened in 1874. But it was for disaster rather than development that Penistone became noted, a rapid succession of accidents giving the place a black name among the contemporary travelling public. The most serious was on 16 July 1884 when 24 passengers died following the collapse of the crank axle on the locomotive of an up express, the whole of the train except for the engine, tender and a horse box being flung from the line. Less than six months later, on 1 January 1885, an axle broke on an up empty coal train and caused the derailment of a passing Rotherham–Liverpool excursion, with the death of four passengers. On 1 September 1886 twenty passengers were injured when through coaches for Huddersfield ran back into the buffers after being detached from a main line train. Yet another axle failure occurred on 30 March 1889 on an engine hauling a Liverpool–King's Cross excursion, the wreckage being run into by a King's Cross–Manchester mail train, resulting in the death of one passenger. There was one further fatality on 10 October 1897 when a light engine collided with some through Huddersfield coaches.

Changes west of Penistone included the completion of a

MIDLAND RAILWAY.

THE COMMITTEE OF

ST. STEPHEN'S YOUNG MEN'S SUNDAY SCHOOL

Respectfully announce to their friends and the public that they have made arrangements for their annual TRIP TO

SKIPTON, LANCASTER,

AND

MORECAMBE

FOR 1, 3, 5, OR 9 DAYS,

ON MONDAY, JULY 5, 1875

Affording facilities for visiting Belfast, Isle of Man, Barrow, Blackpool, Fleetwood, Windermere, Piel Pier, &c. Within an easy distance there is Fresh Water and good Sea Fishing.

TIME OF STARTING.	A.M.	1 DAY.	3, 5, OR 9 DAYS.
Sheffield, Midland Statn.	6.15		
Attercliffe Road -	- 6.20	**4s.**	**5s. 6d.**
Brightside - -	- 6.26		
Masbro' - -	- 6.45		

First Class :— Fares for 1 day, 8s.; 3, 5, or 9 days, 11s.

CHILDREN UNDER 12 YEARS OF AGE, HALF-FARES.

Returning same day from Morecambe at 6.50 p.m., and on Wednesday, Friday, or Tuesday following by Ordinary Trains leaving Morecambe at 11.10 a.m., Lancaster 11.25 a.m., and Skipton 1.30 p.m.

Conductors :—Messrs. ROBINSON and EYRE.

Tickets may be obtained previous to the day of the trip at the following places : Mr. J. Eyre, 7 Dairy Bank; Mrs. Lodge, Fawcett Street; Mr. Smeaton, 17 Netherthorpe Place; Mr. Goodison, News Agent, Infirmary Road; Mr. I Plant, Butter Merchant, Devonshire Street; Mr. Mellor, Little Tea Shop, Meadow Street; Mr. T. Plant, Butter Merchant, Wicker; Mr. Goodwin, Grocer, 309 High Street, Attercliffe; Mr. Clifton, Langsett Road; Mr. Ward, 91 Broad Street, Park; Mr. Ingham, Printer, Sheffield Moor; and at the Stations on the morning of the trip.

Remember the Grand Trip to BLACKPOOL, on Monday, July 26th.

D. T. Ingham, Machine Printer, South Street, and Matilda Street, Sheffield.

Sunday school seaside trip. A Midland Railway excursion bill of 1875

large sorting yard at Dunford Bridge in December 1901. What might be termed a subhuman development was the opening in 1899 of a signal box inside the up bore of Woodhead tunnel in an attempt to increase line capacity. It was approached by one of the manholes, but in such appalling working conditions it is understandable that it was difficult to find men to operate even a reduced shift of six hours. As a result the box closed about 1909.

A number of improvements to increase track capacity took place in the Sheffield area at the turn of the century. An ambitious scheme commenced by the Midland in 1899 involved the original lines between Sheffield and Dore & Totley being allocated primarily to Manchester traffic. New main lines were then constructed to the east of these, a burrowing junction being built near Queen's Road goods depot to bring the new down main line into the west side of the station at Pond Street. Here the station was extended and rebuilt to become the largest on the Midland, a new and somewhat uninspiring arcaded frontage being erected to the designs of Charles Trubshaw. Another important part of the scheme was the opening up of the artificial tunnel under 'The Farm'. The entire project was completed in stages between the end of 1900 and the beginning of 1905.

The Great Central also made several Sheffield area improvements. Widening from Darnall junction to Treeton Colliery junction involved the opening out in 1912 of the 374yd (340m) Handsworth tunnel. Another short tunnel opened out was that at Bridgehouses, to the west of the original SA & M terminus, the operation being completed in 1909. The construction of the company's brave London extension, although in itself outside the scope of this volume, had a considerable influence on traffic working at Sheffield. It was opened for freight from Beighton as far south as Annesley in October 1892, and from 5 December was used by L & NW goods trains which worked into Sheffield from Colwick Yard, near Nottingham, via the GN's Leen Valley line. A daily express freight from Camden to Sheffield also followed the same route. These running powers gave the 'Premier Line' two possible approaches to the city of steel, although it had only used the Woodhead route for freight traffic and special summer passenger workings between Sheffield Victoria and the Lancashire and Welsh holiday resorts. The company became increasingly competitive after it opened its own goods depots in Sheffield in 1895 and 1903. On 27 December 1899 it began through coal workings from Colwick to Mexborough and Dovecliffe, near Barnsley, via the Darnall curve.

Completion of the Marylebone extension altered the pattern of London–Sheffield–Manchester workings. On 2 July 1883 an accelerated Manchester service had been put on from King's Cross via Retford hauled by MS & L locomotives from Grantham, but this practice ceased in April 1899 following the introduction of GC expresses to and from Marylebone on 15 March. The company had staved off GN opposition to the London extension by granting it extensive running powers, from Sheffield west to Manchester and south to Nottingham, and the GN therefore now commenced to run through from King's Cross to Manchester via Nottingham in competition with the GC. A third choice for London–Sheffield passengers continued to be the Midland which had come into its own with the opening of its extension to St Pancras in 1868.

During this period Sheffield in fact gradually lost its former almost exclusive domination by the Midland and the MS & L. The Lancashire & Yorkshire Railway began to run into Victoria from Huddersfield on 1 December 1882, while the North Eastern gained access to both the principal stations. On 1 July 1901 it introduced a summer service into Victoria from Scarborough and Bridlington which lasted until the end of the 1911 season. Workings into the Midland station began on 1 July 1898 when the company commenced to run through from York. These were augmented on 1 July 1903 following the introduction of two trains each way daily from Hull via Ferrybridge, these later running in competition with an H & B service to Sheffield via Cudworth. This was inaugurated on 2 October 1905, discontinued on 1 January 1908, resumed on 1 October of the same year and finally withdrawn on 1 January 1917.

THE SHEFFIELD DISTRICT RAILWAY

A most surprising company to gain running powers into Sheffield was the Great Eastern, for the nearest metals it wholly owned were at Peterborough, almost a hundred miles away. Its entry was closely tied up with the story of the Sheffield District Railway, a system which has a historical complexity out of all proportion to its 'main line' of only 3½ route miles (5·6km).

The story begins on 5 August 1891 with the incorporation of the ill-fated Lancashire, Derbyshire & East Coast Railway, authorised to spend no less than £5 million on the construction of some 170 miles (272km) of line. It was to run from a deep-water dock on the Manchester Ship Canal at Warrington via Macclesfield, Buxton, Chesterfield and Lincoln to new docks at Sutton-on-Sea, but in the event the only portion constructed was that from Chesterfield to Lincoln, together with a branch from Langwith Junction to Beighton so as to serve Sheffield. The Great Eastern, which had no collieries on its own system, saw in the LD & EC a means of gaining access to the Nottinghamshire coalfield via the GN & GE Jt and Lincoln, and therefore put forward substantial monetary support in return for running powers over LD & EC lines.

The Sheffield District as originally conceived represented a nominally independent northwards thrust of the LD & EC, running from its Beighton branch at Killamarsh through Hackenthorpe, Handsworth and Darnall before curving westwards to terminate at Attercliffe. The 1896 incorporation Act provided for the two sponsors of the line, the LD & EC and the GE, to run over it, but did not sanction several connecting spurs or sought-after running powers into Sheffield Victoria. In the following session the Midland promoted a competitive Bill for a railway from the North Midland route at Treeton to the former S & R at Brightside, thus giving it similar direct access from the south to the substantial freight traffic stemming from the Attercliffe area. After negotiations between the various parties it was agreed that the two schemes should be combined. The SD sponsors would have running powers over the Midland from Beighton to Treeton, but would build the line from here to Brightside instead of the Midland (which would, however, have running powers over it). From Brightside the sponsors would be able to run southwards over the Midland to Grimesthorpe, where a short SD branch into a goods depot at Attercliffe would represent the only surviving portion of the line as first incorporated. The Midland also offered running powers for passenger traffic from Grimesthorpe into its station at Pond Street, and the SD sponsors decided to utilise these rather than again seek access to Victoria.

Engineering works on the SD included the short 80yd (73m) Tinsley Wood tunnel, a nine-arch viaduct over the river Rother at Catcliffe and a six-arch viaduct plus a lattice girder bridge across the Don at Brightside. Construction of the 40-acre Attercliffe goods depot involved two diversions of the Don and filling-in to a depth of 125ft (39m) with 250,000cu yd (190,000cu m) of soil. Opening of the LD & EC's Beighton branch and the SD took place simultaneously in May 1900. A service of six trains each way, operated by LD & EC engines and rolling stock, was put on between Sheffield and Langwith Junction, and an advertising campaign mounted to stress how the line opened up access to the Dukeries. The June 1900 *Railway Magazine* commented: 'It is essential to the welfare of the smoke-begrimed town [of Sheffield] that its workpeople should have their lungs purified by the rare ozone to be found on the city's borders; the Sheffield District Railway will quickly remove the teeming thousands into a purer and brighter atmosphere.' On the freight side the majority of workings over the new line were by the LD & EC, as the GE after having so elaborately gained access to Sheffield made little if any use of its powers.

The Midland gradually played an increasingly prominent role in the affairs of the SD. From 1 July 1903 it utilised its running powers for passenger traffic by putting on a service of four trains each way between Sheffield and Mansfield, hauled by its own locomotives but consisting of LD & EC rolling stock. In 1906 some complex legislation saw the LD & EC being absorbed by the GC, which with the Midland

L

was granted joint use of the SD. At the same time the GN was given running powers over the District line for goods and mineral traffic to and from Sheffield. A special provision of these arrangements was that the GC would not run off the SD into the station at Pond Street, Sheffield, so long as the Midland continued to operate a service over the same route. As might be expected, scrupulous care was taken to ensure that such a lapse never occurred. The District line continued to provide uneasy common ground for rival main line companies until 1923 when, indicative of its complex antecedents, it became an LNER line connecting at each end with LMS metals.

MODERNISATION

The Sheffield area is a classic example of unplanned growth in the heyday of railways. Wherever the Midland went the GC, like Mary's little lamb, was also sure to go. This not only applied to duplicate main lines, such as those northwards up the Don Valley from Sheffield, but also to innumerable collieries and steelworks where both companies provided duplicate siding facilities. Yet in the whole of the area there were no junctions between the two that were really adequate for exchange purposes. Unfortunately, the LMS and LNER continued to engage in wasteful competition until the slump of the 1930s forced them to enter into arrangements for pooling traffic.

An important post-Grouping development at last came in 1936 when the LNER started work between Sheffield Victoria and Manchester London Road on what was to be the first electrification scheme in Britain catering for all classes of traffic. Erection of the 1,500 volt dc overhead equipment was well in hand when the war halted the project, and was quickly resumed on the cessation of hostilities. The major operation which began in 1948 was the building of a new double line Woodhead tunnel, necessitated by the fact that the old single line bores had insufficient headroom for overhead wires and were in any event by now in appalling condition. The new tunnel cost £4¼ million and took six years to complete, but the loss of life was reduced to six. At 3 miles 66yd (4·89km) it equals the original Standedge tunnel in length. Even with modern machinery the work provided employment for 1,100 men who were accommodated in a latterday shanty town at Dunford Bridge with its own cinema, hospital, shops and inn. The new bore never saw regular steam workings for its opening on 14 June 1954 also marked the commencement of full electric working between Manchester and Penistone. Gangers, who had sometimes become invalids after only six years in the smoke and darkness, especially welcomed the closure of the old tunnels in which the average life of track was only 3–3½ years compared with 15–17 years in the open. The north bore was later used to carry high-voltage electric cables when permission for a surface line through this part of the Peak District National Park was refused; the five year operation, which involved the laying of a 2ft (0·61m) gauge railway for maintenance purposes, was finished in June 1969 at a cost of £2¾ million. The overhead wires from Penistone through to Sheffield Victoria were energised on 20 September 1954, the express steam timings of 65 minutes for the 41¼ miles (66km) of the Woodhead route being cut to 56 minutes and the passenger traffic increasing by 37 per cent in six weeks. A major work on this stretch had been completed on 3 October 1948 with the opening of the new 350yd (329m) single line tunnel at Thurgoland. The original double track bore was henceforth used solely for the up line, enabling it successfully to accommodate overhead wires. The scheme was completed on 3 January 1955 when electrification was extended eastwards to Rotherwood Sidings near Woodhouse junction in order to facilitate through freight working.

Other developments in the period of electrification tended to be negative rather than positive. They included the closure of the 1 in 36 spur from Wicker to Bridgehouses, which put an end to the spectacular sight of transfer trains rushing the gradient. The ex-S & R line from Holmes to Rotherham Westgate was completely closed, except for the first half mile (0·8km) serving industrial sidings, in 1952, the main reason being the need to renew the wooden bridge over the river Don.

Even as late as the mid-1950s the Sheffield rail network was much the same as it had been in pre-Grouping days.

It was not until 1961 that work was started on a £11 million comprehensive rationalisation scheme designed to save £1,200,000 per annum and give Sheffield 'a more modern rail layout than any other industrial area in the country'. The hub of the project was the transformation of the greater part of the SD 'main line' into the gigantic Tinsley marshalling yard, a BR showpiece. This site was selected because, although the topography was distinctly unfavourable, it provided access in all directions to both the ex-GC and Midland main lines. A new west to north curve had to be constructed on to the North Midland route at Treeton and the existing connection realigned, while at the west end it was necessary to combine a pair of locks on the Sheffield Canal in order to construct two spurs on to the ex-GC Sheffield–Rotherham line. Further afield a scissors crossing was provided at Aldwarke junction, the point where the GC and Midland Don Valley routes were closest to each other north of Parkgate. This was to enable trains from the north to be diverted to either the east or west approaches to the yard, and for heavy trains to be diverted from the more steeply graded ex-GC line.

Parliamentary powers for Tinsley yard were obtained in the British Transport Commission Act of 1960, and work on moving no less than $3\frac{3}{4}$ million tons of earth from the site started in August 1961. The double-direction yard of 11 reception sidings, 53 main sorting sidings and 25 secondary sorting sidings was designed to handle 275 freight trains every 24 hours in round-the-clock working, a computer being installed to give automatic speed control of wagons with the aid of over 20,000 Dowty booster/retarder units. Another associated work was the extension of 1,500 volt electrification into the yard from Woodburn and Darnall junctions. Freight traffic from former Midland lines was transferred to Tinsley on 12 July 1965, and the yard was formally opened on 29 October.

Another important scheme was the construction of a centralised freight terminal at Grimesthorpe, on the site of the old locomotive depot, to handle all small consignments from the Sheffield, Chesterfield, Rotherham and Barnsley areas. It comprised a goods shed covering 25,000sq yd (21,000 sq m) and a warehouse of 15,000sq yd (12,600sq m), the major part of it coming into use simultaneously with the first phase of the Tinsley yard. Later modernisation saw complete resignalling throughout much of the Sheffield area, the first stage coming to fruition on 22 January 1973 when the Sheffield Signal Centre was brought into operation.

On the passenger side a policy was instituted of concentrating all traffic at Sheffield (Midland), the long standing unofficial name for the station at Pond Street which was formally adopted in 1951. A first stage was the construction in 1965 of a connection from Nunnery Single Line junction on to the former GC about $\frac{3}{4}$ mile (1·2km) west of Victoria, enabling services such as those from King's Cross and Lincolnshire to be diverted into the Midland station. This meant that virtually all London trains now used Midland, through expresses between Victoria and Marylebone, apart from one night train, having been withdrawn on 4 January 1960. A second stage in the change-over was the concentration of all Don Valley services on the Midland line from 5 September 1966, those from Doncaster using the new Aldwarke junction. The third and final alteration was intended to follow fairly quickly, BR publishing its proposals in January 1967. These involved the withdrawal of electric passenger trains between Victoria and Manchester, and the substitution of a new diesel-hauled service from Sheffield (Midland) via the Hope Valley. Apart from the need to centralise passenger facilities in Sheffield, the main argument put forward by BR was that the special locomotives and time-table paths needed by the relatively few electric passenger workings handicapped a line which had to carry a very heavy freight traffic. The proposals created such fierce opposition, especially in Penistone, that BR was forced to retain part of the Woodhead route for a new Sheffield (Midland)–Penistone–Huddersfield service, operated by DMUs which reversed after traversing the Nunnery curve. This was introduced in 1970, when the remaining proposals were finally implemented and Victoria station closed after a life of almost 120 years.

TRAIN SERVICES

The comparison already made between Sheffield and Leeds is reflected in the pattern of train services. Sheffield, by virtue of the slow development of certain key routes, did not initially attract such keen inter-company competition as its rival town astride the Aire. A choice of routes to London became available in the early 1850s, but it was not until the very end of the Victorian era that services from Sheffield to such key centres as Hull and Manchester were really competitive.

Until the outbreak of World War I the GN narrowly held the edge as regards London services. In April 1910, for instance, the best timings over the three possible routes were: GN via Retford, 2hr 58min; Midland, 3hr 2min; GC, 3hr 15min. Earlier, on 1 July 1903, the GC had introduced a non-stop working from Sheffield Victoria to Marylebone in 3hr 10min, and in 1905 both the GC and GN were running to Sheffield in 2hr 50min. As a wartime measure through services to King's Cross ceased in 1916 and were not reinstated until 2 June 1924 when the LNER launched its unsuccessful all-Pullman working to Sheffield via Nottingham. It was diverted via Retford and extended to Manchester Central on 1 April 1925 before being taken off altogether on 21 September. Ordinary services maintained the King's Cross–Sheffield link until it again became a casualty of war in September 1939. In 1947 the popular morning express from Victoria to Marylebone was named 'The Master Cutler' and accelerated to perform the journey in 3hr 35min, at that time the fastest train on any route. A headboard of Sheffield stainless steel was made and presented by the Master of the Company of Cutlers. In 1958 the train was diverted to the GN route, covering the $161\frac{1}{2}$ miles (258km) in a record $2\frac{3}{4}$ hours, and at the same time becoming an all-Pullman diesel-hauled service. Alleged mounting losses brought about the withdrawal of the Pullman on 7 October 1968, and St Pancras became the only London terminus for trains from Sheffield.

Services between Sheffield and Leeds have been described

in chapter one. Between Sheffield and Hull the MS & L, and later the GC, always provided the most frequent if not necessarily the fastest workings. A through cross-country service from Liverpool began on 1 August 1874, and this gave the company a headstart which enabled it to counter later competition from the North Eastern, the Midland via Milford Junction and the H & B. Inter-company rivalry between Sheffield and Manchester did not begin until the opening of the Hope Valley line in 1894. An interesting if short-lived through coach working between Manchester Central and Harwich Parkeston Quay was introduced by the Midland on 1 July 1903. The coach was worked along the Hope Valley on a fast Sheffield train, attached to a new through express to Lincoln via the SD and LD & EC, and then worked forward by the GE on the same train that carried through GC coaches from Liverpool and Manchester London Road. Another competitive service stimulated by the Hope Valley line was that between Sheffield and Llandudno, the GC introducing a through summer working in 1905 and the Midland following suit with a service via Buxton in 1910. The Edwardian traveller from Sheffield could also choose between the GC and the Midland when journeying to such varied destinations as Deal, Bournemouth and Bristol.

Further summer workings of note by the GC included a service put on in 1900 from Leicester to Fleetwood in connection with the Isle of Man steamers, and a through carriage from Leicester to Aberystwyth via Sheffield, Manchester and Wrexham, introduced in 1904. A Leicester–Scarborough express, avoiding Sheffield via the Darnall curve, had first appeared in the timetables in 1899, and in 1901 this was extended to form a Marylebone to Scarborough working which ran into Victoria. Two trains each way between Sheffield and Blackpool were introduced in 1900, a through Liverpool–Yarmouth service in 1902 and a Scarborough–Southampton Dock working in 1903. On 1 May 1906 the GC inaugurated a York–Cardiff service (later extended north to Newcastle and west to Swansea), and on 1 July 1909 this began to convey through carriages from Hull. In 1911 an existing through express to Bristol, consisting of Halifax and Leeds portions which combined at Sheffield, was extended to Ilfracombe. The NE started a through Sheffield–Edinburgh service, worked by Midland locomotives as far as York, in the summer of 1898.

MINOR LINES

Perhaps the most interesting of the independent lines in the Sheffield area was the Stocksbridge Railway, built to serve the ironworks which were founded by Samuel Fox in 1842. Initial attempts to get MS & L support for the scheme were unsuccessful, the main line company insisting that it would not be interested unless the railway was laid out as part of a future relief route along the Little Don Valley. Samuel Fox therefore decided to go it alone and, after the first Bill of 1866 had been withdrawn, the line obtained one of the few incorporation Acts for a purely industrial railway on 30 June 1874. Extending west from Deepcar for just under two miles (3·2km) it was opened on 14 April 1877, the main engineering work being a 56ft (17·3m) high viaduct over the river Don. Passengers, who were almost entirely Fox employees and Penistone Grammar School pupils, travelled free and at their own risk until these services were withdrawn in 1931. In September 1898 Sheffield Corporation completed a three mile (4·8km) extension of the line for the construction of Langsett Reservoir; this work was finished in 1904 but the track was not lifted until about 1912.

Another line made by the Corporation was that for the building of the Broomhead and Moor Hall reservoirs in the Ewden Valley. It left the GC at Wharncliffe Wood, between Deepcar and Oughty Bridge, and descended to the Don by a zig-zag and a 1 in 26 gradient. The line was built in 1913–14, and was in operation until the inauguration of the reservoir works in October 1929.

Away to the west, the Hepworth Iron Company established works on the 1,000ft (305m) contour at Crow Edge in 1858. A Bill for a Hazlehead & Hepworth Railway was deposited in 1860 but withdrawn, although the company proceeded to construct a rope-worked incline climbing at 1 in 17 from the MS & L's Hazlehead Bridge station. The discovery of extensive beds of clay led to the building of a $\frac{1}{4}$ mile (0·4km) tunnel in order to ease the gradient to 1 in 23/25; this permitted the introduction of locomotive working which continued until the line was closed in 1969.

CHAPTER VII

Barnsley

KING COAL

Barnsley has long been regarded in Yorkshire as something of a music hall joke. The image is no longer justified, but the popular impression still lingers of a community dominated by cloth-cap and muffler, beer-swilling men, and women permanently enshrouded in hair curlers. Even the local newspaper once admitted that 'Barnsley is not a pretty town and doesn't pretend to be anything other than a town with its sleeves rolled up'. Completing the unfortunate mental picture is the deeply ingrained soubriquet of 'Black Barnsley', a long-standing corruption of 'Bleak Barnsley' in reference to its situation on a steep north-east facing slope above the river Dearne.

The allusion to blackness stems from a lengthy enslavement to king coal. One of the earliest records of coal mining in the West Riding comes from Barnsley, and concerns the purchase of a pit by the Cluniac monks of Pontefract in 1491. A little over 200 years later Daniel Defoe noted that the town had 'a smoaky aspect', but it was not until the 1840s that large-scale collieries were established to tap the ten feet (3m) thick Barnsley seam which proved particularly suitable for both coking and steam-raising. This was the prime area in the West Riding where technological developments in the coalfield were gestating at the same time as the Railway Mania, a coincidence which had two key results. The first was that the Barnsley area possessed an exceptionally high proportion of lines built with just one aim in mind—that of moving 'black diamonds' from pit to port or consumer. The second was that Barnsley rapidly became the recognised centre of the Yorkshire coal trade; in 1874 its 55 collieries produced $3\frac{1}{2}$ million tons of fuel, the highest amount of any area in the county. It was not until the turn of the century that development of deep-level mining techniques caused the centre of the active coalfield to move eastwards towards Doncaster, and even then another fifty years elapsed before the Barnsley seams began to be worked out. Closures commenced soon after nationalisation and were accelerated in 1965, the last pit within the Barnsley Borough being shut down in 1970.

Another mineral present in the Barnsley district was ironstone, an iron foundry being established as early as 1380. This, together with the coal and an abundance of local limestone, stimulated the development of two important canal undertakings and quite extensive connecting tramroads. The Barnsley Canal, which branched off the Aire & Calder Navigation at Wakefield, was opened as far as Barnsley in 1799 and extended westwards for a further three miles (4·8km) to Barnby Basin by the beginning of 1802. A two-mile (3·2km) tramroad from the basin to serve coal pits at Silkstone village was opened in 1810, and was laid to a gauge of about 4ft (1·22m) on exceptionally large stone blocks weighing at least 200lb (90kg). There were a number of short branches, and about 1830 the 'main line' itself was extended by a private company for a further $1\frac{1}{4}$ miles (2km) in order to serve pits at Silkstone Moor End. The entire railway was abandoned about 1860.

The second canal to serve the Barnsley area was the Dearne & Dove, which extended from the Don Navigation at Swinton and was opened throughout in 1804. It included a branch to a basin at Worsborough (now spelt Worsbrough), and from here a three mile (4·8km) private tramroad to pits at Ratten Row, east of Thurgoland, was opened about 1821. A $1\frac{1}{2}$ mile (2·4km) branch from a junction at Rockley Smithies to coal and ironstone pits at Pilley was brought into use about 1832. The Worsborough railway was built as a plateway of approximately 4ft 3in (1·29m) gauge, and was finally abandoned about 1920.

Another branch of the Dearne & Dove Canal terminated at Elsecar, from where the $2\frac{3}{4}$ mile (4·4km) Elsecar & Thorncliffe waggonway was built about 1837 to serve the famous Milton Ironworks at Hoyland, the Thorncliffe Ironworks at

Chapeltown and several collieries and ironstone pits. It was laid on stone sleepers and worked by a combination of stationary engines and horse haulage; the western section closed in 1879, but the remainder was relaid as a standard gauge colliery line in 1886 and was in use until 1911.

The presence of these three early railways, and the numerous undertakings they served, is indicative of an era of intense local expansion, and indeed by the 1830s the region stretching from Silkstone to Chapeltown was one of the most highly industrialised in England. Thorncliffe Ironworks had an annual output of 7,000 tons of pig iron and Milton Ironworks was producing 3,200 tons of castings per year, while both Silkstone and Worsborough collieries were capable of turning out 600 tons of high-quality coal per day. Yet the coming of the railway age quickly saw these industries go into decline owing to the limited transport facilities; the Barnsley Canal achieved its maximum coal tonnage in 1839 and was then hit by the movement into South Yorkshire of rail-borne coal from County Durham. The coalmasters and ironmasters rallied to the opportunity offered by the Railway Mania, and vigorously promoted numerous different schemes. They may even have been inspired by one of Barnsley's most famous townsmen, Joseph Locke, who was at this time battling against adversity at Woodhead. He was born at Attercliffe Common, near Sheffield, on 9 August 1805, and came to Barnsley with his parents at the age of five; he is commemorated by a statue in the town's Locke Park.

THE NORTHERN EXIT

There was a Barnsley station prior to the Railway Mania, but it was sited three miles to the north-east of the town centre, and could only be conveniently reached by horse-drawn omnibus. It was an intermediate stopping point on the North Midland main line, opening with the company's Rotherham–Leeds section in 1840. Barnsley, like Sheffield and Wakefield, was a victim of George Stephenson's policy of adhering to minimal gradients at the expense of by-passing important settlements. The station was the scene of a bad accident directly due to George Hudson's take-over of the

North Midland and his instant dismissal, on Christmas Eve 1842, of all drivers and firemen who had protested about his proposed reduction in wages. On 12 January 1843 a luggage train, running four hours late and in the so-called charge of a driver of only three weeks' experience, collided with the rear of a stationary passenger train causing the death of a commercial traveller. Hudson was severely censured by both the coroner's jury and the Board of Trade. The first Barnsley station was renamed Cudworth in 1854.

Conflicting promotions of the Railway Mania period caused considerable delay in the completion of an east–west line serving the centre of Barnsley, but a north–south scheme was successful at its first attempt. It was incorporated in 1846 with the extraordinarily long-winded title of the Sheffield, Rotherham, Barnsley, Wakefield, Huddersfield & Goole Railway, but was authorised to extend for no more than twenty miles (32km) from the Midland's Sheffield & Rotherham line at Wincobank to the Manchester & Leeds Railway at Horbury. To give direct access to Goole for coal traffic, it was agreed in October 1846 that the section from Barnsley northwards should be leased to the M & L and this took effect from 11 May 1847. The history of the portion south of Barnsley is detailed below under 'Links with Sheffield'.

During the post-Mania recession the proposed double line was reduced to single track and a connection facing solely towards Wakefield replaced the intended double junction at Horbury. The main engineering work was the 1,745yd (1·59km) Wooley tunnel taking the line through the ridge separating the Dearne and Calder valleys. Opening took place in 1850, simultaneously with a branch to Silkstone Colliery. Coal traffic to Goole built up so rapidly that the single track was soon inadequate and a second line was opened on 21 April 1855, although the tunnel remained as a single track bottleneck. The sale of the line to the L & Y took effect on 1 January 1858.

The reports of the Great Northern Railway for 1855 show that the company was then working through from Knottingley via Wakefield to collieries at Gawber Hall, near Darton, and Silkstone. The West Yorkshire Railway was granted running powers from Wakefield to Barnsley in 1863,

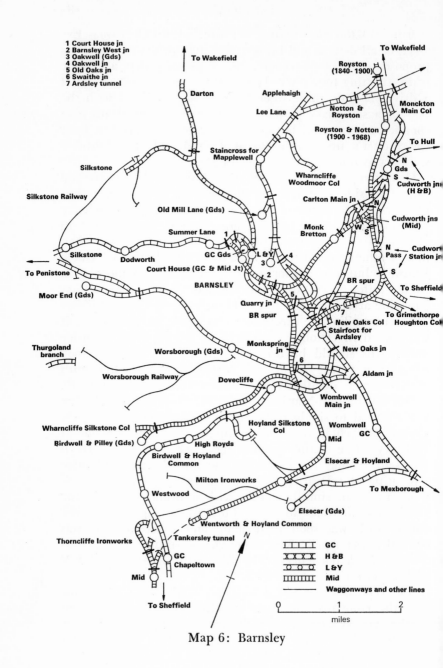

1 Court House jn
2 Barnsley West jn
3 Oakwell (Gds)
4 Oakwell jn
5 Old Oaks jn
6 Swaithe jn
7 Ardsley tunnel

To Wakefield

To Wakefield

Royston
(1840- 1900)

Darton

Applehaigh

Monckton
Main Col

Lee Lane

Notton &
Royston

Royston & Notton
(1900 - 1968)

To Hull

Staincross for
Mapplewell

Silkstone

N
Gds
S

Cudworth jns
(H &B)

Wharncliffe
Woodmoor Col

Silkstone Railway

Old Mill Lane (Gds)

Carlton Main jn

N

Cudworth jns
(Mid)

W   S

Summer Lane

Monk
Bretton

Silkstone

Dodworth

GC Gds

L &Y

3

4

N
Pass
S

Cudworth
Station jn

To Penistone

Court House (GC & Mid Jt)

2

BR spur

To Sheffield

BARNSLEY

Moor End (Gds)

Quarry jn

5

To Grimethorpe
Houghton Col

BR spur

7

Thurgoland
branch

Worsborough (Gds)

Monkspring
jn

New Oaks Col
Stairfoot for
Ardsley

New Oaks jn

Worsborough Railway

Dovecliffe

6

Aldam jn

Wombwell
Main jn

Wharncliffe Silkstone Col

Hoyland Silkstone
Col

Wombwell
GC

Birdwell & Pilley (Gds)

High Royds

Mid

Birdwell & Hoyland
Common

Elsecar & Hoyland

Milton Ironworks

To Mexborough

Westwood

Elsecar (Gds)

Wentworth & Hoyland Common

N

Thorncliffe Ironworks

Tankersley tunnel

GC

GC
Chapeltown

Mid

	GC
XXXXX	H &B
ooo	L &Y
	Mid
—	Waggonways and other lines

To Sheffield

0   1   2
miles

Map 6: Barnsley

and these were apparently exercised by the GN which took over the WY two years later. Another company interested in the coal measures was the NE; it gained running powers to Barnsley and Silkstone, also in 1863, in exchange for giving the L & Y access to Hull from Goole. In 1892 the L & Y obtained powers to build a second Wooley tunnel as well as a south to west curve from Crigglestone to the Calder Valley main line at Horbury & Ossett. The new tunnel was opened on 2 March 1902 when goods workings over the curve also commenced. Other twentieth century changes to Barnsley's northern rail exit have been of only a minor nature.

LINES EAST AND WEST

The first move towards the promotion of an east–west line serving Barnsley came in 1842, when Joseph Locke was asked to survey the Barnsley Junction Railway, extending from the Sheffield, Ashton-under-Lyne & Manchester Railway at Oxspring to the North Midland at Royston. The Bill was thrown out on standing orders in the session of 1844, and was again unsuccessful the following year when the SA & M re-submitted it with an extension to Pontefract. The scheme bobbed up again in 1846, this time starting at Penistone and terminating at Cudworth, and now in competition with proposals put forward by the Midland and the Huddersfield & Sheffield Junction railways. All three Bills failed to receive parliamentary sanction, the same fate befalling a new venture which was of more than usual interest. This was the South Yorkshire Coal Railway, a rare collusion of railway and canal factions. As originally proposed it was to run from the H & SJ near Shepley & Shelley through Barnsley, Wath and Mexborough to Doncaster, and was backed on the railway side by the SA & M and the GN. The canal support came from the Don Navigation which foresaw that the line would largely supplant the Dearne & Dove Canal it was then in the process of absorbing. It therefore decided to strengthen its position by adhering to the old adage, 'if you can't beat 'em, then join 'em', but opposition from the powerful Aire & Calder Navigation, and not competing railway schemes, caused the Bill to be lost.

During the next twelve months the Don Navigation managed to placate its neighbouring waterway, and in 1847 the section of line extending eastwards from Barnsley to Doncaster was authorised as the South Yorkshire, Doncaster & Goole Railway. The GN was granted running powers over it, and there were to be branches from near Wombwell to Elsecar and Silkstone Moor End (not to be confused with the L & Y Silkstone branch). The Act provided that amalgamation with the Don Navigation should not take place until half the railway's capital had been raised and expended. This stage was reached on 19 April 1850 when the name of the company was changed to the South Yorkshire Railway & River Dun Navigation (Dun, an otherwise archaic spelling of Don, was retained in legal documents).

Barnsley now had the blessing of Parliament to move its sea-borne coal via the L & Y or along the SY and the Don Navigation. The SY and the GN would provide a direct route to London, but access westwards to Manchester and the potentially vast market in Lancashire was still denied. For the fourth consecutive session a Bill for this purpose was put forward in 1847; it was suspended in the Lords and not until 1848 did the MS & L finally obtain powers for a line from Penistone to Barnsley. The SY put forward its own Bill for an extension to Penistone in the same year, but this was thrown out and the company instead given running powers over the MS & L.

As described in chapters six and eight, the first portion of these east–west lines came into use in 1849 when the SY was opened from the Midland at Swinton through Mexborough to Doncaster. A single line from Mexborough to Elsecar, crossing the Dearne & Dove Canal by a lifting bridge, was brought into use for mineral traffic in 1850. The Elsecar branch achieved its greatest prominence through being the nearest rail-head to the Wentworth Woodhouse seat of Earl Fitzwilliam, chairman of the SY from 1845 to 1851. He had a covered platform within his Elsecar Ironworks close to the branch terminus and a special train was put on to take his house party to Doncaster races. The same arrangements were employed when the Prince of Wales (later King Edward VII) stayed at Wentworth.

A further single track extension of the SY westwards from Elsecar junction as far as collieries on the Silkstone Moor End branch was in use for mineral traffic by June 1850. Laying of a second track from Mexborough to the divergence point of this branch at Aldam junction, together with construction of the remaining portion of the main line from this junction to Barnsley, commenced in the autumn of 1850 and was completed in time for a GN-worked passenger service from Doncaster to begin in 1851. At Barnsley the SY terminated by an end-on junction with the northern section of the SRBWH & G, immediately south of the existing station. Among the more infamous intermediate stations was Ardsley, rebuilt and renamed Stairfoot in the 1870s but originally described as 'a miserable affair six feet by seven feet with room for three persons to sit and two to stand by courtesy of the station master'.

The SY, with its lucrative coal traffic, was a constant source of what today would be termed take-over rumours. Joint leasing by the GN, MS & L and Midland was mooted in June 1851, and the end of the company seemed imminent when leasing solely by the GN was authorised on 30 June 1852. In order to prevent monopoly control the Act laid down that, if the Midland so requested, a west to south curve was to be built at Adwick for the exchange of traffic from the SY on to the Midland main line (a spur was ultimately built here in the 1870s—see reference section). Partly because of this proviso, the GN backed out of the amalgamation and a period of protracted litigation followed. A comic result was that the GN gave the SY a day's notice of its intention to reduce the Doncaster–Barnsley passenger service to a token one train each way from 1 August 1853. The SY had to make frantic arrangements to hire carriages from the Midland and provide motive power from its own meagre stud of nine locomotives. A more fruitful outcome of the 1852 flirtation was that it gave the GN ideas of extending westwards from Barnsley to Manchester. This proposal came to the notice of the MS & L whose own scheme for a Penistone–Barnsley line had, for financial reasons, lain dormant since the passage of its Act. Deputations from Barnsley residents and coal owners, angry that an essential link with Lancashire

M

first mooted ten years earlier was still moribund, had failed to influence the company, but now it was suddenly galvanised into action.

To save time and cost, the line was initially constructed with just a single track and was opened in stages, passenger trains reaching Summer Lane on the western outskirts of Barnsley in 1855. From here the final section of line descended on gradients as steep as 1 in 50 in almost continuous cutting averaging 53ft (16·5m) in depth. Owing to the heavy works involved, it was not until 1857 that completion of the line throughout was marked by celebrations at the MS & L's Barnsley goods depot. An 1853 Act had permitted the company to connect with and use the existing passenger station and also to have running powers from here over SY metals, but a protracted dispute over signalling arrangements at the junction meant that this desirable development did not come to pass for another two years. Summer Lane remained the enforced passenger terminus until 1 December 1859, when MS & L trains at last entered what had now become the L & Y station and also began to work through to Doncaster. Doubling of the Penistone–Barnsley line was completed in 1871.

Barnsley passenger station, with its single platform, rapidly proved inadequate for the trains of three companies, operations being hampered by the increasing volume of westbound coal traffic passing through, and its facilities became the subject of frequent abuse. Barnsley Town Council unashamedly referred to 'that disgraceful and beastly hole called the railway station', while more brickbats were hurled during the parliamentary session of 1863. Disparaging remarks were made about its 'execrable accommodation', and particularly about what 'by a very gross abuse of language' was called a ladies' waiting-room—it was allegedly so small that 'one lady of modern dimensions would occupy a very considerable portion of it'. Apparently the only consoling factor was that 'under no combination of circumstances could the accommodation be worse'.

The occasion was the promotion of a successful Midland Bill for a branch from a double junction at Cudworth to Barnsley which would give the town a second station as well as more immediate access to a north–south main line. The branch was routed to pass close to Mount Osborne and Oaks collieries, then respectively producing 162,000 and 182,000 tons per annum, and its main engineering feature was the 1,087ft (335m) long Barnsley or Oaks viaduct which eventually spanned two railways, a main road, the river Dearne, the Dearne & Dove Canal and the Barnsley Canal! From here the line continued westwards parallel to the SY and eventually crossed it to join the MS & L west of its junction with the L & Y.

The new route was closely affected by an Act of 1864 which authorised the leasing of the SY to the MS & L, a position only reached after more than three years of haggling over the possibility of a joint lease with the GN. In 1861 the tonnage of coal carried by the SY just topped the million mark for the first time, and the lease clearly represented a milestone in the development of the MS & L. An incidental provision of the Act was that it gave the Sheffield company running powers over the L & Y from Barnsley to Wooley Colliery at Darton and also over the Silkstone branch.

The lease paved the way for an important MS & L Act of 5 July 1865 which provided for an extensive interchange of running powers with the Midland. The MS & L was to be able to run from Barnsley on to the Midland main line by means of the new branch to Cudworth, and then continue northwards almost to Oakenshaw to gain access to the West Riding & Grimsby Railway (about to become joint GN/MS & L). Further running powers from this point right through to Skipton were also granted but never exercised. In return the Midland was to be able to work traffic west from Barnsley through Penistone and Woodhead to Manchester. Provision was also made for the Barnsley station on the Cudworth branch to be the joint property of the Midland and MS & L. The two companies agreed to install a connecting junction east of Barnsley where the branch and the SY ran parallel to one another, so that the MS & L would no longer have to depend on the L & Y in order to reach its newly leased metals and could instead use the western end of the Midland line. The company would thus be saved the payment of tolls to the L & Y, its passengers would be spared the evils of the much maligned earlier station, and its drivers would no longer have to face the perils of the sharply curved 1 in 50 start on to the Penistone line.

It all sounded like the start of a new era, but once again there was to be an outbreak of animosity. According to official records goods traffic over the Midland branch commenced in June 1869, but it must have been of a restricted nature for the company was in dispute with the MS & L over connecting junctions. The *Sheffield Telegraph* of 11 March 1870 noted: 'Some time ago the points at the junction were torn up by the servants of the [MS & L] but their opponents had them replaced. Within the last few days this has been repeated and it is said that a staff of men are kept on watch day and night to prevent Midland goods trains from passing onto the Penistone branch.' Soon afterwards the dispute was healed, but a defective embankment further delayed the commencement of regular goods traffic until 1 April. This included a through Midland service from Leeds to Manchester, which lasted until the opening of the Hope Valley line in 1893. As mentioned in chapter one, a similar if short-lived through passenger working began in August, Midland local services to Barnsley having commenced in May.

At this eleventh hour the L & Y offered to improve the earlier Barnsley station providing the MS & L paid half the cost, but it was too late and from 1 June 1870 the only passenger trains using the 'beastly hole' were those from Wakefield via Horbury Junction. On this date all MS & L services were transferred to the station on the Midland line which was then only a temporary structure. In 1871–2 the old Barnsley Court House, built in 1861 by Reeves, was adapted to form the permanent station and the name was retained.

Developments of the 1870s included the inauguration on 1 August 1874 of the through MS & L Liverpool–Hull service, some of the trains travelling via Barnsley. In March 1873 agreement was reached for the North Eastern to run over the Midland from Normanton to collieries on the Barnsley branch in order to obtain locomotive coal, but this arrangement lapsed in 1875. The SY was formally vested in the MS & L in 1874, its closing years being marred by a disastrous accident on 12 December 1870. Fifteen people were killed and fifty injured when ten wagons ran away during shunting at Barnsley and buried themselves in the rear of a passenger train standing at Stairfoot.

The MS & L felt impelled to do something about the more disgraceful SY stations, and as a result new structures at Wath and Wombwell (as well as at Silkstone on the Penistone line) were opened in 1877. Another improvement completed in the same year was the doubling of the Silkstone Moor End branch as far as New Sovereign Colliery. The terminus of this branch was little more than a mile (1·6km) from the MS & L's Penistone line, and the company took the obvious step of constructing a connection so that the ever-increasing volume of Lancashire-bound coal traffic could bypass Barnsley. Although the distance was short the vertical separation was in the region of 200 feet (61m) and heavy engineering works were involved in order to keep the climb out of the Wentworth valley down to what was still an exceptionally steep 1 in 40. Known as the Wentworth or Worsborough bank, it left the original Silkstone Moor End branch half a mile (0·8km) before the terminus and was opened to goods traffic in 1880.

Virtually all the twentieth century developments to the east–west lines in the Barnsley area were concerned with speeding up the working of coal traffic. In April 1905 the GC agreed to spend £190,000 on the construction of a hump marshalling yard at Wath, almost at the geographical centre of the South Yorkshire coalfield. Partially opened on 19 August 1907, it was brought into full operation on 4 December and was the first power-operated gravitation yard in the country. It extended for almost a mile (1·6km) on the south side of the line between Wath and Elsecar junction, contained 110 roads and 15 reception sidings, and its throughput was estimated at 5,000 wagons every 24 hours with 35 men per eight hour shift. It was worked by four 0–8–4Ts specially built by Beyer Peacock & Co of Manchester (two more were added by the LNER). The North Eastern commenced to operate through coal trains between Wath and Hull on 9 February 1912.

In 1925 the LNER built a one-off 2–8–8–2 Beyer-Garratt

locomotive, No 2395, for banking the 850 ton coal trains up Wentworth bank. It was the first Garratt to be used by a British main line railway company and, with a tractive effort of 72,940lb (32,823kg), was the most powerful steam locomotive in the country. The engine worked twenty out of every twenty-four hours, and its crew were provided with respirators to cope with what must have been appalling conditions inside the 220yd (200m) West Silkstone tunnel. One train after another struggled up the 1 in 40, often double-headed at the front and banked by a conventional engine and the Garratt at the rear. They created spectacular sound effects which could be heard in Barnsley and took something like 2¼ hours to cover the 19 miles (30km) from Wath to Dunford Bridge. It was an exceptionally difficult line to work, and conditions could become chaotic when greasy rails caused trains to slip to a standstill on the bank. It is scarcely surprising that the Manchester–Sheffield electrification scheme, more fully described in the previous chapter, should have been planned also to extend to Wath, and that the section between there and Dunford Bridge should be the first to be inaugurated. This took place on 4 February 1952, after experimental working between Wath and Barnsley junction had begun on 2 September 1951. A single electric locomotive at the front, with an additional one at the rear to guard against breakaways, proved capable of working the coal trains up Wentworth bank at 30mph (48kmph), and reduced by half the time taken to reach Dunford Bridge. Traffic increased to such an extent that in 1961 over 80 trains daily were being worked westwards over Woodhead to Mottram where they were remarshalled for destinations in Lancashire.

All the east–west routes had lost their regular passenger services by the 1960s. That between Barnsley and Cudworth was withdrawn on 9 June 1958, the famous Barnsley viaduct being demolished ten years later. The local service between Doncaster and Penistone ceased on 29 June 1959, and the sole surviving regular passenger working over this line west of Mexborough was withdrawn in 1970.

LINKS WITH SHEFFIELD

As already noted, a line from Horbury through Barnsley to join the Midland at Wincobank was incorporated in 1846 as the Sheffield, Rotherham, Barnsley, Wakefield, Huddersfield & Goole Railway, and the portion north of Barnsley leased to the M & L in the following year. So as to consolidate under one management all lines within the local coalfield, it had previously been agreed in May 1846 that the section south from Barnsley should be taken over by the SY.

Much of the route was in the Blackburn Valley, which under the original proposals was to be reached by a line passing close to Worsborough and then piercing the watershed by a 1 mile 518yd (2·08km) tunnel at Birdwell. Work on this started in July 1847, but after three shafts had been sunk to full depth, six nearly to the top of the tunnel and some 6,000cu yd (4,587cu m) of material excavated, the onset of hard times caused the operations to be suspended in April 1848. They were never resumed. William Shaw, the contractor, claimed damages of £100,000, but according to his obituary received only £55,000. Powers were obtained in 1851 for a deviation which would be longer and more steeply graded, but would cost less and would also serve collieries at Blacker and Hoyland. The route now left the SY main line at Aldam junction by a connection facing towards Wath, climbed at 1 in 63 to Birdwell and then swung through a right angle to descend into the Blackburn Valley at 1 in 62. The single line was completed in December 1853, but owing to a dispute with the Midland at the Sheffield end was not opened until September 1854. A through passenger service was introduced between Barnsley and Sheffield, all trains having to reverse at Aldam junction or Wombwell. Coal traffic provided the bulk of the revenue, this being increased by constructing a number of short colliery branches.

In 1862, 22 trains each way were being worked over the single line, each accompanied by a pilotman or in SY parlance a 'travelling porter'. Doubling was not put in hand until the 1870s, the operation being completed in 1876. The Sheffield–Barnsley passenger services continued to reverse en route until 1879 when the opening of a curve between

Wombwell Main and New Oaks junctions permitted direct running (Sunday trains reversed at Wombwell until World War I). The final development here occurred in 1906 when the layout of the eastern end of the line to Worsborough and Penistone was altered so that it diverged at Wombwell Main junction instead of Aldam junction, thus allowing coal traffic from Stairfoot and points north to work directly towards Penistone without reversal.

In the meantime a second route had been thrust through the narrow confines of the Blackburn Valley. It started off as an insignificant Midland branch from Wincobank to serve the ironworks at Chapeltown and Thorncliffe; never more than $\frac{1}{4}$ mile (0·4km) from the parallel MS & L line, it was brought into use for mineral traffic in 1893. The line was elevated to importance when it was extended from a junction near Chapeltown, just over a mile (1·6km) short of the Thorncliffe Ironworks terminus, through to the Cudworth–Barnsley route. It thus provided a Midland Sheffield–Barnsley link of 16 miles (25·6km) compared with the existing 20¾ miles (33·2km) via Rotherham, and a passenger service between the two towns over this route commenced in 1897. North of Chapeltown the line threaded the ¾ mile (1·2km) Tankersley tunnel before passing close to Elsecar and then turning through a right angle to go beneath the MS & L between Dovecliffe and Wombwell Main junction. At this point a branch diverged on the down side and paralleled the MS & L in order to serve the Barrow, Rockingham and Wharncliffe collieries and a goods depot at Birdwell & Pilley.

A further rise in status came when a line from Monkspring junction, between Wombwell and Barnsley, to Cudworth Station South junction was opened in 1899. This completed what was termed the Chapeltown loop, an alternative route for traffic between Sheffield and Leeds. Although much more steeply graded than the main line, it was used by a number of expresses as it avoided the congested junctions around Rotherham and Swinton.

Both the MS & L and Midland routes through the Blackburn Valley had a relatively uneventful twentieth century existence up to nationalisation, and the obvious step of eliminating duplicate passenger facilities was not taken until 1953, when those on the earlier line were withdrawn. Trains from Sheffield via the Midland's Blackburn Valley route formed virtually the only passenger traffic into Barnsley Court House after the withdrawal of the Doncaster–Penistone local services in 1959. The older Barnsley station, which gained the suffix Exchange in 1924, was still being used solely by trains from Wakefield, and a combination of passenger facilities was therefore an urgent need. It was made even more imperative by the fact that the southern approaches to Court House required renewal at an estimated cost of £200,000. To achieve this unification, a south to west connection was constructed at Quarry junction, the SY main line being lifted by no less than fourteen feet (4·3m) in order to link up with the ex-Midland Sheffield route and allow traffic from the south to work into Exchange station. The new arrangements came into operation on 19 April 1960, when a through Leeds–Barnsley (Exchange)–Sheffield DMU service was instituted and Court House officially closed to passengers, although the last train ran four days earlier. The Chapeltown loop ceased to be an alternative route to the main line in 1967 when the section north from Monkspring junction to Ardsley was abandoned. As is mentioned below, the remaining portion was utilised to form a direct Stairfoot–Cudworth link.

LATER MINERAL LINES

Although both of the lines which left the Barnsley area in a north-easterly direction carried a meagre passenger service, they conformed to the local pattern in that coal was the primary traffic. The first to come into being had the mundane title of the Barnsley Coal Railway, this concealing territorial ambitions of the highest importance. Its Bill for an extension from the SY at Ardsley (later Stairfoot) to Wakefield came before Parliament in 1861, but owing to opposition from the Wooley estate was trimmed at its northern end so that the line rather incongruously terminated at Applehaigh Lane, near Notton. Attempts in 1862 and 1863 to obtain powers for an extension to Wakefield were unsuccessful, as was a scheme promoted by the Bradford, Wakefield & Leeds Railway in 1863 for a link to the truncated northern end of the Barnsley line, which in the same year was purchased by the SY. In the background of all these schemes was the MS & L, desperately eager to reach Wakefield. This ambition was largely achieved in 1865 when it gained running powers over the Midland main line, and henceforth the BC became much less significant. Construction did not begin until two years later, and it was 1870 before opening took place.

In 1873 the MS & L made a further attempt to extend what had become known as the 'Barnsley Stump' towards Wakefield, but once more ran into difficulties with the Wooley estate. Powers were finally obtained in 1874, the Act also authorising a west to north curve at Stairfoot which would permit trains from Barnsley to run direct on to the BC. The extension commenced at Lee Lane, just over half a mile (0·8km) short of Applehaigh, although it seems probable that the final section of the original line was already disused. It terminated by a double junction with the West Riding & Grimsby at Nostell, and included a west to north curve on to the Midland main line at Royston junction. Goods and mineral traffic commenced to use both the extension and the Stairfoot curve in August 1882, the first passenger trains running over the line from the following month when a service was instituted from Barnsley Court House to Leeds Central. It survived until 1930.

The second line to occupy the north-east orbit around Barnsley had even more ambitious territorial aims. This was the Hull, Barnsley & West Riding Junction Railway & Dock, more fully described in the next chapter, which in 1880 asked for powers for a main line extending from the Humber port through Cudworth to junctions with the Midland at Monk Bretton and the MS & L at Stairfoot. Running powers were sought into both Barnsley stations, and then westwards over Woodhead to Manchester and through to Liverpool via the Cheshire Lines. A spur was to connect with the Midland main line a mile north of Cudworth so as to permit through running into Sheffield. This attempt to gain access to the greater part of industrial Lancashire and Yorkshire was ruthlessly dealt with by Parliament, only the powers over the

Midland into Barnsley surviving the passage through the
Commons and even these becoming a casualty in the Lords.

The company thus found itself in the embarrassing position of having no effective terminus at the western end of
its main line, a fact which led its opponents to dub it the
'Hull and Nowhere Railway'. There were frequent jibes
about the railway petering out among the spoil heaps west
of Cudworth, while the *Barnsley Chronicle* cuttingly
remarked: 'The term Hull and Barnsley is a misnomer and
as regards the vast majority of the public, it has never been
anything else than an abstraction'. In an attempt to seek a
way out of its difficulties the H & B turned to the Midland,
almost alone in maintaining reasonable relations with the
Hull company, and the two reached an agreement described
in the parliamentary session of 1882 as 'the first recognition
of a railway Ishmael'. An Act of that year authorised a line
which would leave the principal trunk of the H & B at Cudworth South junction and extend to the Midland main line
just south of Cudworth station where separate facilities for
the Hull company would be provided. Colonel Gerard
Smith, the redoubtable H & B chairman, had successfully
pleaded to the Commons that these arrangements were
necessary in order 'to get a home somewhere in South Yorkshire'. From the opening in 1885, passenger trains terminated
at a single platform station at Cudworth which formed part
of the more substantial Midland station. Short branches to
collieries in the locality helped to provide much of the coal
traffic which was the mainstay of the H & B.

As outlined in the next chapter, traffic between Hull and
Cudworth was progressively reduced after the Grouping and
all through workings ceased in 1958. Closure of the greater
part of the Cudworth to Stairfoot section took place in 1967
when a new route, more favourably graded and less affected
by subsidence, was created between these points by linking
the northern end of the Chapeltown loop with the nearby
southern part of the ex-H & B line at Ardsley. By the following year this tiny fragment was about the sole surviving local
remnant of a brave company's ambitious network, all its
other lines in the area apart from some sidings at Cudworth
having been abandoned.

CHAPTER VIII

Doncaster and the Concealed Coalfield

Scenically, the region centred around Doncaster is somewhat monotonous. It comprises an area where the Pennine slopes merge into the southern end of the Vale of York, the undulating foothills quickly giving way to a vast area of low-lying and almost flat arable and marsh land. The geology is more inspiring than the landscape might suggest, for east of a line drawn almost due south from Pontefract lies the so-called concealed coalfield. Here very substantial coal measures exist at considerable depth beneath the limestone, but owing to the technical problems of extraction their exploitation did not begin until the dawn of the twentieth century. The high finance involved ushered in the era of the 'giant pit', causing colossal pithead works and spoil heaps to sprout incongruously in the former cornfields and woodlands.

Unlike the rest of south and west Yorkshire, the railways of this area were not greatly constrained by physical features, and thus the first impression is of a network of lines crisscrossing at random with little apparent sense of purpose. In fact chronologically there are two systems, one superimposed on top of the other. The first, occupying the initial three sections of this chapter and stemming from the period 1845 to 1880, was centred on Doncaster itself and built to provide essential radial links for both passenger and goods traffic. The second, covered by the last three sections and dating from 1880 onwards, was created primarily to open up new workings in the coalfield and transport its products to the coastal ports.

Doncaster has always been a traveller's town, its foundation dating from the Roman period when it was a bridging point on the lower Don. From medieval times its economy was dominated by the Great North Road, while by the early nineteenth century it was famous for horse racing and was noted as 'one of the most clean, airy and elegant towns in the British dominions'. For these reasons aristocratic Doncaster did nothing to encourage the coming of railways, typical of the town's attitude being its rejection of the 1830 Sheffield & Goole Railway as 'wholly unnecessary and uncalled for'. As a result there were no lines of any importance in the region until as late as 1848.

Lines which did materialise prior to this date were very minor indeed. The $7\frac{1}{2}$ mile (12km) Heck Bridge & Wentbridge Railway was built to link stone quarries in the Went Valley with the Knottingley & Goole Canal. One of its most substantial contributions to posterity is its incorporation Act of 5 May 1826 which manages to extend to 70 pages and includes a provision that 'persons damaging the line [are] liable to be sentenced to transportation for seven years'. No opportunity to inflict such a dire punishment ever arose for finance ran out in the autumn of 1829 before regular traffic commenced. The plate railway, which was laid to a gauge of about 3ft 6in (1·07m) on stone sleeper blocks, was authorised to be sold in 1833. At Conisbrough some limestone quarries on the banks of the Don were connected with kilns $\frac{1}{4}$ mile (0·4km) away by means of a primitive stone railway. Blocks of stone were chiselled to form parallel grooves, although in this case the flanges were on the outside of the blocks in contrast to the better known and earlier Haytor tramway on Dartmoor. The gauge of the line was approximately three feet (0·9m) and it went out of use about 1902; its building date is not known.

THE EAST COAST ROUTE

The evolution of the original and indirect East Coast Route, which by 1840 extended from London (Euston Square) as far as York via Rugby, Derby and Normanton, has already been outlined. This had a heyday of only ten years before it was eclipsed by the present main line running north from

King's Cross through Peterborough and Doncaster, where almost overnight it transformed the coaching town into a key railway centre. Doncaster, at first reluctant to recognise railways, expanded enormously once it had yielded to them, although its initial apathy meant that the town was avoided by some of the early proposals and came dangerously close to being relegated to a small market settlement. An abortive survey for a line from London to York via Lincoln was completed in 1827, and the railway boom of 1836 saw two Bills coming before Parliament. One was for the Northern & Eastern Railway via Peterborough and the other for the Great Northern Railway via Lincoln, but both were rejected in favour of the lines through the Midlands which served a greater density of population.

The Railway Mania brought a plethora of schemes, culminating in one of the greatest of all parliamentary battles. The first proposal, in 1843, was for the Direct Northern Railway to York via Lincoln and Thorne. The following year saw a revival of the two 1836 schemes which united as the London & York Railway, passing through Grantham and Gainsborough and initially intending to go to the east of Doncaster. A change was made at the instance of Edmund Denison, in many ways the creator of the southern portion of the present East Coast Route. He was born in Doncaster, was MP for the West Riding and successfully pressed for the route to be changed so that it would better serve both his constituents and his town.

As the line would shorten the rail journey from London to York by thirty miles (48km), it naturally encountered the full wrath of George Hudson. He denounced it as 'the most complete monopoly ever sought to be established', promoted a series of blocking lines and employed obstructionist tactics to such effect that the committee examining the Bill sat for seventy days. Finally, he managed to prevent its passage through the Lords by using questionable methods to uncover errors in the subscription contract. The Direct Northern was also thrown out, so in the session of 1846 the two amalgamated and revived the title of the Great Northern. This time Hudson resorted to even more desperate tactics, assuming the chairmanship of the Eastern Counties Railway in

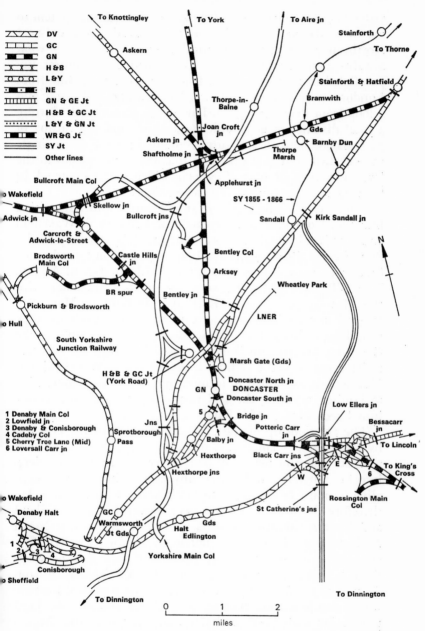

Key:

ZZZZ	DV
⊥⊥⊥⊥	GC
▬▬▬	GN
XXXX	H & B
○○○○	L & Y
▬▬▬	NE
▥▥▥▥	GN & GE Jt
▦▦▦▦	H & B & GC Jt
····	L & Y & GN Jt
▬▬▬	WR & G Jt
═══	SY Jt
———	Other lines

To Knottingley

To York

To Aire jn

Stainforth

To Thorne

Askern

Stainforth & Hatfield

Bramwith

Thorpe-in-Balne

Joan Croft jn

Gds

Barnby Dun

Askern jn

Thorpe Marsh

Shaftholme jn

Bullcroft Main Col

Applehurst jn

SY 1855 - 1866 →

To Wakefield

Skellow jn

Sandall

Kirk Sandall jn

Adwick jn

Bullcroft jns

Carcroft & Adwick-le-Street

Bentley Col

Brodsworth Main Col

Castle Hills jn

Arksey

BR spur

Bentley jn

Wheatley Park

Pickburn & Brodsworth

LNER

To Hull

South Yorkshire Junction Railway

Marsh Gate (Gds)

H & B & GC Jt (York Road)

Doncaster North jn
DONCASTER
Doncaster South jn

Low Ellers jn

1 Denaby Main Col
2 Lowfield jn
3 Denaby & Conisborough
4 Cadeby Col
5 Cherry Tree Lane (Mid)
6 Loversall Carr jn

GN

5

Bridge jn

Potteric Carr jn

Bessacarr jn

Jns

Sprotborough Pass

Balby jn

To Lincoln

Hexthorpe

Black Carr jns

To King's Cross

Hexthorpe jns

W

E

6

To Wakefield

St Catherine's jns

Rossington Main Col

Denaby Halt

GC
Warmsworth Jt Gds

Gds

1
2 3 4

Halt Edlington

Conisborough

Yorkshire Main Col

To Sheffield

To Dinnington

To Dinnington

0   1   2
miles

Map 7: Doncaster

order to promote further blocking routes from this system to his own Midland lines. It was to no avail, for the Great Northern Bill received the royal assent in 1846 after what a subsequent directors' report described as 'a contest un-paralleled in railway annals'. It authorised a main line from London to York via Grantham, Retford and Doncaster and a loop from Peterborough to Bawtry via Boston and Lincoln, a total distance of $285\frac{1}{4}$ miles (456·4km), and the raising of £5,600,000. Both these figures remained records for a single railway Bill, and it is probable that the same applies to the legal expenses of over £400,000 which were incurred in fighting Hudson during the two sessions.

A setback was the rejection of a separate Bill authorising branches from Bawtry to Sheffield and Arksey to Wakefield and Leeds, although this was mitigated by the Wakefield, Pontefract & Goole Railway obtaining sanction for a branch linking its main line at Knottingley with the GN at Askern. The WP & G had by this time agreed to amalgamate with the Manchester & Leeds Railway, which on 1 May 1847 entered into an important agreement with the GN for reci-procal use of lines. The M & L was to be able to run over the GN from Askern into Doncaster, and in return the GN was to have use of WP & G lines from Askern to Wakefield and Methley. As explained in chapter one, this encroachment led to Hudson granting the GN running powers from Methley into Leeds over the Midland.

The relationship of the 'Railway King' with the GN was by now quietly changing. A man of his astuteness must have realised that the new line had thrust a critical blow deep into his kingdom, and that if any part of it was to be kept alive he must be prepared to sacrifice the weakest links. He therefore decided to give up his command of the Midland and Eastern Counties railways, and graft the York & North Midland and lines to the north on to the GN. His first cunning move was the 1847 promotion of a line no more than 3 miles (4·8km) long from the Y & NM at Burton Salmon to the WP & G at Knottingley. Its supposed purpose was to tap limestone quarries in this area and link the local population with Leeds and Hull, and its momentous impor-tance as the vital connection in a new East Coast route did not at first dawn on Midland shareholders. Hudson then commenced secret negotiations which would allow the GN to run over the new line to Burton Salmon and on to York, providing the company abandoned its own approach to the city and also allowed the Y & NM to run south from Knottingley into Doncaster. It was a tempting offer, for after its bitter parliamentary struggle the GN was decidedly impoverished. After some hesitation over loss of independence the company finally accepted, although the formal agreement was not confirmed until 29 November 1850. Thus it came about that the GN main line terminated not at York but by an end-on junction with the WP & G (later the L & Y) at Askern. In a famous phrase attributed to Edmund Denison, its first chairman, the GN ended 'in a ploughed field four miles north of Doncaster'.

In the meantime the company had been having its problems on the other side of Doncaster. With the rejection of the branch to Sheffield from Bawtry it was no longer necessary for the Lincoln loop to join the main line at this point, and therefore a Bill was promoted in 1847 to move the point of junction north to Rossington. This was unexpectedly thrown out on the grounds that the new route would interfere with fox-hunting, although another portion of the Bill providing for the main line to pass through the western instead of the eastern side of Doncaster was sanctioned.

In 1848 the GN made a second attempt to deviate the northern end of the loop, but was again unsuccessful and so concluded arrangements with the MS & L to use its line from Gainsborough to Retford. In June of the same year a mere $2\frac{1}{4}$ miles (3·6km) of the new trunk route were brought into use when the L & Y instituted services from Knottingley to Askern and over the GN as far as Stockbridge (later Arksey). Omnibuses ran from this point to Doncaster until the line was extended to a temporary station here north of the later site in September 1848.

Opening of the section from Retford to Doncaster in September 1849 completed a through route from Peterborough to Leeds via Lincoln just in time for that year's St Leger traffic. As explained in chapter one, a regular service to Leeds did not begin until October when the GN took over

N

St Leger crowds at Doncaster's first temporary station in September 1849. The present day permanent

from the L & Y all passenger services between Doncaster and Knottingley. Freight workings from Doncaster to Leeds were similarly transferred on 1 July 1850. Opening of the link to Burton Salmon was delayed by difficulties with Robert Stephenson's tubular bridge over the Aire at Brotherton, although in April 1850 the Board of Trade sanctioned the use of a single line temporary bridge providing every train was conducted over it by a pilotman. This enabled the GN to begin a through London–York service in August on completion of the southern end of its main line. The first tube of the Brotherton bridge was passed for passenger traffic in July 1851, the completion date of the second tube was October 1852 (both were replaced by a girder bridge in 1902). At Doncaster itself work on constructing a permanent station started in March 1850, the structure being ready for use by mid-September of the same year. The final development in this period was the opening to passengers of the direct 'towns line' from Peterborough to Retford in 1852. The GN, almost strangled at birth only six years previously, was now a fighting force which quickly captured all through traffic from the former Midland route to York. In the words of its later historian, Charles H. Grinling, the company had in Doncaster control of 'the key to the whole of the north'.

Hudson's role in aiding the GN to enter both Leeds and York could not be concealed from Midland shareholders indefinitely, and it ultimately played a major part in the events of 1849 which culminated in his 'dethronement' and disappearance from the railway scene. The pact between the GN and the Y & NM was instrumental in the formation of the Euston Square Confederacy, more fully explained in the Introduction. One of its members was the L & Y, which in January 1852 gave notice that it would stop GN trains working north of Askern unless the company paid the maximum parliamentary toll. The GN had to apply to the Court of Chancery for protection, but relations between the two companies slightly improved and in 1853 they agreed to set up a joint committee for the management of Knottingley station. It was rebuilt as a four platform structure with overall roof, joint working commencing in 1854.

The major changes stemming from the opening of the

GN occurred in Doncaster itself, for despite some local opposition the town was in 1851 selected as the site of the company's locomotive works. It was felt to be a more suitable centre for obtaining labour, coal and iron than the existing temporary location at Boston. The initial plans envisaged expenditure of some £45,000, but it was soon decided to provide additional facilities for the construction and repair of carriages. What was always known as the Plant was partially brought into use at the end of June 1853 and was in full operation by 9 August. Some 900 workmen were transferred from Boston, and with their families added more than 2,500 to the population of Doncaster which between 1851 and 1861 increased from 12,052 to 16,406. Edmund Denison repeatedly told shareholders that he would not be a party to bringing so many additional people into the town without making some provision for their education and spiritual welfare. In 1854 he induced the company to vote £1,000 for the provision of schools, and when opened in January 1855 these were attended by 246 children. Much more controversial was his Bill of 1855 for the construction and endowment of a church, which in the end he had to withdraw owing to mounting opposition from shareholders over the use of company funds for religious purposes. Instead, St James's church was built by subscription and completed in 1858 to the designs of Denison's son, E. B. Denison, later Lord Grimthorpe. Substantial extensions to the works were made in 1855, and 1865–6 when locomotive building began on the appointment of Patrick Stirling. A new erecting shop was completed in 1890–1, a new carriage shop in 1897–8 and additional repair shops in 1900–1, while wagon shops were built on the Carr in 1889. By the turn of the century the combined works covered 200 acres, was surrounded by 60 miles (96km) of sidings and employed 4,500 men.

The Plant played a major role in handling the traffic for a traditional event which the railway revolutionised—the St Leger. This originally attracted a relatively small and most elite gathering, but the opening of the GN brought crowds from a distance and turned it into a popular festival. In 1864 over 70 special trains arrived in Doncaster on St Leger Day, and by the turn of the century this number had grown to the 150 mark. The locomotive and carriage shops were closed for the week and all goods workings suspended so as to clear as many sidings as possible for stabling purposes. Excursions were worked in by all the main line companies which had access to Yorkshire, and also by such strangers as the North Staffordshire Railway, and in the evening were dispatched at the rate of one a minute for over two hours.

Work on enlarging Doncaster station at a cost of £20,000 began in 1873 and was completed by the end of 1877. As a result of becoming a joint partner in most of the 1879 Market Harborough–Newark line, the L & NW received running powers north to Doncaster and commenced to run through freight and coal trains between here and Camden and Willesden on 1 December 1879. These workings were drastically reduced in 1892 when the 'Premier Line' instead began to pick up South Yorkshire coal at Colwick following the opening of the first stage of the MS & L's London extension. Developments to the south of Doncaster at this time included the enormous Decoy marshalling yards, named after the wild-duck shooting popular here in pre-railway days, the down yard being opened on 25 May 1891 and the up yard in November 1895. In the meantime considerable changes had been taking place on the Askern–Knottingley line which gradually lost much of its importance. The first blow fell in February 1866 when the GN transferred its Leeds services to the new West Riding & Grimsby joint line (see below), a substitute Doncaster–Knottingley–Wakefield local service being put on by the L & Y from 1 March of the same year. Then, in 1871 the NE opened a cut-off from Chaloner Whin junction, York, through Selby to Shaftholme junction, ten chains (0·2km) south of the end-on Askern junction with which it is frequently confused. By agreement with the NE, the GN commenced to work all through traffic as far as York over the cut-off, and thenceforth the Knottingley line saw few expresses except for an L & Y Liverpool–Harwich boat train and the North Country Continental to York which were respectively routed this way until 1914 and 1939. However, on 1 July 1902, the GN commenced a service of three expresses each way between King's Cross and Harrogate via Knottingley, Church Fenton and Tadcaster, and the Harrogate Pullman also followed this route from 1925 to 1928. Further variety at Knottingley was provided by an H & B service to the town from Hull via Hensall junction, which first appeared in the timetable in April 1886 and was terminated on 25 April 1912. Regular passenger services between Doncaster and Knottingley were withdrawn in 1948, the last King's Cross to Harrogate working via this line having ceased on 11 July of the previous year.

FROM THE COALFIELD TO THE COAST

Until the opening of the L & Y branch from Knottingley in 1848, the nearest station to Doncaster was on the North Midland at Swinton. Connections from here were provided both by coaches and by a service of fast passenger boats, known as aquabuses, on the Don Navigation. These lasted from 1840 until the opening in 1849 of the first section of the South Yorkshire, Doncaster & Goole Railway from Swinton to Doncaster. As outlined in the previous chapter, the purpose of the SY was to provide an outlet from the Barnsley coalfield to London, by connecting with the GN, and to the Humber estuary by transferring traffic to the Don Navigation at Doncaster.

The early SY arrangements at Doncaster are rather obscure, but it seems that the initial Midland-worked passenger service from Sheffield (Wicker) which began in 1849 terminated at a rudimentary station at Cherry Lane (or Cherry Tree Lane) on the west side of the GN main line. The GN, which was still using a small temporary station at Doncaster, would not be keen to accommodate additional traffic, and in any event was distinctly at odds with the Midland as a result of the Euston Square Confederacy. Contemporary issues of the *Doncaster Chronicle* make it clear that from the outset the SY had accommodation in both the temporary and permanent GN stations, but this was probably for office purposes rather than for handling Midland trains. The *Barnsley Chronicle* of 21 September 1850 states that the SY station was separate from the GN, and it seems that Cherry Lane remained a passenger terminus until about 1852 when it was leased to the Midland as a goods depot and the Sheffield trains were admitted to the main line station. In the meantime the GN-worked Doncaster–Barnsley service had commenced on 1 July 1851, the same date as the opening of a short SY branch to Strawberry Island on the Don for interchange of coal traffic with the Navigation.

The GN admittance of the Midland was possibly connected with the fact that at this time the company was anxious not to upset the SY. Its friendly relations culminated in the 1852 leasing Act, an event of enormous importance for by now the GN was working an almost hourly service of coal trains south from Doncaster which were bringing in some £2,000 per week. This is why such lengthy and bitter litigation followed the collapse of the leasing arrangements for reasons noted in the previous chapter. The bitterness reached its peak early in 1853 when from 22 to 24 February the SY stopped all GN coal trains from going on to its metals until such direct action was prevented by a court injunction. Edmund Denison complained: 'There were 500 or 600 colliers out of work; the trains were all stopped; our engine-drivers were playing marbles or snowballs or something of that sort; the engines were standing idle; people were calling out for coals, but coals they could not get.' Even after some degree of harmony had been restored in 1854, a proper working relationship was never really established, and this helped the Derbyshire coalfield to gain something of an edge over that of South Yorkshire.

One of the numerous SY legends relates that at Doncaster the company's first locomotive water supplies were drawn from a pump in the garden of a cobbler who lived near the line. Access to it was by means of a gate which could only be unlocked by the cobbler, who became over-awed with his position of power and was most reluctant to perform this simple operation! Such an archaic practice would no doubt be swept away when the MS & L leased the SY in 1864.

At Hexthorpe were extensive sidings to which the NE was granted access for coal and coke traffic by agreement of 5 October 1869. Here too was the ticket platform for Doncaster, the scene on 16 September 1887 of the worst accident in the history of the MS & L. A Midland excursion from Sheffield, packed with race-goers, was standing at the platform when it was run into by an MS & L express from Liverpool, killing 25 people and injuring 94. The company was faced with claims exceeding £30,000, many of its employees offering to defray a week's wages in order to meet the costs. The offer was declined by the directors, who did not however defend the driver and fireman when they were charged with manslaughter. This was done by the then infant ASLEF, and with their acquittal the union's membership leapt by over 2,000.

It was not until twenty years after its opening that the SY was effectively extended north-east from Doncaster to the Humber estuary. A direct link from South Yorkshire to Goole and Hull was obviously highly desirable, but all earlier attempts to build such a route were unsuccessful. The first SY venture in this direction was indeed modest, taking the form of a single track line to Thorne from the terminus of the earlier branch to the Don Navigation at Strawberry Island. So that it could be built without an Act, it was constructed on the bank of the Navigation and then paralleled the Stainforth & Keadby Canal, also owned by the company. The line made coal transport easier by shifting trans-shipment to Thorne and thus cutting out a section of waterway prone to drought problems, but it was extremely tortuous and on at least one occasion caused an engine to be derailed and plunge into the water! Opening to the main terminus at Thorne Lock took place for passengers in July 1856, the trains connecting with canal packets to Keadby where Gainsborough–Hull boats completed a somewhat inadequate link with the Humber port. In January 1856 a branch had been brought into use to Thorne Waterside, with its large warehouse and coal staithes alongside the Don. A tale is attached to the official inspection of the Thorne line which on almost any other railway but the SY would not be credible. Just before the arrival of the government inspector it was realised there was no run-round loop at the terminus, so some wagons attached to the train were filled with resplendently attired navvies as if to celebrate the occasion. On arrival at Thorne the inspector was hurried into the nearest hostelry, so that the navvies could turn the train round by bodily lifting the locomotive off the track and pushing the coach and wagons

Victorian tragedy at Hexthorpe, near Doncaster. In September 1887 an MS & L express ran into the back of a Midland excursion crowded with race-goers. Twenty-five passengers were killed and 94 injured

past it. This operation had been performed by the time the official emerged, and no awkward questions were asked!

An extension from Thorne to Keadby was opened in 1859, and was of the same pattern in that it was a single line built alongside the canal without an authorising Act. It was constructed for less than £3,000 per mile, and was initially traversed by three mixed trains each way. To coincide with the opening, Thorne Lock terminus was replaced by a new through station at Orchard Street, ¼ mile (0·4km) nearer Keadby. Beyond Maud's Bridge, two miles (3·2km) east of Thorne, the new line was reasonably straight, but the whole route up to this point from Doncaster was little more than a glorified waggonway.

Change seemed imminent in 1861 when the SY, along with the GN, backed a Thorne–Goole–Hull link. The scheme was withdrawn in favour of proposals promised by the NE, which duly appeared in the next session along with lines put forward by the SY, L & Y and the independent Hull & West Riding Junction Railway. The result of this sudden and conflicting scramble to carry South Yorkshire coal to the Humber was that none of the Bills was successful, but the three established companies were not deterred and again put forward proposals in 1863. This time the NE and SY came to an agreement under which the former was to stop short at Thorne its proposed line to Doncaster from a junction at Staddlethorpe on the Hull–Selby route. The SY was to form 'a First class double line of Railway' between Doncaster and Thorne and abandon its intended extension from here to Hull. The two companies would exchange running powers into Hull and Doncaster, where NE traffic would be admitted into the main line station in return for giving the GN access to Hull. Traffic concessions were also offered to the L & Y which accordingly withdrew its competing Bill.

In the following year the MS & L leased the SY and hence took over construction of the deviation line from Doncaster. This forked at Thorne junction, one portion continuing eastwards to link up with the original Keadby branch at Maud's Bridge. It included a new station at Thorne (now Thorne South) and was opened in 1866, the improved route rapidly assuming great importance as a result of the establishment of Scunthorpe Ironworks in 1864 and the opening of an extension across the Trent at Keadby. The second portion of the fork made an end-on junction with the NE link from Staddlethorpe and Goole just south of Thorne (now Thorne North), the town's fourth passenger station in fourteen years. Both lines were opened simultaneously in August 1869, and on 1 November the MS & L commenced to run through to Hull. The GN did not exercise its running powers until July 1897 when it put on a summer boat train from King's Cross to Hull in connection with the Norwegian steamers.

As traffic increased, the MS & L was increasingly handicapped by the fact that its South Yorkshire–Humberside route cut across the GN at Doncaster on the level. By the turn of the century there were some 700 conflicting train movements a day at this point, and the problem seemed likely to increase with the construction of the GC docks at Immingham. The problem was solved with the opening in 1910 of the 'Doncaster Avoiding Line' which ran from Hexthorpe junction to a flying connection with the Thorne route at Bentley junction, crossing not only the GN but also two main roads and a flood drain. It therefore had to be built entirely on embankment, consuming a million cubic yards (765,000cu m) of earth and costing over £160,000. Traffic continued to expand, and in 1912–17 the GC quadrupled the greater part of its lines from Wath to Thorne.

JOINT PASSENGER LINES

There were three important joint main lines in this area, all of them in one way or another born out of necessity rather than a genuine desire for co-operation. The first to be formed was the West Riding & Grimsby Joint, seemingly a strange name for a line whose prime purpose became the conveyance of GN traffic between Doncaster and Wakefield. Yet it accurately indicates its origins, for it was initially promoted by the SY in 1862 as the West Riding, Hull & Grimsby Railway, extending from Wakefield to a junction with the company's pending Doncaster–Thorne direct line at Stainforth, and including a branch from Adwick to Doncaster. It was seen as providing a direct link between the West Riding and Hull, by means of the line which the SY was then hoping to make to the Humber port, and also to Grimsby by already mooted extensions of the Keadby route. 'Hull' had been dropped from the title by 7 August 1862 when the company was incorporated despite opposition from the NE and L & Y.

The GN must have been more than a little chagrined at this parliamentary victory, for in 1857, 1860 and 1861 its own schemes for a Doncaster–Wakefield link had been thrown out. Now that both the Leeds, Bradford & Halifax Junction and the Bradford, Wakefield & Leeds railways were being worked by the company, and were about to be absorbed by it, the need for access to this area independent of the L & Y became imperative. As described below, the L & Y played a major part in the Great Eastern proposals of 1862–5 for a new trunk route from the south to Doncaster. The GN realised the danger of its position and attempted to buy the West Riding & Grimsby, even though the SY supported the trunk proposals. A further complication was that the SY was at this moment in the process of being leased by the MS & L, also well-disposed towards the GE schemes, which insisted that purchase of the line could only be on a joint basis. Little progress was therefore made until the trunk route had been rejected, and the way cleared for an 1866 Act authorising the WR & G to be jointly vested in the GN and MS & L. It gave the Sheffield company running powers over existing GN lines north-west of Wakefield, including access to Leeds Central, and permitted the GN to work from Stainforth to Grimsby—which it never did except for excursions and special traffic.

In the meantime the Doncaster–Adwick–Wakefield portion of the WR & G had been opened in February 1866. The section from Adwick junction to Stainforth junction (originally Parkswood or Haggswood junction) could not be brought into use until completion of the Doncaster–Thorne direct line. It was opened in November 1866, crossing the Don Navigation by means of a swing bridge (eliminated when a $\frac{1}{2}$ mile (0·8km) deviation was brought into use on 14 November 1955). Initially visualised as the main line, it was now of lesser importance than the branch to Doncaster, but it did carry a heavy freight traffic as well as a passenger service from

Leeds Central to Grimsby and Cleethorpes and, in later years, holiday workings from several West Riding towns. In 1882 the L & Y was granted running powers over the WR & G between Wakefield and Doncaster in return for giving the GN access to Halifax via the Calder Valley, but these were only regularly exercised for coal traffic. Local passenger services over this portion of the line were withdrawn on 6 November 1967.

The Great Northern & Great Eastern Joint had even more protracted and turbulent origins. After its formation in 1862, the GE was described by GN counsel as being 'in the painful position of having a great deal of railway which had cost a great sum of money, but very little traffic'. It was particularly short of coal, and therefore in the year of its incorporation promoted the March & Askern Coal Railway so as to gain access to South Yorkshire. This was withdrawn, although in the following year the GE sought running powers over existing lines to Askern. In retaliation the GN revived its Gainsborough–Doncaster direct line thrown out in 1847 and 1848, but once again Parliament regarded the fox-hunting in the area as sacrosanct. Both companies' Bills were rejected, yet strangely in 1864 a complete reversal occurred. The GN Bill was authorised at the expense of a new GE proposal for the Great Eastern Northern Junction Railway, extending from Long Stanton, near Cambridge, to a junction with the WR & G near Adwick. The GE scheme came up again in the next session, this time in concert with the L & Y which felt aggrieved at progress made by the GN in the West Riding and was keen to win a share of the London coal traffic. It would have joined the L & Y at Askern, but once again was stillborn.

This consistent failure led the GE to consider working agreements with the GN and MS & L, under which it would have shared the cost of constructing the Gainsborough–Doncaster line and have been given running powers over the WR & G to Wakefield. Bills for this purpose were put forward in 1866, but withdrawn owing to alterations in the GE Board leading to policy changes. It was therefore a wholly GN line which opened the following year from Gainsborough to a junction with the East Coast route at Black

Carr. Negotiations between the GN and GE, including amalgamation proposals, continued over the next decade as the
companies' relations varied from harmonious to a state of
total war. During a low ebb the GE attempted once more
to reach Askern, and when this was rejected in 1878 it
quickly capitulated. An 1879 Act authorised the formation
of the Great Northern & Great Eastern Joint Committee
which was empowered to take over the Gainsborough–Black
Carr section and other routes to the south, thus creating a
joint main line from March to Doncaster. This took effect
on 1 August 1882 when the GE became the sixth company
working into the single Doncaster station (the others were
the GN, L & Y, Midland, MS & L and NE). A month afterwards through services were inaugurated between Liverpool
Street and Doncaster, and in 1883 the North Country Continental was put on from Harwich, both these workings
being extended to York when GE passenger traffic was
admitted to the NE capital on 1 November 1892. The distance
from Liverpool Street was 214¾ miles (344km) compared with
188 miles (301km) from King's Cross, so in an attempt
to minimise the disadvantage the GE gave great publicity
to what it termed 'The Cathedrals Route'. The ancient
edifices at Ely, Lincoln and York were not however able to
compensate for the longer journey, and the service succumbed during World War I. Since then there have been
few changes to the GN & GE Joint, which continues to carry
a steady volume of traffic from the north to Lincolnshire and
East Anglia.

The third of the joint main lines, the Swinton & Knottingley, was distinct from the other routes in that it was not
centred on Doncaster. Although geographically part of the
area under consideration, its main purpose was as a cut-off
for traffic from Sheffield and the south to York and the north.
The line was the strange result of early attempts by the
MS & L to gain an independent route towards London. In
1872 the Sheffield company unsuccessfully promoted an
extension for this purpose from Doncaster to Market Harborough, and in the following year joined forces with the
Midland to put forward a similar scheme, although this time
including a connection with the NE at Askern. The Bill

was so mauled during its parliamentary passage that it was withdrawn, whereupon the NE suggested to the Midland that a better direct connection between the two systems would be provided by a link from Swinton to a junction with the Knottingley–Burton Salmon line at Ferrybridge. The NE had spare track capacity north of this point owing to the diversion of London–York trains to the new Selby route. Hence the two companies agreed jointly to promote in 1874 the S & K, something of a misnomer in that it did not actually enter Knottingley.

The MS & L, perhaps rather aggrieved at being left out in the cold at this stage, promoted the rival Leeds, Pontefract & Sheffield Junction Railway jointly with the GN. Neither Bill was at first successful, but the MS & L and GN agreed to a re-commital of the S & K provided that they received running powers over it and that provision was made for a south to west spur on to the L & Y at Pontefract so as to give access to Castleford. The line accordingly received its Act, which incorporated the Midland and North-Eastern Railway Companies Committee, and was opened in 1879. Besides the main line and the Pontefract curve, there were also connections with the MS & L at Mexborough and the WR & G at Moorthorpe. A north to west spur on to the MS & L at Wath was opened in 1882, one half of it belonging to the Sheffield company and the remainder to the S & K.

Operationally, the S & K was truly a joint line in that it was used by a multiplicity of services. The Midland was very much the dominant member of the owning partnership, and from the opening commenced to work its trains through to York. This not only cut $4\frac{1}{2}$ miles (7·2km) off the former route via Normanton, but also eliminated delays caused by changing engines at this congested junction. From 1 July 1881 to 31 December 1889 the company operated a connecting service from Milford Junction to Hull. It was not until 1 July 1898 that the NE entered the picture when, as noted in chapter six, it began to work its own passenger trains between York and the Midland station at Sheffield. As mentioned in chapter one, the MS & L, and for a brief period the GN, ran through trains from Sheffield Victoria to Leeds Central over the S & K and then on to the WR & G at Moor-

Map 8: Wath to Wrangbrook

thorpe. The other curve here was used by the GN until World War I for Doncaster–York locals, some of its King's Cross–Harrogate services and in summer one Scottish express each way. The MS & L worked excursions through to York, a regular service commencing on 15 March 1899 following the completion of the London extension. A fifth company to appear on the scene was the L & Y which used the Pontefract curve and the Dearne Valley Railway to gain access to collieries on the line. The curve at Pontefract was also used by Midland and MS & L race specials working into the L & Y station here, and by the NE service from Leeds New to Pontefract S & K via Garforth and Castleford.

After the Grouping the LNER made an interesting use of the line for excursions from Manchester to York and the north, travelling via Barnsley Exchange and the Wath curve so as almost entirely to avoid LMS metals. From 1968 colliery subsidence on the Midland main line forced Sheffield–Leeds passenger trains to be diverted via the S & K and on to the WR & G at Moorthorpe, but in 1973 the pattern was reversed. The Leeds services reverted to their traditional route, and Sheffield–York expresses were diverted via Normanton because of increasing subsidence problems on the S & K.

Following the passage of the Light Railways Act of 1896, it at one point seemed likely that the S & K would become a springboard for some ambitious lines of this kind. The Yorkshire District Light Railway Syndicate Ltd first put forward its proposals for the Brackenhill Light Railway in May 1899, and after modification these received Board of Trade approval in 1901. The line, which was not opened for goods and mineral traffic until 1914, ran for under three miles (4·8km) from a junction with the S & K south of Ackworth to Hemsworth Colliery, with a short branch to a goods depot at Ackworth Moor Top. The NE took an interest in the railway, but wished to avoid a formal working agreement which would have required Board of Trade approval. It was therefore arranged that although the line was 'in point of fact worked by North Eastern [it was] ostensibly worked by Brackenhill'. It never carried a regular passenger service, and after being absorbed by the LNER at the Grouping survived

o

until 1962 when it was completely closed. A more striking proposal was the Ackworth & Lindsey Light Railway of 1904 which envisaged a 53¾ mile (86km) line to Killing-holme, the object apparently being to convey coal from the Hemsworth and Pontefract district direct to Immingham docks. The first 4¾ miles (7·6km) to a junction with the H & B near Kirk Smeaton were sanctioned in 1907 as the Ackworth Light Railway, but even in this greatly reduced form it failed to materialise.

CHALLENGING A MONOPOLY

The considerable network of predominantly mineral lines around Doncaster dates from the promotion in 1880 of the Hull, Barnsley & West Riding Junction Railway & Dock, a cumbersome title mercifully shortened to the more familiar Hull & Barnsley Railway in 1905. Its origins lay not in the West Riding but almost entirely in Hull, where the whole of the docks were under one ownership and the railways serving the town belonged to the NE. This led to increasing resentment, culminating in the promotion of the H & B in an attempt to break both monopolies. Strongly supported by Hull Corporation, it was conceived primarily for conveying South Yorkshire coal to Hull for shipment through the company's own Alexandra Dock and was thus aimed at the MS & L just as much as the NE. The Bill optimistically provided for running powers to Sheffield, Leeds, Bradford, Huddersfield, Halifax and, as indicated in the previous chapter, Manchester and Liverpool, but these had all been struck out when it received the royal assent in 1880.

Construction took five years, lack of funds halting work from July to November 1884 and putting almost 6,000 navvies out of work. Lax management was a prime reason for the total expenditure on the railway exceeding £4 million, a figure double the original estimate and even then not including the dock. The cost of the line itself averaged almost £60,000 per mile, making it the most expensive rail-way of any substantial length to be built in Britain. This was despite the fact that after leaving the Wolds the route passed through level countryside until it began to climb away from the plain at Kirk Smeaton, penetrating the ridge of magnesian limestone by a 1,226yd (1·12km) tunnel officially known as South Kirkby but always referred to as Barnsdale (a name formally adopted by the LNER). Five miles (8km) later came the 685yd (623m) Brierley tunnel, approached from the west by a maximum gradient of 1 in 110 against loaded coal trains. The entry into Cudworth and Stairfoot has already been described in the previous chapter.

The line was opened in 1885, an immediate rate war breaking out with the Hull Dock Company which resulted in the railway falling deeper and deeper into debt. A further difficulty was that the NE managed to starve the line of traffic, and so amalgamation with this company or the Midland was frequently mooted but always opposed by Hull Corporation. A working arrangement was finally patched up in 1899, H & B finances rapidly improving once co-operation replaced futile competition. By the early 1900s the line was conveying some 45 coal trains and 20 goods trains each way daily.

Contributing substantially towards this traffic were two important extensions opened at the turn of the century. The first was the South Yorkshire Junction Railway, proposed in 1888 by the Denaby & Cadeby Colliery Company then starting to exploit the concealed coalfield just to the north of Conisbrough. The line was the first of several built in the area to connect 'giant pits' with a port, in this case by means of a rather sinuous single track joining the H & B at Wrangbrook junction between Upton and Kirk Smeaton. The Bill was authorised at its second attempt in 1890, a further Act of 1891 permitting the H & B to work the line which was opened for goods and mineral traffic in September 1894. Passenger services to and from Carlton on the main line commenced in December, but their withdrawal was proposed as early as September 1895 and they lasted only until 1903. The southern terminus of the SYJn at Denaby was only yards from the much earlier main line of the South Yorkshire Railway, but it was not until 1908 that the GC inserted a connecting junction in order to run over the SYJn as far as Brodsworth Colliery.

The second important additional line was the Hull &

South Yorkshire Extension Railway, incorporated in 1897 and taken over by the H & B the following year. It too started at Wrangbrook junction, and after passing a number of collieries terminated at Wath. Again, a connection with the earlier South Yorkshire line was authorised, but this time was never made despite the powers being renewed in 1908. Goods and mineral traffic commenced in March 1902, passenger services to and from Kirk Smeaton beginning in August.

The H & B amalgamated with the NE nine months in advance of the Grouping in April 1922, but the SYJn which had remained an independent company was not absorbed into the LNER until 2 July 1924 owing to legal difficulties. On the main line 1932 saw the withdrawal of through passenger trains from Hull to Cudworth; these had always been something of an embarrassment west of Howden and an obstacle to efficient freight working. Bus competition brought the end of the Wath passenger service in 1929, the whole of this line south of Moorhouse being abandoned in 1954. Through mineral workings over the main line ceased on 29 November 1958 and complete closure east of Wrangbrook junction was effected the following year. Coal traffic from the two extension lines continued to be taken out via Cudworth, involving reversal at Wrangbrook, but in 1963 the section of the Wath line north of Moorhouse was abandoned (the portion through the station itself was still served from the WR & G line). Finally, the greater part of the Denaby extension and the remaining section of the main line east of Cudworth were closed in 1967. The railway which bravely set out to challenge a monopoly had finally succumbed, the only portion surviving in the area being a now isolated branch to Frickley Colliery which is reached from the former WR & G at South Elmsall.

THE DEARNE VALLEY

Another important line sponsored by coal owners was the Dearne Valley Railway, promoted by the managers of the Hickleton Main, Houghton Main and Carlton Main (Cudworth) collieries. It was incorporated in 1897 to run from the H & B near Hemsworth to the GN and GN & GE Joint at Black Carr, south of Doncaster. A strangely feudal provision of the Act for so late a date was that a station had to be constructed at Barnbrough (now Barnburgh), where the owner of Melton Hall could stop any train provided that thirty minutes' notice was given to the station master and that his passengers were travelling first class!

The DV considered aligning with each of the three established companies with which it connected, opting in 1898 for the fairly obvious choice of the H & B so as to have a direct outlet to Hull. A five year working agreement was sealed and running powers exchanged. Rather surprisingly, the company then made an approach to the L & Y which after some hesitation agreed to work the line and to build a connection to it from the Wakefield–Goole route at Crofton. As can be imagined, this sudden shift of allegiance caused considerable friction with the H & B. The main line of the DV, together with its numerous colliery branches and a spur on to the S & K at Hickleton, was opened for mineral traffic in stages between 1902 and 1909, the L & Y connection being brought into use in 1905. The most impressive section was between Cadeby and Edlington where the line was carried across the Don at a height of 113ft (35m) by the superb Conisbrough viaduct with its twenty-one arches and 150ft (47m) central span. This was followed by a 70ft (22m) deep cutting through magnesian limestone, authorised in 1905 in substitution for an intended tunnel at an estimated saving of £26,200.

At first the DV was single track throughout, but rapidly increasing traffic caused the greater part of it to be doubled from 1912 when a steam rail-motor service was introduced between Wakefield and Edlington. Rail-level halts, each consisting of a shelter converted from an old carriage, were provided along the line, the service continuing right through LMS days until the withdrawal of the latterday push-and-pull workings in 1951. The ex-L & Y connecting line and a large proportion of the DV, including Conisbrough viaduct, were abandoned in 1966 on the opening of new curves on to the Midland main line near Houghton.

JOINT MINERAL LINES

A very considerable tract of South Yorkshire, bounded to
the east and west by the GN and Midland main lines and to
the north and south by the South Yorkshire and Sheffield &
Lincolnshire Junction routes, remained devoid of railways
until the first decade of the twentieth century. This was
despite the known existence of coal measures and numerous
attempts from 1874 onwards to penetrate this quite hilly and
once very rural area. None of these schemes materialised,
but by the turn of the century pioneer sinkings in the concealed coalfield close to rail access had more than proved
themselves. The decision was therefore taken to open up
what may be termed the untapped quadrangle, and this led
to rival railway promotions on the grand scale. It is wholly
appropriate that the final section of this book should feature
the last of the inter-company conflicts which so epitomised
West Riding railway construction. By now, however, it was
too late for sustained war, and every line opened in this area
was jointly owned by two or more partners.

In the early months of 1900 work began on sinking Silverwood Colliery, north-east of Rotherham, with a planned production of 5,000 tons a day, and building the privately owned
Roundwood & Dalton Railway to link it to the Don Valley.
The other major contemporary sinking was at Dinnington,
where the colliery proprietors were granted the Wales &
Laughton Light Railway Order in 1901 so as to form a
connection with the GC's Sheffield–Retford route.

The main line companies now cast their covetous eyes on
Silverwood and Dinnington, and began to gather round like
birds of prey. The NE proposed to reach both pits by acquir-
ing the Isle of Axholme Light Railway and building an
extension from Haxey, while the H & B put forward a complex scheme which had Hickleton & Thurnscoe on the
Wrangbrook junction–Wath line as its jumping-off point.
Both Bills were withdrawn, but the GC and Midland
approach from the south materialised in 1901 in the form of
the nominally independent Shireoaks, Laughton & Maltby
Railway. Despite its title, the powers were limited to a line
from a double junction at Brantcliffe, a mile (1·6km) west

of Shireoaks, to Dinnington & Laughton. The Dinnington Colliery proprietors agreed to withdraw their own light railway scheme, providing that the line from Brantcliffe was extended to the GC at Conisbrough. A GC Act of 1902 placed the SL & M under control of the Sheffield & Midland Committee (later the Great Central & Midland Joint Committee). The portion north of Rotherham Lane, including the branch to Dinnington Colliery, was transferred to the South Yorkshire Joint Railway by mutual agreement (see below). Opening of the SL & M and the transferred portions for mineral traffic took place in 1905.

The H & B South Yorkshire Extension Lines Act of 1902 authorised a route from Hickleton through Mexborough and Braithwell to a junction at Laughton East with the SL & M, a fact which may well have made the GC reluctant to fulfil its promise of extending to Conisbrough. Activity was renewed with the incorporation in 1905 of the independent Rotherham, Maltby & Laughton Railway, leaving the Don Valley between Aldwarke and Kilnhurst by junctions with both the GC and Midland lines and taking over part of the private Roundwood & Dalton Railway in order to reach Silverwood Colliery. From here it was to continue through Braithwell and Laughton to join the SL & M at Anston junction, south of Dinnington. It thus goaded the GC into action, and at the same time irritated the H & B by duplicating part of its already authorised route. The result was an agreement that the RM & L powers be transferred to the GC, and that the duplicated portion between Northern junction (Braithwell) and Southern junction (Laughton West) be joint GC and H & B. An Act of 1907 provided for the Midland to be brought in as an additional partner to the whole of the line which was opened for mineral traffic in October 1909. Abandonment of the section between Silverwood and Thurcroft collieries took place in 1967–9.

The second phase of the joint mineral lines stemmed from what seemed likely to be a major inter-company conflict in 1902. Apart from the H & B South Yorkshire Extension lines mentioned above, other Bills of that year included an L & Y and NE joint line from Thorne and Askern to Dinnington and Silverwood collieries; GN branches to the same collieries

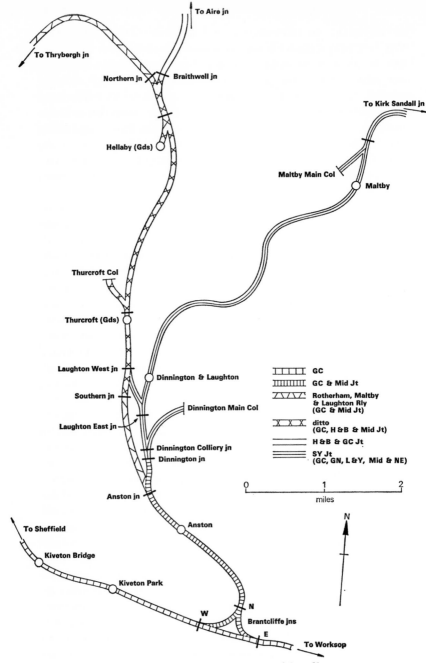

Map 9: Brantcliffe to Braithwell

from Scrooby and Bessacarr; a GC and Midland extension from Laughton to Kirk Sandall; and the Sheffield, Rotherham & Bawtry Railway running from Darnall, Rotherham and Thrybergh to Bawtry via Maltby. Wisely, competition gave way to co-operation and in April 1902 agreement was reached for building a single joint line which would be common to the GC, GN, L & Y, Midland and NE. After some complex legislation, the South Yorkshire Joint Railway was created in 1903, the Act providing for an exchange of running powers to Thorne at one end and over the SL & M at the other.

The SYJt, the fourth line in the West Riding to have South Yorkshire as part of its title, was opened for mineral traffic in January 1909. All five companies used the predominantly single track route which climbed steeply to Maltby on gradients up to 1 in 113. There were connections with both the DV and the GN main line, that at Potteric Carr being used by a passenger service from Doncaster to Shireoaks, introduced in 1910. The working of the four trains each way was initially shared by the GC and GN, but the latter withdrew on 2 October 1911. The GC carried on alone, reducing the workings to a Saturdays only basis from 1 June 1917, and then restoring weekday trains and extending them to Worksop on 1 April 1920. The service was finally withdrawn in 1929. Two further additions to the SYJt were commenced during World War I, but not completed until long afterwards. A line from a double junction at Tickhill to Harworth Colliery was authorised by an NE Act of 1914 and opened throughout in 1929, while the Firbeck Light Railway from a junction west of Harworth to Firbeck Colliery was approved in 1916 and opened in 1927.

The third and final phase of the joint mineral lines stemmed from a northwards extension of workings in the concealed coalfield and the sinking of Bentley, Bullcroft and Yorkshire Main collieries. In order to serve these pits the H & B decided to abandon its line authorised in 1902 from Hickleton towards Dinnington, and instead construct the 21 mile (34km) double track Gowdall & Braithwell Railway. As built, this left the H & B main line at Aire junction, near the crossing of the L & Y Wakefield–Goole line, and after avoiding all settlements of any size joined the Rotherham, Maltby & Laughton Railway at Braithwell junction.

At the time it seemed the coalfield was on the point of being extended even further north from Bentley towards Selby, and so great interest was shown in the new line. The authorising Act of 1909 gave running powers over differing sections to the GN, L & Y, Midland and NE, although these were never exercised. It also gave the GC an option of a third share in the new line, but the company felt impelled to keep out the NE and so increased this to a half share under a GC Act of 1910 which set up an H & B & GC Joint Committee. The Midland was also very keen, its 1910 Act laying down that construction of the line could not be postponed without its consent and that it would provide the necessary capital if the GC failed to do so. The company did in fact advance the considerable sum of £250,000 to the H & B to encourage it to proceed with the venture, although problems in obtaining labour and materials delayed the opening until 1916. Apart from the main line there were several colliery branches, two connections with the GC's 'Doncaster Avoiding Line' at Sprotborough and a branch to York Road, Doncaster, where a proposed passenger station never proceeded beyond the platform stage.

The last of the joint mineral lines, and the last railway of any real significance to be built in the West Riding, never really lived up to expectations. The anticipated extension of the coalfield did not then materialise, and so the intermediate stations which had been built in the hope of serving new colliery villages remained silent and forlorn. After a life of only twenty-seven years parts of the Gowdall & Braithwell Railway were in 1942 reduced to the role of wagon stabling. The section south from Warmsworth was allowed to become completely derelict, the sleepers being virtually eaten away by dry rot and having sizeable trees growing between them by the time the track was lifted in 1970. The greater part of the remaining portion of the line was closed in 1958 after a survey had shown that £11,000 per annum was being spent on maintenance, while abandonment would produce an annual loss of revenue of only £100!

CHAPTER IX

The Future

Forecasting the future pattern of any railway network is a hazardous occupation. Especially is this the case in an area like South and West Yorkshire where growth or contraction is dependent on so many complex factors, but nevertheless certain trends are clearly apparent.

On the freight side there is little scope for further large-scale rationalisation. Almost all outlying goods depots have been closed and superseded by centralised freight-handling facilities. Traffic flows have now been concentrated on a limited number of key routes, and few if any additional through lines are ripe for closure. The most radical changes are likely to stem from rolling stock developments, with even further emphasis on block loads and liner trains. An indication of things to come has already been provided by the 'merry-go-round' trains, conveying coal from South Yorkshire pits to the new power stations at Ferrybridge 'C', Eggborough and Drax 'A', all approached by the Wakefield–Goole route. In each case trains of thirty 26-ton hopper wagons, hauled by diesel locomotives fitted with a special low-speed device, crawl round a reverse loop and discharge coal without actually stopping. A typical week in 1973 saw 228 trains move just under 200,000 tons of coal to the three power stations from thirteen collieries. The annual input of about 19 million tons will be increased by another five million when Drax 'B' comes into operation. Weekly timetables are prepared by the BR computer at Crewe, and the locomotives are serviced at a purpose-built depot at Knottingley.

The future role of passenger services within the region depends on continued acceptance of the principle of grant-aid. By 1972, 452 miles of line serving 78 stations were receiving a grant subsidy of £2 million a year. Even the Leeds–Bradford local service, linking two large cities, had to be aided to the tune of £294,000. These figures prompted the Eastern Region to promote a special campaign, designed to safeguard the future of West Riding rail services and launched under the slogan, 'Take a new look at your local railway system'. Extensive publicity and numerous cheap fare facilities brought a 2·2 per cent increase in patronage and an 8·9 per cent upsurge in receipts within eight weeks. Forecasts on the future of the area's suburban services have ranged from extreme pessimism to relative optimism. A detailed analysis was undertaken as part of the 1969 West Yorkshire Transportation Study, which found that only two per cent of the one million working population travelled to work by rail. The study saw little future for local passenger services and in general advocated their replacement by express bus services running on new or improved roads. Only four routes were recommended for development—those radiating from Leeds to Bradford Exchange, Harrogate, Selby and York.

Since 1969 the concept of subsidising railways in order to reduce road congestion and environmental damage has rapidly gained ground, and at the time of writing no local services are in imminent danger of withdrawal. Indeed, development rather than contraction of the system is being seriously urged in many quarters. The successful reopening of Baildon station in 1973 unleashed a flood of demands for similar action in other localities as well as the provision of new, unstaffed halts at strategic points. The introduction of a rapid transit system has also been put forward on many occasions, but this would face the same problems which afflicted the original railway network more than a century ago. A region with no clearly defined centre, and possessing numerous small towns providing employment for their own population, does not generate the density of passenger movement ideally required for rapid transit. Nevertheless, the creation of the West Yorkshire Passenger Transport Execu-

tive as part of the 1974 reorganisation of local government
may bring some developments in this direction. At the time
of writing, the Executive is undertaking a study to show
where new rail/bus stations could be built, 'to fit in with
the integrated pattern of a new rail network working closely
with bus services in the West Yorkshire area'. Closed rail
connections would be reopened where necessary. Similar
plans are being formulated by the South Yorkshire PTE.

Medium and long-distance passenger services appear to
have good prospects. If the mooted electrification of the East
Coast route and the main cross-country link from Bristol and
Birmingham to Leeds and York should come to fruition, it
will bring substantial improvements in schedules. So too will
the advanced passenger train, reducing the journey time from
Leeds to London to little more than $1\frac{1}{2}$ hours. Massive
resignalling at present taking place will also play a vital role
in ensuring a competitive future for these services.

Given continued government and trade union support,
the railways of South and West Yorkshire would seem to be
moving with reasonable self-assurance into the electronic age.
Computers, automation and concrete architecture will help
to present the general public with a picture of radical if
faceless efficiency, but will never compensate the railway
enthusiast for the vanished glories of yesteryear.

One looks back, and is overwhelmed with memories: of
watching N1 tanks blasting up the 1 in 43 from Batley to
Howden Clough under grimy skies; of waiting for the hoot
of an A4 chime whistle as one of Gresley's masterpieces
rounded the curve into Doncaster and rushed north with the
non-stop 'Elizabethan'; of waving to the crews of local trains
busily shuttling to and fro past the bramble woods of Burley-
in-Wharfedale; of whiling away the night hours at Leeds City
and wondering what exotic motive power would be pulling
the Swansea mail; and of wishing longingly that one's child-
hood had been fifty years earlier in the era of North Western
blackberry black, Midland red and the great days of a truly
fascinating railway network. No matter how promising the
future, it will never completely erase the past.

Reference Section

This reference section gives the basic details of all railways in South and West Yorkshire (for space reasons, minor mineral lines under a mile in length are excluded). It should be used in conjunction with the folding map and the detailed sectional maps in the text. The section is sub-divided to accord with the chapters in the book, and in each division the lines are listed chronologically (not all of them are necessarily mentioned in the text). The information given is as follows:

1. The portion of line opened. Stations and goods depots within the area covered by this volume are given in capitals.
2. Length of line to nearest $\frac{1}{4}$ mile (0·4km) (lines less than $\frac{1}{4}$ mile in length are shown to nearest $\frac{1}{8}$ mile (0·2km)).
3. Ownership of line at date of authorisation. If the ownership was different at the Grouping, 31 December 1922, this is indicated in parenthesis (for this purpose, the earlier amalgamation of the H & B with the NE and the L & Y with the L & NW is ignored). See list of company abbreviations.
4. ACT(S): Authorising Act(s) of Parliament. If the Act relates to the incorporation of the company, amalgamation or was obtained by another company, this is shown in parenthesis.
5. LRO: Light Railway Order (date of confirmation by Board of Trade).

6. OPD (Opened): Date of opening of line to freight and/or passenger traffic. If neither category is indicated, then opening is to all traffic. Where a line opened piecemeal, dates are given in sectional rather than chronological order. To save space, repetition is avoided, eg:

   OPD: Doncaster North jn–Sandall 1 December 1866; –Maud's Bridge 10 September

   means that the line was opened from Doncaster North jn to Sandall on 1 December 1866, and from Sandall to Maud's Bridge on 10 September 1866. All the dates are based on contemporary sources and have been carefully checked; in some cases they correct those previously accepted. Where two or more official sources differ, the most likely date is given first, followed by the alternative.

7. CSD (Closed): As above, except relates to closure. All passenger closure dates apply to regular traffic only; many lines remained open for seasonal traffic after all-the-year-round services had been withdrawn. In some cases all traffic ceased prior to the official closure date. With some freight branches, the terminal goods depot has closed but the line has remained open for traffic to private sidings. This is indicated by 'Depot closed'.

8. STNS (Stations): All passenger stations on the line are listed, the name shown being that at the time of opening. Subsequent name changes of a substantial nature are indicated, but minor changes, additions of suffixes and spelling alterations are generally omitted. Where a station is replaced or resited, this also is shown. On lines which extend beyond the confines of this volume, only stations actually in the area under review are listed.

   Where a station is known to have opened at a later date than the line on which it is situated, this is indicated. However, this information should be used with care as with some early lines documentary evidence of station openings is almost entirely lacking. Bradshaw, often the only source of dates, did not at first always list intermediate stations.

   Station closures are not generally given as this information is readily obtainable from the *Register of Closed Passenger Stations & etc* (see bibliography). The same applies to closures followed by a subsequent reopening. Stations which remain open are shown in capitals, while stations which were noteworthy in closing prior to nationalisation, 1 January 1948, are shown in italics. In addition, the closure dates of stations of major importance or interest (eg Sheffield Victoria) are given.

It should be stressed that all station dates relate to passenger traffic only.

Abbreviations

amalg	amalgamation
appr	approved
c	circa
csd	closed
E	east
G or Gds	goods and mineral
Inc	incorporated
jn(s)	junction(s)
Jt	joint
LRO	Light Railway Order
N	north
opd	opened
P or Pass	passenger
perm	permanent
ren	renamed
reop	reopened
repl	replaced
S	south
stn(s)	station(s)
t	first appearance in timetable—usually Bradshaw
temp	temporary
W	west

SECTION ONE: LEEDS

MARSH LANE—Selby   20 miles (32km)
L & S (NE)
ACTS: 29 May 1830 (Inc; formerly a controversial date, but see
  evidence presented by J. Whitaker—bibliography); 6 April
  1841 (lease to Y & NM); 23 May 1844 (vesting in Y & NM); 28
  July 1891.
OPD: P—22 September 1834, G—15 December; Csd: Marsh
  Lane–York Jn, P—9 November 1840, G—July 1848, reop G—
  July 1850, P—November 1850.
STN: Marsh Lane (csd 1 April 1869, repl by stn on line to
  Leeds New—qv).

———

Derby–HUNSLET LANE
(See Section Six)

———

WELLINGTON–BRADFORD (MARKET STREET)
(See Section Two)

———

Leeds jn–Hunslet jn   1¼ miles (2km)
Whitehall jn–Engine Shed jn   ¼ mile (0·4km)
L & B (Mid)
ACT: 4 July 1844 (Inc).
OPD: P—1 July 1846, G—September. Whitehall jn–Engine
  Shed jn not used by regular P traffic after 1901.

———

LEEDS CENTRAL (Pass)–Three Signal Bridge jn
                                                           ¼ mile (0·4km)
GN, L & NW, L & T & L & Y Jt (GN, L & NW, L & Y & NE Jt)
ACTS: 22 July 1848 (Leeds Central Station); 10 July 1854 (LB
  & HJ); 2 July 1855 (GN); 4 July 1870 (L & NW).
OPD: P—18 September 1848.
CSD: 1 May 1967.
STN: Leeds Central (Opd as temp terminus 18 September 1848,
  completed August 1857. Used by owning companies as
  follows: GN: 1 October 1849–13 May 1850, and from 1
  August 1854; L & NW: 18 September 1848–30 September 1850;
  L & Y: From 18 September 1848; L & T: 10 July 1849–30
  April 1850. Csd 1 May 1967).

———

P

Three Signal Bridge jn–Dewsbury jn (Thornhill)
(See Section Four)

———

Three Signal Bridge jn–Thirsk   38¼ miles (61·2km)
Holbeck jn–Geldard jn   ⅛ mile (0·2km)
L & T (NE) (Three Signal Bridge and Holbeck jns–Wortley jn
   joint with GN)
ACTS: 21 July 1845 (Inc); 3 July 1851 (change of name to LN);
   31 July 1854 (amalg to form NE); 2 July 1855 (GN).
OPD: 10 July 1849 (northern portion of line opd earlier).
CSD: Three Signal Bridge jn–Geldard jn: P—14 May 1850, reop
   1 July 1899, csd 1 January 1908, reop 1 July 1923, csd 1 May
   1967; G—2 March 1970. Holbeck jn–Geldard and Wortley
   jns: 1 May 1967.
STNS: Holbeck (interchange with GN high-level lines opd 2 July
   1855); *Royal Gardens* (opd June 1857(t)); HEADINGLEY;
   Woodside (opd July 1850(t), ren Horsforth Woodside July
   1857(t)); HORSFORTH; Pool (ren Arthington February
   1852(t), resited ¼ mile (0·4km) to S 1 February 1865).

———

Geldard jn–WELLINGTON STREET (NE Gds) ½ mile (0·8km)
L & T (GN & NE Jt/NE)
ACTS: 21 July 1845 (L & T); 22 July 1848 (Leeds Central
   Station); 2 July 1855 (GN).
OPD: G—18 February 1850.

———

Branch to WELLINGTON STREET (GN)   ¼ mile (0·4km)
GN
ACTS: As above.
OPD: P—14 May 1850, G—1 July.
CSD: P—1 August 1854.
STN: *Wellington Street* (csd 1 August 1854, temp terminus).

———

Copley Hill jn–Whitehall jn   ½ mile (0·8km)
LD & M (L & NW)
ACT: 30 June 1845.
OPD: 1 October 1850. Csd: P—1 March 1882, reop on new
   alignment 18 December 1966.

———

LEEDS CENTRAL (L & NW & L & Y Jt Gds)–Three Signal
   Bridge jn
L & NW & L & Y Jt   ¼ mile (0·4km)
ACTS: 30 June 1845 (LD & M); 22 July 1848 (Leeds Central
   Station).
OPD: G—about 1851.
CSD: 2 March 1970.

Three Signal Bridge jn–Bowling jn (Bradford)
(See Section Three)

Branch to HUNSLET (Mid Gds)   ¼ mile (0·4km)
Mid
OPD: G—c 1854. (Goods depot given suffix 'Balm Lane' c 1904).

Wortley East jn—Ings Road jn (Wakefield)
(See Section Three)

Farnley jn–Farnley Siding   1¼ miles (2km)
L & NW
ACTS: 7 August 1862; 18 July 1881.
OPD: G—2 April 1866 (new east-facing connnection on to main
   line opd 31 May 1885).

MARSH LANE–LEEDS NEW–Leeds jn   1 mile (1·6km)
L & NW & NE Jt/NE
ACTS: 5 July 1865 (Leeds New Station); 5 July 1865 (NE); 16
   July 1874 (New Station enlargement); 28 July 1891 (NE).
OPD: 1 April 1869.
STNS: Marsh Lane (repl L & S terminus); Leeds New (enlarged
   5 January 1879, combined with Wellington to form LEEDS
   CITY 2 May 1938, rebuilt 13 May 1967).

Branch to WHITEHALL ROAD (Gds)   ¼ mile (0·4km)
L & NW & L & Y Jt
ACT: 19 July 1875 (L & NW).
OPD: G—1 December 1880.

Canal jn–Farnley North jn   1¾ miles (2·8km)
L & NW
ACT: 17 June 1878.
OPD: 1 March 1882.
CSD: 18 December 1966. Reop Canal jn–Geldard Road jn 1
    May 1967.
STN: Wortley & Farnley (ren Farnley & Wortley 1 April 1891
    (t)).

———

Lofthouse North jn–ROTHWELL   3 miles (4·8km)
E & WYU
ACTS: 2 August 1883 (Inc); 25 June 1886; 24 July 1888; 26 July
    1889 (GN); 25 July 1890.
LRO: 7 June 1901.
OPD: G—20 May 1891; P—Robin Hood–Rothwell, 4 January
    1904.
CSD: P—30 September 1904; G—3 October 1966.
STNS: *Robin Hood*; *Rothwell*.

———

ROTHWELL–Stourton jn   2¼ miles (3·6km)
SLJ (E & WYU)
ACTS: 24 August 1893 (Inc); 2 July 1896 (amalg with E &
    WYU).
OPD: G—to private sidings at Stourton 6 April 1895, connection
    with Mid at Stourton jn 1 November 1903; P—4 January 1904.
CSD: P—30 September 1904; G—c February 1962 (official date
    3 October 1966).
STN: *Stourton*.

———

ROBIN HOOD–Royds Green Lower   1¾ miles (2·8km)
E & WYU
LRO: 14 December 1897.
OPD: G—By end of 1898.
CSD: 9 December 1963.

———

Neville Hill West jn–HUNSLET (NE Gds)   1½ miles (2·4km)
NE
ACTS: 29 June 1893; 31 July 1894.
OPD: G—2 January 1899.
CSD: Depot csd 5 September 1966.

Beeston jn–HUNSLET (GN Gds)   3¾ miles (6km)
Hun (GN)
ACTS: 27 July 1893 (Inc); 3 July 1894 (amalg with GN); 3 June
   1897.
OPD: G—3 July 1899.
CSD: Beeston jn–Parkside jn 3 July 1967; –Hunslet 3 January
   1966.

———

Branch to CARDIGAN ROAD (Gds)   ⅛ mile (0·2km)
NE
OPD: G—19 May 1900.
CSD: 4 September 1972.

———

SECTION TWO: AIREDALE AND WHARFEDALE

LEEDS (Wellington)–BRADFORD (Market Street)
                                          13½ miles (21·6km)
L & B (Mid)
ACTS: 4 July 1844 (Inc); 30 June 1845; 24 July 1851 (vesting in
   Mid).
OPD: P—1 July 1846; G—7 September.
CSD: P—Wellington (City North)–Leeds jn, 13 June 1966.
STNS: Wellington (temp stn repl by perm structure 1 October
   1850, combined with Leeds New to form Leeds City 2 May
   1938, csd 13 June 1966); Holbeck (Mid platform opd 2 June
   1862); Armley (opd September 1847); Kirkstall (opd by September 1846); *Kirkstall Forge* (opd 1 July 1860); Newlay (opd
   by September 1846); Calverley (opd by September 1846);
   Apperley Bridge (opd early 1847); *Idle* (opd second half of
   1847); SHIPLEY (opd by September 1846, repl by new stn
   ⅛ mile (0·2km) to S February 1875); Frizinghall (opd 1 February 1875); Manningham (opd 17 February 1868); BRAD-
   FORD (Market Street) (repl by new stn and suffix dropped
   2 March 1890, suffix 'Forster Square' added 2 June 1924).

———

Shipley (Leeds jn)–Colne   26¼ miles (42km)
Bradford jn–Bingley jn (Shipley)   ¼ mile (0·4km)
L & B (Mid)
ACT: 30 June 1845.
OPD: Shipley–Keighley 16 March 1847; –Skipton 8 September;
    –Colne 2 October 1848.
CSD: Skipton–Colne 2 February 1970.
STNS: Saltaire (opd 1 January 1859); BINGLEY (new stn to S
    of original site opd 24 July 1892); *Thwaites* (opd 1 June 1892);
    KEIGHLEY (new and resited stn opd 7 April 1883); Steeton &
    Silsden (opd c December 1847, new and resited stn opd 1
    March 1892); Kildwick & Crosshills (repl by new stn ¼ mile
    (0·4km) to W 7 April 1889); Cononley (opd c December 1847);
    SKIPTON (repl by new stn ⅛ mile (0·2km) to N 30 April
    1876).

ARTHINGTON–OTLEY   3½ miles (5·6km)
NE
ACT: 11 July 1861.
OPD: P—1 February 1865; G—1 October 1866.
CSD: P—22 March 1965; G—5 July.
STNS: Pool; Otley.

Apperley jn–Burley jn   6 miles (9·6km)
Menston jn–Milner Wood jn   ½ mile (0·8km)
Mid
OTLEY–ILKLEY   6 miles (9·6km)
O & IJt
ACTS: 11 July 1861 (Mid); 11 July 1861 (NE).
OPD: P—1 August 1865; G—1 October 1866.
CSD: Menston jn–Milner Wood jn: P—25 February 1957; G—
    5 July 1965. Otley–Burley jn: P—22 March 1965; G—5 July.
STNS: GUISELEY; MENSTON (opd 1 November 1875); *Men-
    ston Junction* (opd 1 March 1873); BURLEY; BEN RHYDD-
    ING (opd 1 July 1866); ILKLEY.

Arthington (North to West curve)   ¼ mile (0·4km)
NE
ACT: 11 July 1861.
OPD: G—1 October 1866; P—1 August 1877.
CSD: P—25 February 1957; G—5 July 1965.

KEIGHLEY–OXENHOPE 4¾ miles (7·6km)
K & WV (Mid)
ACTS: 30 June 1862 (Inc); 11 August 1876 (purchase by Mid);
18 July 1881 (vesting in Mid).
OPD: P—15 April 1867; G—1 July. Csd: P—1 January 1962;
G—18 June. Reop: 29 June 1968 by Keighley & Worth Valley
Railway Preservation Society.
STNS: INGROW; DAMEMS (opd 1 September 1867); OAK-
WORTH; HAWORTH; OXENHOPE.

Shipley (Guiseley jn)–Esholt jn 3½ miles (5·6km)
Mid
ACT: 25 July 1872.
OPD: P—4 December 1876; G—13 December.
STNS: BAILDON; *Esholt*.

ILKLEY–SKIPTON 11½ miles (18·4km)
Mid
ACT: 16 July 1883.
OPD: Ilkley–Bolton Abbey: P—16 May 1888, G—27 August;
–Skipton 1 October.
CSD: P—22 March 1965; G—Ilkley–Embsay jn 5 July.
STNS: Addingham; Bolton Abbey; Embsay (retained after
closure by Yorkshire Dales Railway Preservation Society).

Rawdon jn–YEADON 1¼ miles (2km)
GY & R (Mid)
ACTS: 16 July 1885 (Inc); 5 August 1891 (change of name to
GY & H); 28 June 1892 (amalg with Mid).
OPD: G—26 February 1894.
CSD: 10 August 1964.

Embsay jn–GRASSINGTON 8¾ miles (14km)
YD
ACT: 6 August 1897 (Inc).
OPD: 29 July 1902.
CSD: P—22 September 1930; G—Swinden Siding–Grassington
11 August 1969.
STNS: *Rylstone*; *Grassington*.

SECTION THREE: AIRE AND CALDER WATERSHED

LEEDS (Wellington)–BRADFORD (Market Street)
(See Section Two)

BRADFORD (L & Y)–LOW MOOR   3 miles (4·8km)
WRU (L & Y)
ACT: 18 August 1846 (Inc).
OPD: 9 May 1850
CSD: Exchange (original terminus)–Exchange (new terminus) 15 January 1973.
STNS: Bradford (L & Y) (suffix 'Exchange' added April 1867 (t), csd 15 January 1973); BRADFORD (Exchange) (new terminus opd 15 January 1973); Bowling Junction (opd 1 February 1902).

BATLEY (L & NW)–BIRSTAL   2 miles (3·2km)
LD & M (L & NW)
ACTS: 30 June 1845; 27 July 1846.
OPD: 30 September 1852.
CSD: P—1 January 1917; G—18 June 1962.
STNS: *Carlinghow* (opd 1 April 1872); *Birstal.*

Leeds (Three Signal Bridge jn)–Bowling jn   9¼ miles (14·8km)
LAISTER DYKE–BRADFORD (Adolphus Street)
                                        1¼ miles (2km)
LB & HJ (GN)
ACTS: 30 June 1852 (Inc); 4 August 1853; 10 July 1854; 5 July 1865 (amalg with GN).
OPD: P—1 August 1854; G—7 August.
CSD: Hammerton Street jn–Adolphus Street: P—7 January 1867; G—1 May 1972. Laister Dyke–Bowling jn: P—6 January 1969; reop 31 March, csd 9 June. Three Signal Bridge jn–Holbeck: 1 May 1967.
STNS: Holbeck (interchange with low-level NE lines opd 2 July 1855); Armley & Wortley (ren Armley Moor 25 September 1950); Bramley; Stanningley; NEW PUDSEY (opd 1 May 1967); Laister Dyke; *Bowling*; *Adolphus Street* (csd 7 January 1867).

Leeds (Wortley East jn)–Wakefield (Ings Road jn)

9¾ miles (15·6km)

Wortley West jn–Wortley South jn   ½ mile (0·8km)

BW & L (GN)

ACTS: 10 July 1854 (Inc); 7 August 1862 (WR & G); 21 July 1863 (change of name to WY); 23 June 1864 (WR & G); 5 July 1865 (amalg with GN); 31 May 1867 (WR & G).

OPD: P—5 October 1857 (Wortley West–South jns rarely used by P trains until September 1964); G—12 November.

STNS: Beeston (opd February 1860(t)); Ardsley; Lofthouse (opd 1858); WAKEFIELD (WESTGATE) (repl by GN & MS & L Jt stn ⅛ mile (0·2km) to N 1 May 1867).

LAISTER DYKE–ARDSLEY   10¼ miles (16·4km)

LB & HJ (GN)

ACTS: 4 August 1853; 10 July 1854.

OPD: Laister Dyke–Gildersome: P—20 August 1856; G—1 January 1857. –Ardsley: 10 October 1857.

CSD: P—4 July 1966. G: Dudley Hill–Birkenshaw & Tong 16 March 1968; –Gildersome 31 October 1966; –Morley 16 March 1968; –Ardsley May 1969.

STNS: Dudley Hill (repl by new stn ¼ mile (0·4km) to N 1 October 1875); Birkenshaw & Tong; Drighlington & Adwalton; Gildersome (GN); Morley (GN); Tingley (opd May 1859(t)).

Wrenthorpe South jn–BATLEY   7¼ miles (11·6km)

BW & L (GN)

ACTS: 23 July 1860; 17 May 1861.

OPD: G—Wrenthorpe South jn–Roundwood Col January 1862. P+G: Wrenthorpe South jn–Flushdyke (see Stns) 7 April 1862; –Ossett 2 April 1864; –Batley 15 December. G—South curve at Batley 18 April 1966 (not shown on map).

CSD: P—Wrenthorpe South jn–Runtlings Lane jn 7 September 1964; –Batley 1 July 1909. G—Wrenthorpe South jn–West jn 15 February 1965; –Roundwood Col 1 November; –Runtlings Lane jn 15 February; –Shaw Cross Col 26 March 1956; –Batley 1 May 1972.

STNS: Alverthorpe (opd second half 1972); *Flushdyke* (known as Ossett from opening until line extended 2 April 1864); Ossett; *Chickenley Heath* (opd 2 July 1877).

Adwalton jn–BATLEY   3 miles (4·8km)
LB & HJ (GN)
ACTS: 7 June 1861; 30 June 1862.
OPD: Adwalton jn–Upper Batley 19 August 1863; –Batley 1
   November 1864.
CSD: P—7 September 1964; G—15 February 1965.
STNS: Howden Clough (opd 1 November 1866); Upper Batley;
   Batley (GN) (csd 7 September 1964).

———

Hammerton Street jn–Mill Lane jn (Bradford)   ¾ mile (1·2km)
LB & HJ (GN)
ACT: 14 July 1864.
OPD: 7 January 1867.
STN: St Dunstan's (opd 14 October 1875).

———

Wrenthorpe North jn–Wrenthorpe West jn   ½ mile (0·8km)
GN
OPD: c March 1875.
CSD: P—October 1938; G—1 November 1965.

———

LAISTER DYKE–SHIPLEY (GN)   6¼ miles (10km)
Cutlers jn–Quarry Gap jn   ¼ mile (0·4km)
Branch to SHIPLEY (GN Gds)   ¼ mile (0·4km)
Jn with Mid at Shipley   ⅛ mile (0·2km)
BE & I + I & S (GN)
ACTS: 28 June 1866 (BE & I Inc); 12 August 1867 (I & S Inc);
   24 July 1871 (amalg with GN); 18 July 1872.
OPD: G—c August 1874 (except jn with Mid, 1 November
   1875); P—Laister Dyke–Shipley (GN) 15 April 1875.
CSD: P—2 February 1931. G—Laister Dyke–Quarry Gap jn 31
   October 1966; Cutlers jn–Idle 2 November 1964; –Shipley,
   including branch to gds depot and jn with Mid, 7 October
   1968.
STNS: *Eccleshill*; *Idle*; *Thackley* (opd April 1878(t)); *Shipley*
   (GN).

———

STANNINGLEY–PUDSEY GREENSIDE   1¾ miles (2·8km)
GN
ACT: 24 July 1871.
OPD: G—summer 1877; P—1 April 1878.

CSD: Stanningley–jn with new curve from Bramley 1 November 1893. Remainder: P—15 June 1964; G—6 July.
STNS: Pudsey Lowtown (opd April 1878); Pudsey Greenside.

ST DUNSTAN'S–THORNTON$\qquad$5½ miles (8·8km)
Leeds curve at St Dunstan's$\qquad$⅛ mile (0·2km)
Horton Park jn–CITY ROAD (Gds)$\qquad$1¼ miles (2km)
B & T (GN)
ACTS: 24 July 1871 (Inc); 18 July 1872 (amalg with GN); 16 July 1874.
OPD: G—St Dunstan's–Great Horton and City Road (+ Leeds curve) November 1876; –Clayton 9 July 1877; –Thornton by April 1878. P—14 October 1878 (Leeds curve little used by regular P services).
CSD: P—23 May 1955. G—St Dunstan's–Great Horton 26 August 1972; –Thornton 28 June 1965; Horton Park jn –City Road 28 July 1972.
STNS: *Manchester Road*; Horton Park (opd 1 November 1880); Great Horton; Clayton; Queensbury (opd 14 April 1879); Thornton.

QUEENSBURY–HOLMFIELD$\qquad$2¼ miles (3·6km)
West curve at Queensbury$\qquad$¼ mile (0·4km)
GN
ACT: 5 August 1873
OPD: 1 December 1879.
CSD: P—23 May 1955; G—28 May 1956.

THORNTON–KEIGHLEY (GN Gds)$\qquad$7½ miles (12km)
Branch to Keighley (GN jn)$\qquad$¼ mile (0·4km)
GN
ACTS: 5 August 1873; 6 August 1880; 18 July 1881.
OPD: G—Thornton–Denholme 1 January 1884; –Keighley (GN Gds) 1 April. P—Thornton–Denholme 1 January 1884; –Ingrow 7 April; –Keighley (GN jn) 1 November.
CSD: P—23 May 1955. G—Thornton–Cullingworth 11 November 1963; –Ingrow 28 May 1956; –Keighley (GN jn) 28 June 1965; –Keighley (GN Gds) 17 July 1961.
STNS: Denholme; Wilsden (opd July 1886); Cullingworth; Ingrow.

BATLEY–TINGLEY   3 miles (4·8km)
TINGLEY–Beeston jn   2 miles (3·2km)
GN
ACTS: 18 July 1881; 26 July 1889.
OPD: G—Batley–Soothill Wood Col by April 1888; –Woodkirk
  1 July 1890; –Beeston jn 1 August. P—1 August 1890. (Airey's
  map of 1890 shows a west curve at Tingley, but it is doubtful
  if this was ever laid and virtually certain that it never carried
  any traffic.)
CSD: P—29 October 1951. G—Batley–Woodkirk 6 July 1953;
  –Tingley 30 June 1964; –Beeston jn 6 July 1953.
STN: *Woodkirk*.

Bramley West jn–Pudsey (jn with branch from Stanningley)
                                              ½ mile (0·8km)
PUDSEY GREENSIDE–Cutlers jn   1¾ miles (2·8km)
GN
ACTS: 24 July 1871; 16 July 1885.
OPD: 1 November 1893.
CSD: P—15 June 1964; G—6 July.

Tyersal jn–Broad Lane jn   ½ mile (0·8km)
GN
ACT: 16 July 1885.
OPD: 1 December 1893.
CSD: P—October 1938; G—c 1952.

DUDLEY HILL–LOW MOOR   2 miles (3·2km)
South curve at Dudley Hill   ¾ mile (1·2km)
Branch to LOW MOOR (GN Gds)   ¼ mile (0·4km)
GN
ACTS: 2 August 1883; 5 July 1887.
OPD: P—1 December 1893 (the south curve at Dudley Hill was
  inspected by the Board of Trade in May 1894, but it is doubt-
  ful if it was ever fully brought into use). G—1 December 1894.
CSD: Low Moor (GN Gds) branch: 9 May 1933. Remainder:
  P—31 August 1914; G—1 October 1917.

SECTION FOUR: THE CALDER VALLEY

Derby–NORMANTON–LEEDS (HUNSLET LANE)
(See Section Six)

York–Altofts jn (Normanton) $23\frac{1}{2}$ miles (37·6km)
Y & NM (NE)
ACTS: 21 June 1836 (Inc); 6 April 1841; 31 July 1854 (amalg to form NE).
OPD: 1 July 1840 (northern portion of line opd earlier); csd P—Burton Salmon–Castleford, Whitwood jn–Altofts jn, 5 January 1970, reop 7 May 1973.
STN: CASTLEFORD (repl by new stn $\frac{1}{4}$ mile (0·4km) to W 1871, ren Castleford (Central) 15 September 1952–20 February 1969).

Whitwood jn–Methley jn   1 mile (1·6km)
Y & NM (NE)
ACT: 21 June 1836.
OPD: 27 July 1840. Csd P—1 April 1869, reop Whitwood jn—Methley Joint jn 13 May, csd 2 November 1964, reop throughout 7 October 1968. Csd G—Whitwood jn–Methley Joint jn 27 March 1967, –Methley jn 30 June 1929, reop throughout 31 July 1967.

Manchester–Goose Hill jn (Normanton) $50\frac{1}{4}$ miles (80·4km)
M & L (L & Y)
ACTS: 4 July 1836 (Inc); 5 May 1837; 1 July 1839; 9 July 1847 (change of name to L & Y); 3 July 1851 (GN); 13 August 1859.
OPD: Summit tunnel 1 March 1841; –Hebden Bridge 1 January 1841; –Goose Hill jn 5 October 1840. (The Lancashire portion of the line opd earlier).
CSD: P—Milner Royd jn–Greetland jn, Bradley Wood jn–Heaton Lodge jn 5 January 1970.
STNS: Walsden (opd c November 1845); TODMORDEN; Eastwood; HEBDEN BRIDGE; MYTHOLMROYD (opd May 1847(t)); Luddenden Foot; SOWERBY BRIDGE (repl by new stn $\frac{1}{4}$ mile (0·4km) E 1 September 1876); North Dean (opd 1 July 1844, ren Greetland & North Dean 1 January 1883); Elland (repl by new stn $\frac{1}{8}$ mile (0·2km) E 1 August 1865); Brighouse (repl by new stn $\frac{1}{4}$ mile (0·4km) W 1 May 1893);

Cooper Bridge; MIRFIELD (opd April 1845, repl by new stn ⅛ mile (0·2km) E 5 March 1866); Dewsbury (ren Thornhill January 1851(t)); Horbury; Horbury Junction (opd 1 January 1850, repl by Horbury (Millfield Road) ½ mile (0·8km) W 11 July 1927); WAKEFIELD (KIRKGATE) (L & Y & GN Jt from 23 August 1853).

———

NORTH DEAN–HALIFAX (SHAW SYKE)   1¾ miles (2·8km)
M & L (L & Y)
ACTS: 1 July 1839; 13 August 1859.
OPD: 1 July 1844.
STN: *Halifax (Shaw Syke)* (csd 7 August 1850).

———

WAKEFIELD (KIRKGATE)–Goole   27 miles (43·2km)
WP & G (L & Y)
ACTS: 31 July 1845 (Inc); 9 July 1847 (amalg with M & L); 3 July 1851 (GN).
OPD: 1 April 1848.
CSD: P—Wakefield–Pontefract (jn with Methley branch) 2 January 1967.
STNS: *Crofton* (opd 1 November 1853); Sharlston (opd 1869); Featherstone; Tanshelf (opd c September 1871, ren Pontefract (Tanshelf) 1 December 1936); PONTEFRACT (ren Pontefract (Monkhill) 1 December 1936); KNOTTINGLEY (L & Y & GN Jt from 1 February 1854).

———

MIRFIELD–LOW MOOR   7¾ miles (12·4km)
WRU (L & Y)
ACTS: 18 August 1846 (Inc); 13 August 1859.
OPD: 18 July 1848.
CSD: P—14 June 1965. G—Mirfield–Heckmondwike jn 14 June 1965; north of Cleckheaton for construction of M62 3 October 1970, reop 1 April 1974.
STNS: Northorpe (opd 1 December 1891); Heckmondwike; Liversedge; Cleckheaton; Low Moor.

———

Leeds (Three Signal Bridge jn)–Dewsbury jn (Thornhill)
                                                        10½ miles (16·8km)

LD & M (L & NW)

ACTS: 30 June 1845 (Inc); 27 July 1846; 9 July 1847 (amalg with L & NW).

OPD: 18 September 1848.

CSD: Three Signal Bridge jn–Copley Hill jn, P—1 March 1882, G—18 December 1966; –Farnley North jn, P—1 March 1882, reop 18 December 1966.

STNS: *Wortley* (opd 8 October 1848); *Churwell*; MORLEY; BATLEY; Staincliffe & Batley Carr (opd 1 November 1878); DEWSBURY (ren Dewsbury (Wellington Road) 2 June 1924–20 February 1969); RAVENSTHORPE & THORNHILL (opd 1 September 1891).

TODMORDEN–Burnley   8¾ miles (14km)
M & L (L & Y)

ACT: 30 June 1845.

OPD: 12 November 1849.

CSD: P—Todmorden–Stansfield Hall 9 November 1965.

STNS: *Stansfield Hall* (opd August 1869 (t)); *Cornholme* (opd July 1878(t)); Portsmouth.

PONTEFRACT–Methley jn   4¼ miles (6·8km)
WP & G (L & Y)

ACT: 16 July 1846.

OPD: 1 December 1849 (official L & Y date; GN services commenced 1 October 1849).

CSD: P—Cutsyke jn–Methley jn 7 October 1968.

STNS: Castleford (opd 1860; ren Castleford (Cutsyke) 15 September 1952, csd 7 October 1968); *Methley Junction.*

HALIFAX–LOW MOOR   5¼ miles (8·4km)
WRU (L & Y)

ACT: 18 August 1846 (Inc).

OPD: 7 August 1850.

STNS: HALIFAX (repl Shaw Syke terminus; ren Halifax Old June 1890(t), Halifax Town 30 September 1951, suffix dropped 12 June 1961); Hipperholme; Lightcliffe; Pickle Bridge (ren Wyke 1 March 1882, repl by Wyke & Norwood Green ¼ mile (0·4km) E 23 September 1896).

Milner Royd jn (Sowerby Bridge)–Dryclough jn (Halifax)
$2\frac{3}{4}$ miles (4·4km)

WRU (L & Y)
ACT: 18 August 1846.
OPD: 1 January 1852.
STN: *Copley* (opd November 1855(t)).

———

Branch to HALIFAX (South Parade) (Gds) $\frac{1}{4}$ mile (0·4km)
LB & HJ (GN)
OPD: 1 September 1856.

———

Leeds (Wortley East jn)–Wakefield (Ings Road jn)
(See Section Three)

———

Oakenshaw jn–Oakenshaw South jn (Wakefield) $\frac{1}{2}$ mile (0·8km)
WP & G (L & Y)
ACT: 16 July 1846.
OPD: 16 July 1861.
CSD: P—May 1887, reop 1933, csd by 1938.

———

Hall Royd jn–STANSFIELD HALL $\frac{1}{4}$ mile (0·4km)
L & Y
OPD: c March 1862.

———

Lofthouse North jn–Methley Joint jn   5 miles (8km)
South curve at Lofthouse $\frac{1}{4}$ mile (0·4km)
METHLEY (Joint Line stn)–Lofthouse jn (Methley)
$\frac{1}{4}$ mile (0·4km)

WY (MJ)
ACTS: 21 July 1863; 23 June 1864.
OPD: G—June 1865; P—1 May 1869. Methley (Joint Line stn)
–Lofthouse jn not used by regular P services.
CSD: P—Lofthouse south curve 17 June 1957; Lofthouse North
jn–Methley Joint jn 2 November 1964. G—Lofthouse North
and South jns–jn with Newmarket Silkstone Col branch 5
April 1965; Methley (Joint Line stn)–Methley Joint jn 27
March 1967.
STNS: Lofthouse & Outwood (MJ); Stanley; Methley.

———

Wakefield (Westgate South jn)–Doncaster North jn
(See Section Eight)

Dewsbury East jn–DEWSBURY (Market Place)   1¼ miles (2km)
Curve from Dewsbury West jn   ¼ mile (0·4km)
L & Y
ACT: 7 June 1861.
OPD: G—27 August 1866; P—1 April 1867.
CSD: P—1 December 1930. G—6 February 1961 (reop Dewsbury
   East jn–Headfield jn 15 February 1965).
STN: *Dewsbury (Market Place)* (csd 1 December 1930).

Sandal jn–West Riding jn (Wakefield)   ¾ mile (1·2km)
WR & G
ACT: 7 August 1862.
OPD: G—1 September 1866; P—1 August 1868.
CSD: P—1 January 1917; G—c 1938.

Wrenthorpe South jn–WAKEFIELD (Westgate Gds)
                                            ¼ mile (0·4km)
WR & G (GC & Mid Jt)
OPD: G—1 July 1868.
CSD: Depot closed 5 June 1967.

THORNHILL–HECKMONDWIKE   2¼ miles (3·6km)
L & Y
ACT: 7 June 1861.
OPD: G—10 May 1869; P—1 June.
CSD: P—14 June 1965.
STN: Ravensthorpe (opd July 1869).

Runtlings Lane jn (Ossett)–DEWSBURY   2½ miles (4km)
GN
ACTS: 24 July 1871; 18 July 1872.
OPD: G—by June 1874; P—9 September.
CSD: Dewsbury jn–Dewsbury: P—15 March 1880. Runtlings
   Lane jn–Dewsbury jn: P—7 September 1964; G—15 February
   1965.

Q

STNS: Earlsheaton (opd by January 1875); *Dewsbury* (temp terminus csd 15 March 1880 on opening of extension to Batley Carr).

HALIFAX–HOLMFIELD   2½ miles (4km)
H & OJ (GN & L & Y Jt)

ACTS: 30 June 1864 (Inc); 12 August 1867; 1 August 1870 (vesting in GN & L & Y).
OPD: G—Halifax–North Bridge 17 August 1874; –Holmfield 1 September. P—1 December 1879.
CSD: P—23 May 1955; G—27 June 1960.
STNS: North Bridge (opd 25 March 1880); Ovenden; Holmfield (opd 15 December 1879).

NORTH DEAN (GREETLAND)–Stainland   1½ miles (2·4km)
L & Y

ACTS: 5 July 1865; 16 July 1874.
OPD: P—1 January 1875; G—29 September.
CSD: P—23 September 1929; G—14 September 1959.
STNS: *Rochdale Road Halt* (opd 1 March 1907); *West Vale*; *Stainland.*

Garforth—Castleford (Old Station jn)   6¼ miles (10km)
LC & PJ (NE)

ACTS: 21 July 1873 (Inc); 30 June 1874; 13 July 1876 (amalg with NE).
OPD: G—8 April 1878; P—12 August.
CSD: P—22 January 1951.

SOWERBY BRIDGE–RISHWORTH   3¾ miles (6km)
L & Y

ACTS: 5 July 1865; 20 June 1870.
OPD: Sowerby Bridge–Ripponden: G—15 July 1878, P—5 August; –Rishworth 1 March 1881.
CSD: P—8 July 1929. G—Sowerby Bridge–Ripponden 1 September 1958; –Rishworth February 1953.
STNS: *Watson's Crossing Halt* (opd 1 March 1907); *Triangle* (opd 1 June 1885); *Ripponden*; *Rishworth.*

Dewsbury jn–BATLEY 1¾ miles (2·8km)
GN
ACTS: 24 July 1871; 18 July 1872; 12 July 1877.
OPD: Dewsbury jn–Batley Carr 15 March 1880; –Batley 12
   April.
CSD: P—7 September 1964; G—15 February 1965.
STNS: Dewsbury (ren Dewsbury (Central) January 1951, csd 7
   September 1964); Batley Carr.

CASTLEFORD–Cutsyke jn ¾ mile (1·2km)
LC & PJ (NE)
ACT: 21 July 1873.
OPD: 1 April 1880. Csd P 1 November 1926, reop 5 May 1958,
   csd 2 November 1964, reop 7 October 1968.

Anchor Pit jn (Brighouse)–PICKLE BRIDGE 3¾ miles (6km)
L & Y
ACTS: 11 June 1866; 21 July 1873; 19 July 1875.
OPD: 1 March 1881.
CSD: P—June 1948; G—4 August 1952.
STNS: *Clifton Road (Brighouse); Bailiff Bridge.*

Snydale jn (Normanton)–Don Pedro Col 3¼ miles (5·2km)
Branch to Featherstone Main Col 1¾ miles (2·8km)
Mid
ACT: 12 July 1882.
OPD: G—1 June 1885 (branch by August 1885).
CSD: Snydale jn–Sharlston Col 12 August 1968, –Don Pedro Col
   c 1953. Branch to Featherstone Main Col c 1931.

Low Moor south curve ¼ mile (0·4km)
L & Y
ACT: 2 August 1883.
OPD: 22 April 1886.
CSD: P—1 January 1962; G—19 January 1970.

Hare Park jn–Crofton jn (Wakefield)   1¼ miles (2km)
WR & G
ACT: 2 August 1883 (GN).
OPD: 8 November 1886.

Headfield jn–Dewsbury jn   ½ mile (0·8km)
GN
ACT: 2 August 1883.
OPD: G—October 1887; P—1 December 1893.
CSD: May 1933. Reop G—15 February 1965.

HOLMFIELD–HALIFAX (St Paul's)   3 miles (4·8km)
HHL (GN & L & Y Jt)
ACTS: 7 August 1884 (Inc); 25 September 1886; 5 July 1887
    (GN); 26 July 1889 (GN); 20 June 1892; 3 July 1894 (GN—
    vesting in GN & L & Y).
OPD: G—Holmfield–Pellon 1 August 1890, –St Paul's 5 Sep-
    tember; P—5 September.
CSD: P—1 January 1917; G—27 July 1960.
STNS: *Pellon; Halifax (St Paul's)* (csd 1 January 1917).

Calder Bridge jn–Turners Lane jn (Wakefield)   ½ mile (0·8km)
L & Y
ACT: 31 July 1894.
OPD: G—1 March 1896; P—7 October 1968.
CSD: P—7 May 1973.

Royston jn–Thornhill jn   8 miles (12·8km)
Mid
ACTS: 25 July 1898; 13 July 1899.
OPD: G—Royston jn–Crigglestone 3 July 1905, –Thornhill jn
    10 November; P—1 July 1909.
CSD: P—1 January 1917, reop 3 May 1920, csd 1946, reop 4
    January 1960, csd 13 June. G—Royston jn–Crigglestone
    August 1968; –Thornhill jn 4 May 1968.

Middlestown jn–DEWSBURY (Savile Town) $2\frac{1}{2}$ miles (4·4km)
Mid
ACTS: 30 July 1900; 30 June 1903.
OPD: G—1 March 1906.
CSD: 18 December 1950.

Oakenshaw North jn–Crofton East jn $\frac{3}{4}$ mile (1·2km)
LMS
OPD: G—3 June 1928.

SECTION FIVE: HUDDERSFIELD

Heaton Lodge jn (Mirfield)–Stalybridge $21\frac{3}{4}$ miles (34·8km)
H & M (L & NW) (Huddersfield Station jn–Springwood jn, $\frac{3}{4}$ mile
(1·2km), L & NW & L & Y Jt from 1862).
ACTS: 21 July 1845 (Inc); 27 July 1846; 9 July 1847 (amalg
with L & NW); 13 July 1849 (L & Y); 25 July 1872 (Mid); 17
June 1878.
OPD: Heaton Lodge jn–Huddersfield: P—3 August 1847, G—
16 November; –Stalybridge 1 August 1849.
STNS: *Heaton Lodge*; Bradley (resited July 1849); HUDDERS-
FIELD; Longwood & Milnsbridge; Golcar; Slaithwaite;
MARSDEN.

Springwood jn (Huddersfield)–Huddersfield jn (Penistone)
13 miles (20·8km)
H & SJ (L & Y)
ACTS: 30 June 1845 (Inc); 27 July 1846 (amalg with M & L);
13 August 1859; 30 July 1866 (Mid); 12 July 1882 (MS & L).
OPD: 1 July 1850.
STNS: LOCKWOOD; Berry Brow; HONLEY, BROCK-
HOLES; STOCKSMOOR; SHEPLEY; DENBY DALE.

BROCKHOLES–HOLMFIRTH $1\frac{3}{4}$ miles (2·8km)
H & SJ (L & Y)
ACT: 30 June 1845.
OPD: 1 July 1850; csd 3 December 1865; reop 11 March 1867.

CSD: P—2 November 1959; G—3 May 1965.
STNS: Thongs Bridge; Holmfirth.

BRADLEY–Bradley Wood jn   1¼ miles (2km)
H & M (L & NW)
ACT: 27 July 1846.
OPD: G—26 November 1850; P—1 January 1852.

Deighton (Kirkburton jn)–KIRKBURTON   4¼ miles (6·8km)
L & NW
ACT: 28 July 1863.
OPD: P—7 October 1867; G—1 January 1868.
CSD: P—28 July 1930. G—Kirkburton jn–Deighton 1 February
    1971; –Kirkburton 5 April 1965.
STNS: *Deighton* (opd 30 August 1871); *Kirkheaton*; *Fenay
    Bridge*; *Kirkburton*.

Lockwood (Meltham jn)–MELTHAM   3½ miles (5·6km)
L & Y
ACT: 7 June 1861.
OPD: G—8 August 1868, csd 9 September, reop 6 February,
    1869, csd 17 February, reop 5 July. P—5 July 1869.
CSD: P—23 May 1849; G—5 April 1965.
STNS: *Woodfield* (opd 1 June 1874); Netherton; Healey House;
    Meltham.

Shepley jn–CLAYTON WEST   3½ miles (5·6km)
L & Y
ACT: 11 June 1866.
OPD: 1 September 1879.
STNS: SKELMANTHORPE (opd 1 December 1879); CLAY-
    TON WEST.

Spen Valley jn (Bradley)–Farnley jn (Leeds)   13¼ miles (21·2km)
L & NW
ACTS: 27 June 1892; 6 July 1895.
OPD: G—Spen Valley jn–Northorpe 18 September 1899;
    –Farnley jn 9 July 1900. P—1 October 1900.

CSD: P—2 August 1965. G—11 January 1966 (when Heck-mondwike (L & NW Gds) connected to ex-L & Y line from Thornhill); Spen Valley jn–Heaton Lodge reop 26 April 1970 to form underpass beneath Calder Valley main line.
STNS: Battyeford & Mirfield; Northorpe; Heckmondwike; Liversedge; Cleckheaton; Gomersal; Upper Birstal (ren Bir-stall Town 8 July 1935); *Gildersome*.

Mirfield jn–HUDDERSFIELD (Newtown) (Gds)

$4\frac{1}{2}$ miles (7·2km)

Mid
ACTS: 13 July 1899; 20 July 1906.
OPD: G—1 November 1910; connection with ex-L & NW line at Red Doles jn opd 1 October 1923.
CSD: Mirfield jn–Red Doles jn 12 August 1937; –Huddersfield (Newtown) 5 August 1968.

SECTION SIX: SHEFFIELD AND ROTHERHAM

SHEFFIELD (WICKER)–ROTHERHAM $5\frac{1}{4}$ miles (8·4km)
S & R (Mid)
ACTS: 4 July 1836 (Inc); 23 March 1840; 21 July 1845 (amalg with Mid); 9 July 1847.
OPD: 1 November 1838.
CSD: Wicker–Grimesthorpe jn: P—1 February 1870; G—12 July 1965. Holmes–Rotherham: 6 October 1952 (except for $\frac{1}{2}$ mile (0·8km) stub serving private sidings).
STNS: *Sheffield (Wicker)* (csd 1 February 1870); *Grimesthorpe Bridge*; BRIGHTSIDE; Wincobank (opd 1 April 1868); *Blackburn Forge* (not shown on map); Holmes; Rotherham (suffix 'Westgate' added 1 May 1896, csd 6 October 1952).

HOLMES–Greasbrough Canal   2 miles (3·2km)
S & R (Mid)
ACTS: 4 July 1836; 23 March 1840.
OPD: G—10 August 1839; P—Holmes–Masborough 11 May 1840.

Derby–LEEDS (HUNSLET LANE)   72¾ miles (116·4km)
NM (Mid)
ACTS: 4 July 1836 (Inc); 5 May 1837; 1 July 1839; 23 March
1840 (S & R); 10 May 1841; 10 May 1844 (amlg to form Mid);
9 July 1847; 14 June 1860 (L & NW); 28 June 1861.
OPD: Derby–Masborough 11 May 1840; –Leeds (Hunslet Lane)
1 July.
CSD: P—Chesterfield (Tapton jn)–Rotherham (Masborough) 5
July 1954; Wath Road jn (Swinton)–Goose Hill jn (Normanton) 7 October 1968 (reop 7 May 1973); Hunslet jn–Leeds
(Hunslet Lane) on or about 28 February 1851. G—Leeds
(Hunslet Lane) depot csd 3 January 1972.
STNS: Woodhouse Mill; Treeton; Masborough (ren Masborough & Rotherham 1 May 1896, Rotherham (Masborough)
1 April 1908, ROTHERHAM 20 February 1969); Rawmarsh
(opd May 1853(t), ren Park Gate & Rawmarsh December
1869(t)); Kilnhurst (opd 6 April 1841); Swinton (repl by new
stn ⅛ mile (0·2km) N 2 July 1899); Wath; Darfield (repl by new
stn ½ mile (0·8km) N 30 June 1901); Barnsley (repl by new
stn to S on date unknown, ren Cudworth October 1854(t));
Royston (repl by Royston & Notton 1 mile (1·6km) S 1 July
1900); Sandal & Walton (opd 1 June 1870, ren Walton 30
September 1951); Wakefield (ren *Oakenshaw* 1 March 1841);
NORMANTON; ALTOFTS & WHITWOOD (opd 1 Sep-
tember 1870); Methley; WOODLESFORD; Hunslet (opd June
1854(t), repl by new stn ¼ mile (0·4km) N 14 September 1873);
Leeds (Hunslet Lane) (csd on or about 28 February 1851).

Manchester–SHEFFIELD (BRIDGEHOUSES) 41 miles (65·6km)
SA & M (GC)
ACTS: 5 May 1837 (Inc); 27 July 1846 (amalg to form MS & L);
1 August 1849; 5 July 1865.
OPD: Dunford Bridge–Sheffield (Bridgehouses) 14 July 1845;
throughout 23 December (western portion of line opened
earlier).
CSD: P—Hadfield–Penistone 5 January 1970.
STNS: Dunford Bridge; Hazlehead (opd 1 May 1846, csd 1
November 1847, reop as Hazlehead Bridge 1 November 1850);
PENISTONE (repl by new stn ½ mile (0·8km) to E 1 February
1874); *Oxspring* (opd December 1845(t)); *Thurgoland* (opd
December 1845(t)); Wortley; Deepcar; Oughty Bridge;
Wadsley Bridge; *Neepsend* (opd 1 July 1888); *Sheffield (Bridge-
houses)* (csd 15 September 1851).

Tunnel jn–Wicker jn (Sheffield) ½ mile (0·8km)
S & R (Mid)
ACT: 21 July 1845.
OPD: G—1 January 1847.
CSD: December 1940, reop c 1941, csd 1949.

Thurgoland branch 2 miles (3·2km)
MS & L
ACTS: 9 July 1847; 1 August 1849.
OPD: G—22 or 24 November 1847.
CSD: April 1875.

SHEFFIELD (BRIDGEHOUSES)–Gainsborough
33½ miles (53·6km)
S & LJ (GC)
ACTS: 3 August 1846 (Inc); 27 July 1846 (amalg to form MS & L); 22 July 1848; 1 August 1849; 5 July 1865; 28 June 1866.
OPD: Sheffield (Bridgehouses)–Woodhouse Junction 12 February 1849; –Gainsborough 17 July.
STNS: Sheffield (Victoria) (opd 15 September 1851, csd 5 January 1970); DARNALL; Woodhouse Junction (opd October 1850(t), repl by WOODHOUSE ½ mile (0·8km) to W 11 October 1875); Waleswood (opd 1 July 1907); KIVETON BRIDGE (opd 8 July 1929); KIVETON PARK; SHIREOAKS.

Branch to SHEFFIELD (Park) (Gds) ¼ mile (0·4km)
MS & L (GC)
ACTS: 22 July 1848; 1 August 1849.
OPD: G—September 1854 (Park gds depot opd 1865).
CSD: 1 June 1963.

Woodhouse jn–Birley Col 2¾ miles (4·4km)
MS & L (GC)
ACT: 30 June 1852.
OPD: G—June 1855.
CSD: c 1950.

MEADOW HALL & WINCOBANK–Woodburn jn (Sheffield)
$3\frac{1}{4}$ miles (5·2km)
SY (GC)
ACT: 17 July 1862.
OPD: 1 August 1864.
CSD: P—Meadow Hall & Wincobank–Tinsley 7 December 1953;
–Woodburn jn 5 September 1966.
STNS: Tinsley (opd March 1869(t)); Broughton Lane; *Atter-
cliffe* (opd August 1871(t)).

TINSLEY–Mexborough No 2 jn   8 miles (12·8km)
SY (GC)
OPD: Tinsley–Rotherham 1 August 1868; –Mexborough No 2
jn, G—13 March 1871, P—3 April. (The N end of this line
utilised the Mexborough–Kilnhurst potteries branch, opd G—
August 1863).
CSD: P—5 September 1966.
STNS: Rotherham Central (Perm stn opd 1 February 1874, ren
Rotherham & Masborough January 1889–25 September 1950,
csd 5 September 1966); Park Gate (opd September 1871(t), ren
Rotherham Road 1 November 1895); Aldwarke (opd July
1873(t), ren Parkgate & Aldwarke 1 November 1895); Kilnhurst
(repl by new stn $\frac{1}{2}$ mile (0·8km) to N 1 September 1871); Swinton (opd April 1872(t)).

Holmes jn–Masborough South jn $\frac{1}{4}$ mile (0·4km)
Mid
ACT: 13 July 1876.
OPD: 1 May 1869.
CSD: P—5 July 1954.

Grimesthorpe jn (Sheffield)–Tapton jn (Chesterfield)
$13\frac{1}{2}$ miles (21·6km)
Mid
ACT: 25 July 1864.
OPD: 1 February 1870.
STNS: ATTERCLIFFE ROAD; SHEFFIELD (suffix 'City'
added 25 September 1950, repl by 'Midland' 18 June 1951–5
January 1970); Heeley; Ecclesall (ren Mill Houses & Ecclesall
3 May 1884); Abbey Houses (ren Beauchieff 1 April 1870);
DORE & TOTLEY (opd 1 February 1872).

Branch to SHEFFIELD (Pond Street) (Gds)   ¼ mile (0·4km)
Mid
OPD: G—probably 1 February 1870.
CSD: 19 September 1960.

———

Nunnery Main Line jn (Mid)–jn with MS & L   1 mile (1·6km)
Mid
ACT: 25 July 1864.
OPD: G—c August 1870 (appr by Board of Trade 27 July
   1870); connection at east end with MS & L csd by 1898. P—4
   October 1965, on reop of connection on different alignment.

———

Darnall jn–Attercliffe jn (Sheffield)   ½ mile (0·8km)
MS & L (GC)
ACT: 5 April 1867.
OPD: 25 August 1873 (little used by regular P traffic after 1914).

———

Mexborough No 3 jn–Mexborough No 1 jn   ¼ mile (0·4km)
MS & L (GC)
OPD: 1 June 1874 (little used by P traffic until 1899).
CSD: P—5 September 1966.

———

Tinsley West jn–Tinsley East jn   ¼ mile (0·4km)
MS & L (GC)
ACT: 16 July 1873.
OPD: G—2 July 1875.

———

Branch to SHEFFIELD (Queen's Road) (Gds)   ¼ mile (0·4km)
Mid
OPD: G—6 June 1892.
CSD: 13 May 1963.

———

DORE & TOTLEY–Chinley   21 miles (33·6km)
Dore & Totley south curve   ¼ mile (0·4km)
D & C (Mid)
ACTS: 28 July 1884 (Inc); 24 July 1888 (amalg with Mid).
OPD: G—6 November 1893; P—1 June 1894 (south curve little
   used by P traffic 1914–1968).

———

Woodburn jn–SHEFFIELD (City) (Gds) $\frac{3}{4}$ mile (1·2km)
L & NW
ACT: 27 June 1892.
OPD: G—11 May 1895.
(*N.B.*: The terminus was ren Nunnery on 2 February 1903, the
name of 'City' being transferred to the new L & NW goods
terminal of this date—q.v.).

———

Treeton jn–Brightside jn $3\frac{1}{2}$ miles (5·6km)
Grimesthorpe jn–ATTERCLIFFE (Gds) $\frac{1}{2}$ mile (0·8km)
SD
ACTS: 14 August 1896 (Inc); 15 July 1897; 6 August 1897 (Tree-
ton & Brightside Railway); 12 August 1898; 20 July 1906; 20
July 1906 (GC); 3 August 1916.
OPD: G—28 May 1900; P—30 May.
CSD: P—11 September 1939, reop 6 October 1946, csd 17 March
1947.
STNS: *Catcliffe*; Tinsley Road (ren *West Tinsley* 1 July 1907).

———

Extension to SHEFFIELD (City) (Gds) $\frac{3}{4}$ mile (1·2km)
L & NW
ACT: 27 July 1893.
OPD: G—2 February 1903 (terminus ren Wharf Street 25 Sep-
tember 1950).
CSD: Depot csd 12 July 1965.

———

Branch to Tinsley Park Col $1\frac{1}{4}$ miles (2km)
SD
ACT: 20 July 1906.
OPD: G—20 November 1903.
CSD: 1 March 1958.

———

Nunnery Single Line jn (between ex-Mid and L & NW Nunnery
branches) $\frac{1}{2}$ mile (0·8km)
LMS
OPD: c 1924.

———

Aldwarke jns (between ex-Mid and GC Sheffield–Swinton lines)
BR
OPD: G—7 March 1965, P—5 April.

———

Tinsley Yard curves (north and south curves from ex-GC Shef-field–Rotherham line; north curve from ex-North Midland main line)
BR
OPD: G—12 July 1965.

SECTION SEVEN: BARNSLEY

Derby–BARNSLEY (Cudworth)–LEEDS (Hunslet Lane)
(See Section Six)

HORBURY JUNCTION–BARNSLEY   8¾ miles (14km)
SRBWH & G (L & Y)
ACTS: 7 August 1846 (Inc); 2 August 1858 (amalg with L & Y);
28 July 1863 (NE); 23 June 1864 (SY); 27 June 1892.
OPD: P—1 January 1850; G—15 January.
STNS: Crigglestone; Haigh; DARTON; BARNSLEY (suffix 'Low Town' added 2 June 1924, repl by 'Exchange' 1 August 1924–13 June 1960).

Branch to Silkstone Siding   1¾ miles (2·8km)
SRBWH & G (L & Y)
ACTS: 7 August 1846; 2 August 1858; 23 June 1864 (SY).
OPD: G—15 January 1850.
CSD: 15 December 1937 (except for short stub at E end csd by 1972).

Mexborough No 1 jn–BARNSLEY   8½ miles (13·6km)
SY (GC)
ACTS: 7 August 1846 (SRBWH & G); 22 July 1847 (Inc); 15 July 1850; 3 July 1851 (SRBWH & G); 30 June 1852; 23 June 1864 (transfer to MS & L); 16 July 1874 (vesting in MS & L).
OPD: G—Mexborough No 1 jn–Elsecar jn 1 February 1850;– Aldam jn by June 1850; –Barnsley 1 July 1851. P—1 July 1851.
CSD: P—Mexborough No 1 jn–Quarry jn (Barnsley) 5 January 1970; –Barnsley 1 June 1870, reop 19 April 1960.

STNS: Wath; Wombwell (opd September 1851(t)); Ardsley (opd
   September 1851(t), ren Stairfoot 1 October 1870, repl by new
   stn $\frac{1}{8}$ mile (0·2km) to W 1 December 1871).

———

Elsecar jn–ELSECAR (Gds) $2\frac{3}{4}$ miles (4·4km)
SY (GC)
ACT: 22 July 1847.
OPD: G—1 February 1850.
CSD: Gds depot csd 16 December 1963.

———

Aldam jn–MOOR END (Gds) $6\frac{1}{2}$ miles (10·4km)
SY (GC)
ACTS: 7 August 1846 (SRBWH & G); 22 July 1847.
OPD: G—Aldam jn–Darley Main Cols by June 1850; –Moor
   End April 1852.
CSD: Aldam jn–'Swaithe jn' 30 September 1906; Moor End jn–
   Moor End June 1909.

———

Aldam jn–Blackburn Valley jn (Wincobank) $11\frac{1}{4}$ miles (18km)
SRBWH & G (GC)
ACTS: 7 August 1846 (Inc); 22 July 1847 (transfer to SY); 3 July
   1851.
OPD: 4 September 1854.
CSD: P—Aldam jn–Wombwell Main jn 1 December 1879;
   –Meadow Hall & Wincobank 7 December 1953; –Blackburn
   Valley jn 1 August 1864. G—Rockingham South Col–Smithy-
   wood Col, Ecclesfield 7 March 1966.
STNS: Smithley for Darley Main & Worsborough (ren Dark-
   cliffe October 1859(t), Dovecliffe March 1860(t)); *High Royds*
   (opd July 1856(t)); Hangman's Stone (opd January 1855(t), ren
   Birdwell & Hoyland February 1855 (t)); *Westwood* (repl by
   new stn to S 9 October 1876); Chapeltown & Thorncliffe;
   Ecclesfield (opd November 1854(t), csd October 1856(t), new
   stn opd 1 August 1876); Grange Lane (opd June 1855(t));
   Meadow Hall & Wincobank (opd May 1868(t)).

———

Barnsley jn (Penistone)–BARNSLEY $6\frac{3}{4}$ miles (10·8km)
Branch to BARNSLEY (REGENT STREET) (Gds)
                                          $\frac{1}{4}$ mile (0·4km)

MS & L (GC)
ACTS: 22 July 1848; 4 August 1853.
OPD: G—Barnsley jn–Dodworth 15 May 1854; –Summer Lane
5 December 1855; –Barnsley (Regent Street) 12 February 1857
(terminus later ren Barnsley (Central) (Gds)). P—Barnsley jn
–Dodworth 1 July 1854; –Summer Lane 1 November 1855;
–Barnsley 1 December 1859.
CSD: P—5 January 1970 (Court House jn–Barnsley csd 1 June
1870, reop 19 April 1960). G—Branch to Barnsley (Central)
(Gds) 6 November 1967.
STNS: Silkstone; Dodworth; Summer Lane.

Cudworth South jn (Mid)–Court House jn (Barnsley)
4 miles (6·4km)
Cudworth North jn (Mid)–Cudworth West jn ½ mile (0·8km)
Mid
ACTS: 21 July 1863; 25 July 1864; 5 July 1865 (MS & L).
OPD: G—28 June 1869; P—2 May 1870.
CSD: P—Cudworth South jn–Barnsley West jn 9 June 1958;
–Court House jn 19 April 1960 (Cudworth North jn–West jn
little used by P traffic). G—Cudworth South jn–West jn April
1959; Monk Bretton Col–Oaks Col 5 January 1959, –Barnsley
West jn April 1959, –Barnsley (Court House) 19 April 1960,
–Court House jn 31 January 1966.
STNS: Monk Bretton (opd 1 May 1876); Barnsley (Court House)
(csd 19 April 1960).

Quarry jn–Barnsley West jn ¼ mile (0·4km)
MS & L (GC)
OPD: 31 May 1870.
CSD: 19 April 1960.
(A second spur here, from Quarry jn to Oaks Colliery Siding jn,
was constructed by the Midland under its Act of 25 June 1868,
but was apparently used only for access to Oaks Col. It is not
shown on the map.)

ARDSLEY (STAIRFOOT)–Applehaigh 4¾ miles (7·6km)
BC (GC)
ACTS: 22 July 1861 (Inc); 13 July 1863 (amalg with SY).
OPD: G—28 January 1870; P—Stairfoot–Lee Lane 1 September
1882.

CSD: P—22 September 1930. G—Stairfoot–Wharncliffe Woodmoor Col jn May 1967; –Lee Lane 31 July 1961; –Applehaigh
c 1881.
STN: *Staincross*.

———

GRANGE LANE–Grange Col   1¾ miles (2·8km)
MS & L (GC)
OPD: G—1875.
CSD: 3 December 1958.

———

Adwick curve (Swinton)   ½ mile (0·8km)
MS & L
OPD: G—By February 1875 (actual connection with Mid not
made until c October 1875).
CSD: By 1882 (this line may have succeeded an earlier SY con-
nection, authorised 22 July 1847 and possibly opd in 1850).

———

Wombwell Main jn–New Oaks jn (Stairfoot)   ¾ mile (1·2km)
MS & L (GC)
ACT: 16 June 1873.
OPD: 1 December 1879.
CSD: P—7 December 1953.

———

Moor End jn–West Silkstone jn   2 miles (3·2km)
MS & L (GC)
ACT: 24 July 1876.
OPD: G—2 August 1880.

———

Old Oaks jn (Stairfoot)–Oakwell jn   1 mile (1·6km)
Lee Lane–Nostell North jn   4¾ miles (7·6km)
Royston curve   ¾ mile (1·2km)
Winterset jn–Nostell South jn   ½ mile (0·8km)
MS & L (GC)
ACT: 16 July 1874.
OPD: G—1 August 1882; P—Old Oaks jn–Nostell North jn
1 September.

CSD: P—22 September 1930. G—Old Oaks jn–Oakwell jn 4 May 1959; Lee Lane–Nostell North & South jns 31 July 1961; Royston curve 1897.
STNS: *Notton & Royston*; Ryhill (ren *Winterset & Ryhill* 1 March 1927).

Hull–CUDWORTH
(See Section Eight)

Cudworth South jn (H & B)–STAIRFOOT   3 miles (4·8km)
Carlton Main jn–MONK BRETTON   ½ mile (0·8km)
H & B
ACTS: 26 August 1880 (Inc); 18 August 1882; 16 July 1885.
OPD: G—20 July 1885 (connection with MS & L at Stairfoot opd by mid-August 1885).
CSD: Cudworth South jn (H & B)–Stairfoot 3 July 1967 (N of new jn at Ardsley with Cudworth Station South jn–Monkspring jn line—q.v.); Carlton Main jn–Monk Bretton by November 1939.

STAIRFOOT–Houghton Main Col   3½ miles (5·6km)
MS & L (GC)
ACT: 7 August 1888.
OPD: G—4 July 1892.
CSD: 3 October 1960.

Wincobank Station jn–Thorncliffe Ironworks   5½ miles (8·8km)
Mid
ACTS: 25 July 1890; 11 June 1891.
OPD: G—30 August 1893; P—Wincobank Station jn–Chapeltown 1 July 1897.
STNS: Ecclesfield; CHAPELTOWN.
CSD: Chapeltown–Thorncliffe Ironworks, by 1973.

Branch to OAKWELL (Gds)   ¼ mile (0·4km)
MS & L (GC)
OPD: G—1 July 1896.
CSD: 30 March 1959.

R

Wincobank North jn–Wincobank West jn   ½ mile (0·8km)
Mid
ACT: 20 July 1894.
OPD: G—December 1896.
CSD: 29 September 1969.

___

CHAPELTOWN–Barnsley West jn   7¾ miles (12·4km)
Mid
ACTS: 28 June 1892; 20 July 1894.
OPD: G—12 April 1897; P—1 July.
CSD: New spur to Quarry jn (Barnsley) op 19 April 1960 when
line csd N of this point.
STNS: Wentworth & Tankersley; ELSECAR & HOYLAND;
WOMBWELL.

___

Wharncliffe Branch jn–BIRDWELL & PILLEY (Gds)
                                           3¼ miles (5·2km)
Mid
ACT: 9 June 1893.
OPD: G—probably 12 April 1897.
CSD: Wharncliffe jn–Rockingham Col c 1961; –Birdwell &
Pilley 13 September 1954.

___

Monkspring jn–Cudworth Station South jn   2½ miles (4km)
Mid
ACT: 6 August 1897.
OPD: 11 September 1899.
CSD: 7 September 1964. Reop G, N of new jn with ex-H & B
Cudworth–Stairfoot line at Ardsley, 3 July 1967.

___

Branch to OLD MILL LANE (Gds)   ¼ mile (0·4km)
GC
OPD: G—16 August 1901.
CSD: 30 March 1959.

___

Crigglestone jn–HORBURY & OSSETT   1½ miles (2·4km)
L & Y
ACT: 27 June 1892.
OPD: G—2 March 1902; P—1 July.
CSD: P—11 September 1961 (little used by P traffic after 1939).

___

Wombwell Main jn–'Swaithe jn'   ½ mile (0·8km)
GC
ACT: 14 August 1903.
OPD: G—30 September 1906.

SECTION EIGHT: DONCASTER AND THE CONCEALED COALFIELD

WAKEFIELD (Kirkgate)–Goole
(See Section Four)

KNOTTINGLEY–Askern jn   10¼ miles (16·4km)
WP & G (L & Y)
ACTS: 16 July 1846; 9 July 1847; 3 July 1851 (GN); 17 June
  1852.
OPD: 6 June 1848.
CSD: P—27 September 1948.
STNS: Womersley; Norton; Askern.

London (King's Cross)–Askern jn   160¼ miles (256·4km)
GN
ACTS: 26 June 1846 (Inc); 9 July 1847; 1 August 1849; 15 July
  1850.
OPD: Askern jn–Stockbridge 6 June 1848; –Doncaster 7 September. Retford–Doncaster 4 September 1849.
STNS: Rossington; DONCASTER (temp stn repl by perm stn
  ¼ mile (0·4km) to S September 1850; ren Doncaster Central
  1 July 1923–1 January 1951); Stockbridge (ren Arksey & Stockbridge December 1850(t)).

KNOTTINGLEY–Burton Salmon   3 miles (4·8km)
Y & NM (NE)
ACT: 9 July 1847.
OPD: April 1850 (local traffic); 8 August (GN services).
CSD: P—Knottingley–Ferrybridge 11 July 1947.
STN: Ferrybridge (see Swinton–Ferrybridge below).

Doncaster South jn–SWINTON   8 miles (12·8km)
Doncaster Bridge jn–Hexthorpe jn   1½ miles (2·4km)
SY (GC)
ACTS: 22 July 1847 (Inc); 22 July 1848; 15 July 1850.
OPD: 10 July 1849 (no regular P service Doncaster Bridge jn–
Hexthorpe jn).
CSD: Mexborough No 1 jn–Swinton: 26 July 1965. Mex-
borough No 2 jn–Mexborough No 1 jn: P—5 January 1970.
STNS: *Cherry Lane*; *Hexthorpe* (opd 1 February 1850); *Sprot-
borough* (opd 1 February 1850); CONISBOROUGH (repl by
new stn ⅛ mile (0·2km) to W in 1890s); Mexborough Junction
(opd January 1850, repl by MEXBOROUGH (New) ¼ mile
(0·4km) to E 3 April 1871).

Doncaster North jn–Keadby   20½ miles (32·8km)
Branch to THORNE WATERSIDE
SY
OPD: G—Doncaster North jn–Don Navigation, ½ mile (0·8km),
1 July 1851; –Thorne Lock 11 December 1855; –Keadby Sep-
tember 1859; Thorne Waterside branch January 1856. P—
Doncaster North jn–Thorne Lock 1 July 1856; –Keadby pro-
bably 10 September 1859.
CSD: Doncaster North jn–Sandall 1 December 1866; –Maud's
Bridge 1 October (repl by direct line of 1866—q.v.).
STNS: *Sandall* (opd first half 1857); *Barnby Dun*; *Bramwith*;
Stainforth; *Thorne Lock* (repl by new stn at *Orchard Street*
¼ mile (0·4km) to E September 1859); *Maud's Bridge* (opd c
October 1859).

Branch to DONCASTER (Marsh Gate) (Gds)   ¼ mile (0·4km)
SY (GC)
OPD: G—1856.
CSD: Depot csd 30 April 1971.

Wakefield (Westgate South jn)–Doncaster North jn
                            19 miles (30·4km)
WR & G
ACTS: 7 August 1862 (Inc); 28 June 1866 (joint vesting in GN
& MS & L).
OPD: 1 February 1866.
STNS: Sandall; Hare Park & Crofton (opd November 1885(t));

Nostell; Fitzwilliam Halt (opd 1 June 1937); Hemsworth; SOUTH ELMSALL; Adwick (opd March 1866, ren Carcroft & Adwick-le-Street May 1880(t)).

Doncaster North jn–MAUD'S BRIDGE   11¼ miles (18km)
SY (GC)
ACTS: 17 July 1862; 13 July 1863; 11 June 1866.
OPD: Doncaster North jn–Sandall 1 December 1866; –Maud's Bridge 10 September (Doncaster race traffic), 1 October (regular traffic). (Repl earlier line of 1851–9.)
STNS: Barnby Dun; STAINFORTH & HATFIELD; THORNE.

Adwick jn–Stainforth jn   7 miles (11·2km)
WR & G
ACT: 7 August 1862 (Inc).
OPD: 1 November 1866.

Gainsborough–Black Carr jn   18¼ miles (29·2km)
GN (GN & GE Jt)
ACTS: 25 July 1864; 3 July 1879 (formation of GN & GE Jt Committee).
OPD: G—1 July 1867; P—15 July.

Thorne jn–Thorne   1¼ miles (2km)
SY (GC)
ACT: 13 July 1863.
OPD: 2 August 1869.

Thorne–Staddlethorpe jn   14 miles (20·4km)
NE
ACT: 28 July 1863.
OPD: 2 August 1869.
STN: THORNE.

Shaftholme jn–Chaloner Whin jn (York)   25½ miles (40·8km)
NE
ACT: 23 June 1864.
OPD: 2 January 1871.

Joan Croft jn–Applehurst jn $\frac{1}{2}$ mile (0·8km)
NE
ACT: 23 June 1864.
OPD: G—1 July 1877.

———

Swinton (Wath Road jn)–FERRYBRIDGE 16 miles (25·6km)
Mexborough West jn–Dearne jn 1 mile (1·6km)
Moorthorpe jn–South Kirkby jn $\frac{3}{4}$ mile (1·2km)
South Elmsall jn–Moorthorpe North jn $1\frac{1}{4}$ miles (2km)
Pontefract Station jn–Pontefract East jn $\frac{3}{4}$ mile (1·2km)
S & K
ACTS: 16 July 1874; 13 May 1875.
OPD: G—19 May 1879; P—1 July (Pontefract curve 1 April 1880).
CSD: Mexborough West jn–Dearne jn 4 April 1965 (not used by regular P trains 2 October 1893–15 March 1899). Moorthorpe jn–South Kirkby jn: P—2 October 1893, reop 1 May 1903, csd April 1918, reop 7 October 1968, csd 7 May 1973. South Elmsall jn–Moorthorpe North jn: P—1 January 1917; G—February 1928. Pontefract Station jn–Pontefract East jn: P—1 November 1926, reop 4 January 1960, csd 2 November 1964.
STNS: Hickleton (ren BOLTON-ON-DEARNE 1 November 1879); Clayton (ren Frickley 1 November 1882); MOORTHORPE; Ackworth; PONTEFRACT (ren Pontefract Baghill 1 December 1936); Ferrybridge (opd 1 May 1882).

———

Dearne jn–Wath jn $\frac{3}{4}$ mile (1·2km)
MS & L & Mid & NE Jt
ACTS: 14 June 1875; 8 April 1881.
OPD: G—8 August 1882.

———

Hull–CUDWORTH 53 miles (84·8km)
H & B
ACTS: 26 August 1880 (Inc); 18 August 1882; 16 July 1885; 30 June 1905.
OPD: G—20 July 1885; P—27 July.
CSD: P—1 January 1932. G—Hull–Wrangbrook jn 6 April 1959; –Cudworth 7 August 1967.
STNS: *Kirk Smeaton*; *Upton & North Elmsall*; *Hemsworth & South Kirkby* (opd 1 July 1891); *Cudworth* (H & B).

———

Hemsworth East jn–Hemsworth South jn $\frac{3}{4}$ mile (1·2km)
H & B
ACT: 26 August 1880.
OPD: G—August 1885.
CSD: 7 August 1967.

Moorthorpe (East to south curve from H & B main line to S & K)
$\frac{1}{2}$ mile (0·8km)
H & B
ACTS: 26 August 1880; 20 June 1899 (abandonment).
OPD: Constructed except for actual connection with S & K, but
never brought into use.

Wrangbrook jn–DENABY & CONISBOROUGH
$11\frac{1}{2}$ miles (18·4km)
SYJn
ACTS: 14 August 1890 (Inc); 28 July 1891 (H & B working
agreement); 8 April 1897.
OPD: G—1 September 1894; P—1 December.
CSD: P—2 February 1903. G—Wrangbrook jn–Middleton Sid-
ing 7 August 1967.
STNS: *Pickburn & Brodsworth*; *Sprotborough*; *Denaby & Conis-
borough*.

Wrangbrook jn–WATH $8\frac{1}{2}$ miles (13·6km)
H & SYE (H & B)
ACTS: 6 August 1897 (Inc); 25 July 1898 (amlg with H & B).
OPD: G—31 March 1902; P—23 August.
CSD: P—6 April 1929. G—Wrangbrook jn–Moorhouse & South
Elmsall 30 September 1963; –Wath 31 May 1954.
STNS: *Moorhouse & South Elmsall; Hickleton & Thurnscoe;
Wath*.

Brierley jn–Loversall Carr jn 18 miles (28·8km)
Thurnscoe jn–Hickleton South jn $\frac{1}{2}$ mile (0·8km)
Black Carr East jn–Bessacarr jn $\frac{3}{4}$ mile (1·2km)
DV
ACTS: 6 August 1897 (Inc); 30 July 1900; 31 July 1902 (L & Y);
1 August 1904 (L & Y); 30 June 1905; 20 July 1906 (L & Y).
OPD: G—Brierley jn–Houghton Col jn 19 March 1902; –Hickle-
ton South jn 13 March 1905; –Cadeby Col jn 8 January 1906;

–Edlington 17 March 1909; –Black Carr West jn 19 October 1908 (official date, regular traffic 1 January 1909); –Loversall Carr + Bessacarr jns 17 May 1909. P—Shafton jn–Edlington 3 June 1912.

CSD: P—10 September 1951. G—Thurnscoe jn–Hickleton South jn February 1964. Goldthorpe Col–Edlington 4 July 1966; Brierley jn–Grimethorpe Col jn 11 July (on opening of new curves at Houghton on to ex-Midland main line); Black Carr West jn–Loversall Carr + Bessacarr jns May 1972.

STNS: Grimethorpe Halt; Houghton Halt (ren Great Houghton Halt 24 August 1913); Goldthorpe & Thurnscoe Halt; Harlington Halt; Denaby Halt; Edlington.

Crofton West jn–Shafton jn   8¼ miles (13·2km)
Crofton East jn–Crofton South jn   ½ mile (0·8km)
L & Y
ACT: 26 July 1901 (Dearne Valley Junction Railway).
OPD: G—6 March 1905. P—Crofton West jn–Shafton jn 3 June 1912.
CSD: P—10 September 1951; G—11 July 1966.
STN: Ryhill Halt.

Brantcliffe East jn–Dinnington jn   3¼ miles (5·2km)
Brantcliffe West jn–Brantcliffe North jn   ½ mile (0·8km)
SL & M (GC & Mid Jt)
ACTS: 9 August 1901 (Inc); 31 July 1902 (transfer to GC & Mid Jt); 22 July 1904.
OPD: G—2 October 1905; P—Brantcliffe East jn–Dinnington jn 1 December 1910.
CSD: G—Brantcliffe West jn–North jn April 1914. P—April 1926, reop 25 July 1927, csd 2 December 1929.
STN: *Anston* (opd 20 May 1912).

Castle Hills jn–Brodsworth Main Col   1½ miles (2·4km)
WR & G
ACT: 26 July 1907 (GC).
OPD: G—18 May 1908 (new S curve on to main line opd September 1969).

DENABY & CONISBOROUGH–Lowfield jn   ⅛ mile (0·2km)
GC
OPD: G—13 July 1908.

Black Carr West jn–St Catherine's jn   ¾ mile (1·2km)
L & Y
ACT: 31 July 1902 (NE).
OPD: G—7 October 1908 (official date, regular traffic 1 January
   1909).

Kirk Sandall jn–Dinnington jn   17½ miles (28km)
Potteric Carr jn–Low Ellers jn   ¾ mile (1·2km)
Branch to Dinnington Main Col   1¼ miles (2km)
SYJt
ACTS: 31 July 1902 (NE); 14 August 1903.
OPD: G—Kirk Sandall + Potteric Carr jns–Dinnington &
   Laughton 1 January 1909; –Dinnington jn + Dinnington
   Main Col branch 2 October 1905. P—Potteric Carr jn–Din-
   nington jn 1 December 1910.
CSD: P—April 1926; reop 25 July 1927; csd Potteric Carr jn–
   Maltby 8 July 1929, –Dinnington jn 2 December.
STNS: *Tickhill*; *Maltby*; *Dinnington & Laughton*.

Decoy Down Yard–St Catherine's jn   ¾ mile (1·2km)
GN
ACT: 21 July 1903.
OPD: G—probably 1 January 1909.
CSD: By 1911.

Carcroft jn–Skellow jn   ½ mile (0·8km)
WR & G
ACT: 26 July 1907 (GC).
OPD: G—18 January 1909.

Moorhouse jn–MOORHOUSE & SOUTH ELMSALL
                                          1 mile (1·6km)
WR & G
ACT: 4 August 1906 (GN).
OPD: G—8 March 1909.

Black Carr East jn–St Catherine's jn   ¾ mile (1·2km)
L & Y (L & Y & GN Jt).
ACTS: 31 July 1902 (NE); 3 August 1910 (transfer to joint
    ownership).
OPD: G—17 May 1909.
CSD: c January 1940.

———

Thrybergh jn–Northern jn (Braithwell)   2½ miles (4km)
Roundwood jn (GC)–Don Bridge West jn   ¼ mile (0·4km)
Roundwood Col jn (Mid)–Don Bridge East jn   ¾ mile (1·2km)
Southern jn (Laughton)–Anston jn   1½ miles (2·4km)
RM & L (GC and Mid Jt)
ACTS: 8 August 1902 (H & B); 4 August 1905 (RM & L Inc);
    20 July 1906 (H & B & GC); 9 August 1907 (Mid).
OPD: G—1 October 1909.
CSD: Roundwood jn–Don Bridge West jn March 1914; Round-
    wood Coll jn–Don Bridge East jn 2 August 1966; Silverwood
    Col–Northern jn February 1967 (official date 13 March 1969);
    Southern jn–Anston jn c 1926.

———

Northern jn (Braithwell)–Southern jn (Laughton)
                                               6¼ miles (10km)
Branch to BRAMLEY & MALTBY (Gds) (ren HELLABY 1
    June 1920)   ¼ mile (0·4km)
RM & L (GC, H & B & Mid Jt)
ACTS: As previous entry.
OPD: G—1 October 1909.
CSD: Northern jn–Hellaby jn February 1967 (official date 13
    March 1969); Laughton West jn–Southern jn c 1926; branch
    to Hellaby (Gds) 31 October 1966.

———

Hexthorpe jn–Bentley jn ('Doncaster Avoiding Line')
                                               3¼ miles (5·2km)
GC
ACT: 14 August 1903.
OPD: G—25 July 1910; P—29 July (little used by regular P
    traffic).

———

Laughton East jn–Laughton West jn $\frac{1}{2}$ mile (0·8km)
SYJt
ACTS: 8 August 1902 (H & B); 1 August 1908 (NE).
OPD: G—9 January 1911, csd c 1915, reop c 1923.

Brackenhill jn (Ackworth)–Hemsworth Col   3 miles (4·8km)
Branch to ACKWORTH MOOR TOP (Gds) $\frac{1}{4}$ mile (0·4km)
B Lt
LRO: 19 March 1901.
OPD: G—1 July 1914.
CSD: 1 January 1962.

Knottingley South jn–Knottingley East jn $\frac{1}{4}$ mile (0·4km)
L & Y
ACT: 15 August 1913.
OPD: G—29 March 1915.

Branch to Rossington Main Col $1\frac{1}{4}$ miles (2km)
GN
ACT: 7 August 1912.
OPD: By 1915 (a second connection from near Black Carr East
jn was installed by the LNER).

Aire jn–Braithwell jn $21\frac{1}{4}$ miles (34km)
Bullcroft jn–Bullcroft Main Col   2 miles (3·2km)
Branch to DONCASTER (Gds) (ren Doncaster (York Road) 1
July 1923) $\frac{3}{4}$ mile (1·2km)
Doncaster (Gds) branch south curve $\frac{1}{4}$ mile (0·4km)
Sprotborough jns $\frac{1}{4}$ mile (0·4km)
H & B & GC Jt
ACTS: 16 August 1909 (GC); 16 August 1909 (H & B); 26 July
1910 (GC); 26 July 1910 (Mid); 15 August 1913 (H & B); 31
July 1914 (H & B).
OPD: G—1 May 1916.
CSD: Aire jn–Bullcroft jn 20 October 1958 (reop Thorpe Marsh
Power Station jn–Bullcroft jn c 1961–6 September 1970); Bull-
croft Main Col–Bullcroft jn–Doncaster jn (jn with York Road
branch) 6 September 1970; Sprotborough jn–Warmsworth 3
February 1969, –Northern jn (Braithwell) 13 March (official

date, no traffic after c 1947); York Road branch south curve
1939.

Firbeck jn–Firbeck Col   5¼ miles (8·4km)
South curve at Firbeck jn   ¼ mile (0·4km)
SYJt
ACT: 31 July 1914 (NE).
LRO: 22 February 1916 (Firbeck Lt Rly).
OPD: G—7 April 1924 (temp track); 1 October 1927 (perm line).
CSD: Harworth jn–Firbeck Col December 1968.

Harworth jn–Harworth Col   2 miles (3·2km)
East curve at Harworth jn   ¾ mile (1·2km)
SYJt
ACT: 31 July 1914 (NE); 1 August 1924 (LNER).
OPD: G—15 October 1929.
CSD: East curve at Harworth jn 5 July 1931.

Marshgate jn (Doncaster)–WHEATLEY PARK (Gds)
                                                 2 miles (3·2km)
LNER
OPD: G—1930 (extended by 1 mile (1·6km) 1938).
CSD: August 1971.

West curve at Ferrybridge (from ex-WP & G to S & K)
                                                 ¼ mile (0·4km)
BR
OPD: G—26 July 1965.

COMPANY ABBREVIATIONS

Unless otherwise indicated, all companies have 'Railway' at the
end of their title.

B & T   Bradford & Thornton Railways
BC   Barnsley Coal
BE & I   Bradford, Eccleshill & Idle
B Lt   Brackenhill Light
BR   British Railways
BW & L   Bradford, Wakefield & Leeds

D & C	Dore & Chinley
DV	Dearne Valley
E & WYU	East & West Yorkshire Union Railways
GC	Great Central
GE	Great Eastern
GN	Great Northern
GN & GE Jt	Great Northern & Great Eastern Joint
GY & H	Guiseley, Yeadon & Headingley
GY & R	Guiseley, Yeadon & Rawdon
H & B	Hull, Barnsley & West Riding Junction Railway & Dock (Hull & Barnsley from 30 June 1905)
H & M	Huddersfield & Manchester Railway & Canal
H & OJ	Halifax & Ovenden Junction
H & SJ	Huddersfield & Sheffield Junction
H & SYE	Hull & South Yorkshire Extension
HHL	Halifax High Level & North & South Junction (Halifax High Level from 20 June 1892)
Hun	Hunslet
I & S	Idle & Shipley
K & WV	Keighley & Worth Valley
L & B	Leeds & Bradford
L & NW	London & North Western
L & S	Leeds & Selby
L & T	Leeds & Thirsk
L & Y	Lancashire & Yorkshire
LB & HJ	Leeds, Bradford & Halifax Junction
LC & PJ	Leeds, Castleford & Pontefract Junction
LD & EC	Lancashire, Derbyshire & East Coast
LD & M	Leeds, Dewsbury & Manchester
LMS	London, Midland & Scottish
LN	Leeds Northern
LNER	London & North Eastern
M & L	Manchester & Leeds
Mid	Midland
MJ	Methley Joint
MS & L	Manchester, Sheffield & Lincolnshire

NE	North Eastern
NM	North Midland
O & I Jt	Otley & Ilkley Joint
RM & L	Rotherham, Maltby & Laughton
S & K	Swinton & Knottingley Joint
S & LJ	Sheffield & Lincolnshire Junction
S & R	Sheffield & Rotherham
SA & M	Sheffield, Ashton-under-Lyne & Manchester
SD	Sheffield District
SL & M	Shireoaks, Laughton & Maltby
SLJ	South Leeds Junction
SRBWH & G	Sheffield, Rotherham, Barnsley, Wakefield, Huddersfield & Goole
SY	South Yorkshire, Doncaster & Goole (South Yorkshire Railway & River Dun Navigation from 19 April 1850)
SYJn	South Yorkshire Junction
SYJt	South Yorkshire Joint
WP & G	Wakefield, Pontefract & Goole
WR & G	West Riding & Grimsby
WRU	West Riding Union Railways
WY	West Yorkshire
Y & NM	York & North Midland
YD	Yorkshire Dales

Sources and Bibliography

PRIMARY SOURCES

Minutes and official records housed at British Transport Historical Records

Newspapers etc: *Barnsley Chronicle*; *Dewsbury Reporter*; *Doncaster Gazette*; *Herepath's Journal*; *Leeds Intelligencer*; *Leeds Mercury*; *Railway Times*; *Railway News*; *Yorkshire Post*

Acts of Parliament; Evidence given before Parliament on Railway Bills; Light Railway Orders; Board of Trade reports

Bradshaw's Railway Guide; company timetables

Bradshaw's Railway Manual, Shareholders' Guide and Official Directory, 1848–1923

Airey's and Railway Clearing House Official Railway Maps of Yorkshire; Railway Clearing House Official Railway Junction Diagrams

SECONDARY SOURCES

Secondary source material on the railways of South and West Yorkshire is extremely scattered. On the company side three of the lines in the area, the GC, H & B and L & Y, are now covered by comprehensive modern histories. The NE has Tomlinson's monumental work which is excellent up to 1880, while the GN has Grinling—readable and useful in outline but lacking in detail. Of the many works on the Midland none is wholly satisfactory, but the lines north-west of Leeds are well covered by Baughan (see Airedale and Wharfedale). The L & NW has unfortunately proved too vast and daunting a subject, and up to now no adequate history has appeared. Railway studies on a regional basis are virtually non-existent, and the few booklets and magazine articles have to be supplemented by urban and regional works of a general nature.

In the bibliography below, each section lists railway and non-railway works separately. There is necessarily an element of selection, and attention is therefore particularly drawn to the two published bibliographies which contain additional items. Abbreviations are as follows:

Hal   Halifax Antiquarian Society Transactions
HAS   Transactions of the Hunter Archaeological Society
IBG   Transactions and Papers of the Institute of British
        Geographers
MR   Modern Railways
NEE   North Eastern Express
RCHS   Journal of the Railway & Canal Historical Society
RM   Railway Magazine
RTM   Railway & Travel Monthly
RW   Railway World
TI   Trains Illustrated
TIA   Trains (Illustrated) Annual
TH   Transport History

Bibliographies
Ottley, George. *A Bibliography of British Railway History*
    (1965)
Ward, Clive A. W. 'A Bibliography of the History of Industry in the West Riding of Yorkshire, 1750–1914', Proceedings of the Leeds Philosophical & Literary Society, Literary & Historical Section, 13 Pt 1 (1968), 1–54

General
Ahrons, E. L. *Locomotive and Train Working in the Latter Part of the Nineteenth Century, Vols 1 and 2* (Cambridge 1951–2)
Barnes, E. G. *The Rise of the Midland Railway 1844–1874* (1966)
—— *The Midland Main Line 1875–1922* (1969)
Baxter, Bertram. *Stone Blocks and Iron Rails* (Tramroads) (Newton Abbot 1966)

Biddle, Gordon. *Victorian Stations* (Newton Abbot 1973)

Blower, Alan. *British Railway Tunnels* (1964)

Broadbridge, Seymour. *Studies in Railway Expansion and the Capital Market in England 1825–1873* (1970) (Part 1 is entirely devoted to the M & L and L & Y)

Clinker, C. R. & Firth, J. M. *Register of Closed Passenger Stations and Goods Depots in England, Scotland and Wales* (Harlyn Bay 1971)

Dow, George. *Great Central* (3 vols 1959–65)

Grinling, Charles H. *The History of the Great Northern Railway* (1898, new edition 1966)

Kellett, John R. *The Impact of Railways on Victorian Cities* (1969)

Lambert, Richard S. *The Railway King 1800–1871: A Study of George Hudson and the business morals of his time* (1934, reprinted 1964)

Lewin, Henry Grote. *Early British Railways 1801–1844* (1925)

—— *The Railway Mania and its Aftermath 1845–1852* (1936, reprinted Newton Abbot 1969)

Lewis, M. J. T. *Early Wooden Railways* (1970)

Marshall, C. F. Dendy. *A History of British Railways down to the Year 1830* (1938, reprinted 1971)

Priestley, Joseph. *Historical Account of the Navigable Rivers, Canals and Railways throughout Great Britain* (1831, reprinted Newton Abbot 1969)

Rolt, L. T. C. *George and Robert Stephenson* (1960)

Whishaw, Francis. *The Railways of Great Britain and Ireland* (1842, reprinted Newton Abbot 1969)

Williams, Frederick S. *The Midland Railway: Its Rise and Progress* (5th edition) (1888, reprinted Newton Abbot 1969)

Regional

Appleton, J. H. *The Historical Geography of Railways in Yorkshire* (Kings College, Newcastle, MSc thesis 1956)

—— 'The Railway Network of Southern Yorkshire', IBG, 22 (1956), 159–69

s

Brooke, D. 'The Promotion of four Yorkshire Railways and the Share Capital Market', TH, 5 (1972), 243–72 (includes the L & S and Y & NM)

Elliott, B. J. (edit). *Transport in South Yorkshire* (Sheffield 1972)

Franks, D. L. *South Yorkshire Railway* (Leeds 1971)

Haigh, A. *Railways of West Yorkshire* (Clapham 1974)

Hanson, J. L. *Transport Development in West Yorkshire from the Industrial Revolution to the Present Day* (University of London thesis 1949)

Hoole, K. (edit). *The Hull & Barnsley Railway, Vol 1* (Newton Abbot, 1972)

Hopkinson, G. G. 'Railway Projection and Construction in South Yorkshire and North Derbyshire 1830–50', HAS, 9 Part 1 (1964)

Lawrence, H. S. 'The Great Northern Railway in the West Riding', RM, 25 (1909), 286–93

—— 'The London & North Western Railway in Yorkshire', RTM, 2 (1911), 195–200

Marshall, John. *The Lancashire & Yorkshire Railway* (3 vols, Newton Abbot 1969–72)

Meik, H. H. 'The York & North Midland Railway', RM, 38 (1916), 320–7, 398–402; 39 (1916), 47–51, 113–20

Ross, A. M. 'Rail-Tour of the West Riding', TI, 10 (1957), 199–206 (by 'Yorkshireman'), 254–64, 319–22, 438–41

Scrafton, Derek. *A Study of Public Passenger Transport in the West Yorkshire Conurbation* (University of London thesis 1968, copy deposited at Leeds Central Library)

Speakman, Colin. *Transport in Yorkshire* (Clapham 1969)

Tomlinson, W. W. *The North Eastern Railway: Its Rise and Development* (Newcastle 1915, reprinted Newton Abbot 1967)

Traffic Research Corporation of Toronto. *West Yorkshire Transportation Study* (Wakefield 1969)

———

Cooper, Lettice. *Yorkshire West Riding* (1950)

Fletcher, J. S. *The Making of Modern Yorkshire* (1918)

Hadfield, Charles. *The Canals of Yorkshire and North East England* (2 vols, Newton Abbot 1972–3)

Pevsner, Nikolaus. *Buildings of England: Yorkshire the West Riding* (2nd edit, 1967)

Raistrick, Arthur. *The Making of the English Landscape: West Riding of Yorkshire* (1970)

Singleton, Fred. *Industrial Revolution in Yorkshire* (Clapham 1970)

Victoria History of the County of York (3 vols, 1907–25)

Chapter One: Leeds

Baughan, Peter E. 'The Leeds & Selby Railway', RM, 107 (1961), 392–8

Berrington, G. W. B. 'How Leeds is Catered for by the London & North Western Railway', RM, 23 (1908), 231–6

British Railways Eastern Region. *The New Leeds City Station* (1967)

Bushell, J. & Crew, M. D. *Middleton Colliery Railway, Leeds* (4th edit, Leeds 1968)

Clark, Edward Kitson. *Kitson's of Leeds 1837–1937* (1938)

Field, K. & Wilson, J. P. 'The Origins of Leeds Central', TI, 9 (1956), 223–8

Franks, D. L. *East and West Yorkshire Union Railways* (Leeds 1973)

Hudson, Graham S. *The Aberford Railway and the History of the Garforth Collieries* (Newton Abbot 1971) (Chap 4, 'The Leeds and Selby Railway')

Lawrence, H. S. 'Leeds New Station', RTM, 6 (1913), 25–32

Lawrence, J. T. 'Holbeck Junction' (Curious Railway Stations–4), RM, 11 (1902), 513–17

—— 'The Wellington Station, Leeds' (Notable Railway Stations–22), RM, 13 (1903), 169–77

Lee, Charles E. 'The First Steam Railway: Brandling's Colliery Line between Leeds and Middleton', RM, 81 (1937), 393–7

Redman, Ronald Nelson. *The Railway Foundry Leeds, 1839–1969* (Norwich 1972)

Rimmer, W. G. 'Middleton Colliery, near Leeds (1770–1830)', Yorkshire Bulletin of Economic and Social Research, 7 no 1 (1955), 41–57

Rolt, L. T. C. *A Hunslet Hundred: 100 years of locomotive building by the Hunslet Engine Company* (Dawlish 1964)

Scott, E. Kilburn. *Matthew Murray: Pioneer Engineer* (Leeds 1928)

Thompson, S. P. 'Leeds and its Railways', RM, 37 (1915), 47–52

Whitaker, J. 'The Royal Assent to the Leeds & Selby Railway Bill of 1830', NEE, 12 (1972), 69–72

Beresford, M. W. & Jones, G. R. J. (edit). *Leeds and Its Region* (Leeds 1967) (Chap 14, Dickinson, G. C., 'Passenger Transport Developments')

Briggs, Asa. *Victorian Cities* (2nd edit 1968) (Chap 4, 'Leeds, a Study in Civic Pride')

Chapter Two: Airedale and Wharfedale

Baughan, Peter E. *North of Leeds: The Leeds–Settle–Carlisle Line and its Branches* (1966)

—— *The Railways of Wharfedale* (Newton Abbot 1969)

Biddle, Gordon. 'The Skipton Rock Railway', Transactions of the Newcomen Society, 40 (1967–8), 171–3

Binns, Donald. *The Railways of Craven* (Nelson, 1974)

Povey, R. O. T. *The History of the Keighley & Worth Valley Railway* (2nd edit, Keighley 1968)

Winfield, Norman L. *Last Train to Yeadon: A Survey of the Railways of Aireborough* (MS at Aireborough Public Library, Rawdon)

Chapter Three: The Aire and Calder Watershed

Hutton, C. 'The Railway Services between Bradford and Leeds', RTM, 11 (1915), 367–72

Oxley, J. F. & Smith, D. R. 'The Queensbury Triangle', TI, 9 (1956), 274–81

Thompson, S. P. 'Bradford and its Railways', RM, 35 (1914), 54–8

Fay, C. R. *Round about Industrial Britain 1830–1860* (Toronto 1952) ('Bradford', 114–31)

Hird, Horace. *Bradford in History* (Bradford 1968) (includes a chapter on local railway stations)

Chapter Four: The Calder Valley
Baughan, Peter E. 'Railways of the Spen Valley', RM, 110 (1964), 308–15, 380–5
Baxter, Bertram. 'The Dewsbury and Birstall Railway', RCHS, 5 Pt 1 (1959)
British Railways North Eastern Region. *Healey Mills Marshalling Yard* (1963)
Cook, R. A. 'The Luddenden Valley Railway', RCHS, 18 (1972), 42–4
—— 'The Rishworth Branch', RM, 101 (1955), 202–5
—— 'The Stainland Branch Line', RCHS, 19 (1973), 39–44
Field, K. & Wilson, J. P. 'The Junctions at Methley', RM, 103 (1957), 276–81
Lawrence, H. S. 'Halifax as a "Railway Centre"', RM, 16 (1905), 41–9
Lawrence, J. T. 'Normanton Joint: A Notable Railway Station of 60 Years Ago', RM, 18 (1906), 385–92
Parkes, G. Richard. 'Speed Signalling by the LMS at Mirfield', TIA, 1961, 39–46
Tait, A. F. *Views on the Manchester & Leeds Railway* (1845, reprinted Newcastle 1971)
Wild, J. 'The Halifax High Level Railway', Hal, 1971, 39–66
—— 'Halifax Railway Station', Hal, 1968, 27–35

Dean, David A. *The Economic and Social Development of Dewsbury in the 19th Century* (University of Sheffield thesis 1963; on microfilm at Dewsbury Public Library)
Goodchild, John F. *Coal Mining Industry of the Lower Calder Valley 1750–1860* (MS at South Yorkshire Industrial Museum, Cusworth Hall, Doncaster)
Walker, John. *Wakefield: its history and people* (2nd edit, 2 vols, Wakefield 1939)
Yorkshire and Humberside Economic Planning Council. *Halifax and the Calder Valley: An Area Study* (1968)

Chapter Five: Huddersfield
Allen, G. Freeman. 'The North Western Main Line through the Pennines', TIA, 1958, 26–39

Baughan, Peter E. 'The Clayton West Branch', RM 108 (1962), 84–9

Chadwick, S. *All Stations to Manchester: The Centenary of the Huddersfield and Manchester Railway and Standedge Tunnel* (Huddersfield 1949)

—— *Gateway to the South: the centenary of the Huddersfield & Sheffield Junction Railway* (Huddersfield 1950)

Fraser, Neil. 'Standedge Tunnels', RW, 28 (1967), 58–60

Stocks, William B. 'Huddersfield Station', RM, 102 (1956), 377–80

—— *Pennine Journey: The History of the Railways, Tramways and Canals in Huddersfield and District* (Huddersfield 1958)

'Yorkshireman'. 'The Huddersfield–Penistone Line and its Branches', TI, 12 (1959), 248–55

Brook, Roy. *The Story of Huddersfield* (1968)

Yorkshire and Humberside Economic Planning Council. *Huddersfield and the Colne Valley* (1968)

Chapter Six: Sheffield and Rotherham

Booth, T. 'Sheffield and its Railways', RM, 5 (1899), 345

—— 'The Sheffield District Railway', RM, 4 (1899), 363

—— 'Sheffield (Midland Railway)' (Notable Railway Stations –35), RM, 18 (1906), 449–56

Bowtell, Harold D. 'In the Sheffield Hills', Stephenson Locomotive Society Journal, 44 (1968), 294–307 (Waterworks railways)

British Railways Eastern and London Midland Regions. *Electrification of the Manchester, Sheffield and Wath lines* (1954)

British Railways Eastern Region. *Railway Rationalisation in the Sheffield Area* (1965)

Coleman, Terry. *The Railway Navvies: A history of the men who made the railways* (1965) (Chap 7, 'Woodhead')

Cupit, J. & Taylor, W. *The Lancashire, Derbyshire & East Coast Railway* (Lingfield 1966)

Dow, George. *The First Railway between Manchester and Sheffield* (1945)

—— *The third Woodhead Tunnel* (1954)

Drake, James. *Road book of the Sheffield and Rotherham Railway* (1840)

Dunstan, John. *The Origins of the Sheffield and Chesterfield Railway* (Dore 1970)

Gibbons, V. *The Stocksbridge Railway Company: a brief survey* (Stocksbridge 1955)

Hart, Harold W. 'A Brief Survey of Events leading up to the Opening of the Sheffield & Rotherham Railway', HAS, 9 (1964–9), 269–79

Nicholson, Christopher P. & Barnes, Peter. *Railways in the Peak District* (Clapham 1971)

Rickard, Percy. 'Tunnels on the Dore & Chinley Railway', Proceedings of the Institution of Civil Engineers, 116 (1893–4)

Savill, R. A. 'The Sheffield District of the Eastern Region', TI, 14 (1961), 269–73

Sheffield City Libraries. *A Railway Chronology of the Sheffield Area* (2nd edit, Sheffield 1961)

Sheffield University Working Group. *Passenger Transport Integration Pilot Study: Sheffield Area* (1966)

Snell, Sidney. 'The Sheffield & Rotherham Railway', RM, 83 (1938), 313–18

Warren, K. 'The Sheffield rail-trade 1861–1930: an episode in the locational history of the British steel industry', IBG, 34 (1964), 131–57

Webster, N. W. *Joseph Locke: Railway Revolutionary* (1970) (Chap 6: 'The Driving of the Woodhead')

Linton, David L. (edit). *Sheffield and Its Region* (Sheffield 1956)

Walton, Mary. *Sheffield: its story and its achievements* (Sheffield 1948)

Chapter Seven: Barnsley

Brettle, Roger. 'Routes to Barnsley', TI, 11 (1958), 155–9

Gaitskell, M. H. *Register of Local Events relating to Railways printed in the Barnsley Chronicle* (MS at Barnsley Public Library)

Hewison, C. H. 'The Silkstone Railway', RM, 81 (1937), 159–62

Hewison, C. H. & Lee, Charles E. 'The Worsborough Railway', RM, 89 (1943), 191–3

Lawrence, J. T. 'The Great Central Railway's New Concentration Sidings at Wath', RM, 22 (1908), 177–85

Semmens, P. W. B. 'The Worsborough Bank', TI, 3 (1950), 157–61

Chapter Eight: Doncaster and the Concealed Coalfield

Allen, G. Freeman. 'Doncaster' (Traffic Divisions of British Railways–6), MR, 22 (1966), 28–36, 89–96

Bazin, J. R. 'The Great Northern Railway Works at Doncaster', RM, 32 (1913), 353–74

Boyes, Grahame. *The Heck Bridge & Wentbridge Railway* (Leeds 1973)

Day, J. E. *A History of Doncaster Plant Works from 1853 to the present day* (MS at Doncaster Public Library)

Elliott, B. J. *The South Yorkshire Joint Railway* (Lingfield 1972)

Groves, Philip F. 'Doncaster as a Railway Centre', RTM, 13 (1916), 205–18

Grinling, Charles H. 'A Carnival of the Rail: How the Great Northern Railway works the Doncaster race traffic', RM, 1 (1897), 314

Hemingway, G. Y. 'The Construction of the Gowdall to Braithwell Railway', NEE, 6 (1966), 27–30, 42–5

Lawrence, H. S. 'Doncaster' (Notable Railway Stations–36), RM, 19 (1906), 450–8

Lawrence, J. T. 'The Dearne Valley Railway', RM, 23 (1908), 121–7

Porteous, John D. 'A New Canal Port in the Railway Age: Railway Projection to Goole 1830–1914', TH, 2 (1969), 25–47

Phillips, Ernest & Danby, G. R. H. *The Story of Doncaster* (1921)

Yorkshire and Humberside Economic Planning Council. *Doncaster: An Area Study* (1967)

Acknowledgements

Unravelling and interpreting the history of the West Riding railways has been a daunting six-year task, but one which has been made immeasurably easier by assistance willingly given. I must particularly thank David St John Thomas and Professor Allan Patmore, co-editors of the series, for their advice and encouragement at all times. I am also especially indebted to Dr Arthur Barnett and C. R. Clinker, who painstakingly read through the manuscript and made valuable comments and suggestions. Portions of the MS have also been read by Neil Fraser, Ken Hoole and John Whitaker. Other individuals who have assisted in the preparation of the text have been R. A. Cook, Charles Dodsworth, D. L. Franks, John Goodchild, G. O. Holt, John Marshall, Stuart Rankin, Dr R. W. Rattray, David Sutcliffe and Alwyn Town. I apologise for any names I may have accidentally omitted.

A substantial portion of the research for this book was undertaken at Leeds City Library and the former British Transport Historical Records Office at York, where in both cases the staff could not have been more helpful. Research facilities have also been provided by British Transport Historical Records, London; the public libraries at Barnsley, Bradford, Dewsbury, Doncaster, Halifax, Manchester, Sheffield, Skipton and Wakefield; the former West Riding County Council; and Yorkshire Post Newspapers.

The intricacies of an area as complex as the West Riding would be almost impossible to comprehend without adequate maps, and here I count myself indeed fortunate in obtaining the cartographic services of Tim Hadwin and Geoffrey Hodgson of Leeds University's Department of Geography.

Finally, my deepest thanks go to my wife, Judith, and my son and daughter. They have patiently endured my many absences on research visits and tolerated my withdrawal symptoms during the actual writing. Without their encouragement and understanding, this work would never have been brought to a conclusion.

Index

Lines are indexed under the company authorised to construct them, and cross-referred with the owning company at Grouping. Stations and place names outside South and West Yorkshire are not indexed; nor are junctions, or stations and etc in the Reference Section.